Deconstituting Museums

Deconstituting Museums

Participation's affective work

Helen Graham

UCLPRESS

First published in 2025 by
UCL Press
University College London
Gower Street
London WC1E 6BT

Available to download free: www.uclpress.co.uk

A CIP catalogue record for this book is available from the British Library.

ISBN: 978-1-80008-911-2 (Hbk)
ISBN: 978-1-80008-912-9 (Pbk)
ISBN: 978-1-80008-913-6 (PDF)
ISBN: 978-1-80008-914-3 (epub)
DOI: https://doi.org/10.14324/111.9781800089136

Contents

Acknowledgements

I would like to give my heartfelt thanks to, and recognise the contributions of, the following:

The team at UCL Press. First and foremost Pat Gordon-Smith for managing the tricky task of direct but also supportive feedback at crucial moments. The reviewers of both the manuscript-proposal and of the manuscript for hugely constructive comments. Clifford Hayes for designing the book's front cover. Catherine Bradley for the brilliant and thorough copy-editing. Angela Thompson and Michele Greenbank for stewarding the book through production. Elliot Beck at UCL Press and Ali Kay in the Research Support Team, Leeds University Library, for working through the contracting issues related to UKRI Open Access funding.

The University of Leeds, and especially the School of Fine Art, History of Art and Cultural Studies, for offering me an academic home that has enabled me to pursue more experimental paths that may easily not have felt possible in another academic context. Joanne Crawford and fellow members of the Centre for Critical Studies in Museums, Galleries and Heritage, Nick Cass, Abigail Harrison-Moore, Rob Knifton, Gill Park, Liz Stainforth and Mark Westgarth. Gail Day for reading and responding to the Introduction.

The School of Fine Art, History of Art and Cultural Studies Anti-Racist Organising group, especially Nicola Singh, Maki Fukuoka, Carmen Okome and Zipporah Blake-Gravesande – then third years studying Fine Art and History of Art respectively – for initiating and leading Buyers' Remorse, which investigated white supremacy and racism in our school's teaching and classrooms.

The School of Fine Art, History of Art and Cultural Studies Race Matters module teaching team: Eva Frojmovic, Maki Fukuoka, Gill Park and Claudia Sternberg.

The Hundreds Reading and Writing Group, which ran in the School of Fine Art, History of Art and Cultural Studies 2020–3, for the space that helped me find the registers that in turn have found the page here.

The LAHRI Sadler Seminar 'Writing the Now' 2023–4, convened by Laura Swithenbank and co-facilitated by Laura King, Lone Sorensen, Aylwyn Walsh and Jessica Wright, for establishing a firmer ground for all of our experimental writing within our institution and beyond.

The Participatory Research Group, convened by Alice Borchi (2022–5) and Aylwyn Walsh (2017–24) and based in the University of Leeds School of Performance and Cultural Industries, for offering a brilliant context for discussions and for hosting an event at which I was able to share an earlier version of Chapters 2 and 4. Alice Borchi for reading a draft of Chapter 7 and offering insightful challenges.

The group that came together for 'Loosening the Difficulty' at the University of Leeds in June 2023: Emily Beswick, Solvig Choi, David Farrell-Banks, Cassie Kill, Kirstin Mitchell, Nuala Morse, Kate Noble, Camilla Portesani, Sarah Schroeder, Melissa Strauss, Violeta Tsenova and Hajra Williams – for the depth of discussion about museums and participation, and for responding to an earlier version of the structure of this book's argument.

The Solidarity in Action Network, convened by Bernadette Lynch and Salma Jreige, for thought-provoking conversations about how to frame the politics of museums in the 2020s.

The 'Agonism: Conflicting interpretations of the past' conference at the Luxembourg Centre for Contemporary and Digital History, 7–8 December 2023, convened by Violeta Tsenova, where I presented an early version of Chapter 7 and received very useful responses.

The 'Affect and Ideology: Politics in the impasse' two-day workshop at University of Durham, 11–12 July 2022, convened by Ben Anderson and Anna Secor, where I presented an early version of Chapter 2. Anna Secor for commenting on drafts which turned parts of Chapter 2 into a different, stand-alone article as part of a *New Formations* special issue based on the Affect and Ideology workshop. *New Formations* for arranging in-depth and helpful peer reviews and for Jeremy Gilbert's final feedback, which helped to sharpen up the book's overall project. Thanks to Lawrence and Wishart and *New Formations* for supporting reuse of parts of the article in Chapter 2.

The PhD researchers whom I have had the very good luck to work with – Sue Ball, Dominic Bilton, Solvig Choi, Eleni-Aikaterini Gibson, Samuel McKay, Seb O'Connor, Sarah Richardson, Carley Stubbs, Bing Wang, Amanda Wells and Zejun Yao. Kyle Lee-Crossett for applying abolitionist thinking so powerfully to museums and for the richness of the conversation we had in your PhD viva.

I want especially to mention PhD researchers who later became my colleagues:

Julia Ankenbrand for your wisdom, and for those moments in our action research collaborations when we were lost but then managed to figure something out.

Jade French for the rigour of your facilitation.

Arran Rees for being such an attuned and responsive co-facilitator of action research in the Congruence Engine project.

Liz Stainforth for all our many discussions about heritage, utopian and the speculative.

Laura Swithenbank for your incredible writing which always draws me back out into the world renewed, for all our conversations pondering affect and for reading this whole manuscript when it was in much, much less good shape.

Joanne Williams for your PhD work on museum ontologies and for all the conversations about research and institutions during our collaboration in FAHACS and since.

Victoria Vargas Downing for always having the most brilliant answer to any questions I might ask, for expanding my understanding of decoloniality and for your beautiful writing.

The research collaborations at the heart of The History of Day Centres (Open University/HLF), Art on Tyneside (AH/G000654/1), Ways of Knowing (AH/K006568/1), How Should Decisions about Heritage be Made? (AH/K006754/1), Bradford's National Museum (AH/P008585/1) and Congruence Engine (AH/W003244/1) for all the discussions and experiments. Each project acted as a crucible for the thinking in this book. An Appendix with lists of collaborators can be found at the back of the book. Special thanks to Tim Boon, Mary Dowson, Rhiannon Mason, Seán McLoughlin, Nima Poovaya-Smith, Jo Quinton-Tulloch, Tim Smith and Chris Whitehead for essential discussions about the institutional and political contexts that informed these projects in different ways.

Arran Rees, Katerina Webb-Bourne, Julia Ankenbrand and Alex Fitzpatrick for the discussions that informed our co-writing of 'The Project is Very White' for Congruence Engine.

Nuala Morse for reading the Introduction and for listening to tortured snippets of this argument throughout our friendship. Mark O'Neill for the discussions about the tensions between public service and participation and for reading and responding to aspects of this book's argument.

Phil Bixby for the very long, ongoing conversation and for our set of experiments in engagement and 'making change together' in York. *York Press* once carried an article about our My Future York approach; it attracted a comment below the line which read: 'Sounds like something Neil from the Young Ones would dream up'. Having been given this gift, we often ask, 'What would Neil do?' Maybe if he taught museum studies, the answer might be something like this book.

Mum and Dad for being amazing in all ways, as well as beyond amazing with Eliza.

Katie for being the best sister anyone could ever imagine, for listening more than I had any right to ask for throughout these last years and for only very rarely saying 'you need to finish that bloody book'.

Charlie for the reciprocity of dragons. Eliza for always passing me something and expecting it to be passed back.

This work was supported by the Arts and Humanities Research Council [grant numbers AH/G000654/1; AH/P008585/1; AH/K007459/1; AH/K006754/1; AH/K006568/1; AH/W003244/1; AH/W003244/1]. This book was also enabled by a period of study leave co-funded by the Faculty of Arts, Humanities and Cultures Faculty Study Leave and the School of Fine Art, History of Art and Cultural Studies.

Introduction

I used to work in a museum where most staff had their offices on one of two corridors. The corridors were almost identical, within east and west wings of a Palladian building that was aesthetically committed to symmetry. To walk down each corridor was an uncanny experience, the same and yet somehow different. The difference was not in the blue carpets or the late eighteenth-century and early nineteenth-century pictures on the walls. It was atmospheric; it was in the air. The very world on both corridors was like and yet unlike.

After one particularly difficult meeting a thought occurred. I had been employed to do what other people were employed to stop me doing. I was based in the informal learning team. My role was to work to identify ways of increasing access to the museum. I worked with people who were blind or partially sighted, Deaf networks, adult literacy and numeracy groups and people who had recently arrived in the UK and were learning English. The office I worked in was on a corridor that also included the schools team, press and marketing, exhibitions and digital. The other corridor was home to the curators, conservation, collections management and the director. The institutional functions were divided. Yet they were also structured spatially, as if in balance and as if poised for battle. Two corridors, antagonistically two halves of a whole.

Although that specific museum's architecture and traditions made this division starker than it is in other museums, museums are constituted through tensions.[1] Museums conserve objects for future generations. Museums make objects accessible to everyone now. Museums represent the world. Museums shape the world. In large museums it is very often the case that different aspects of the museum mission are allocated to different teams and different professional roles. The effect of the different purposes being distributed constantly provokes daily skirmishes over fundamental questions: What is the museum? What should we do?[2]

***

Making things happen is never a simple matter. The practical, concrete and actionable are utterly infused with ideas, abstractions, attachments, intensities and imagination.

This is true in particular ways in museums. The museums I have worked in and with have always been full of people trying to figure out the world and their place in it while also figuring out what museums are and can be. The museum teams I worked in, and most closely with, are those concerned with learning, interpretation, access and, more recently, participation. These are all roles that take responsibility for the everyday joining points between the museum and those people it seeks to engage – whether those joins are through collecting, text labels, tours, workshops or participatory projects. The contention of this book is that these practices are illuminating places to investigate the dominant political structure of museums as well as to diagnose – and also to encourage – emerging political tendencies.

This book coins the term 'museum constitution'. I use the term 'museum constitution' to describe a circuit or loop (Massumi 2015b) powered by the tensions that museums generate through their aspirations and abstract constituencies.[3] Such as the claim to be 'For everyone, for ever' (National Trust 2020). The promise of 'unhindered access' (Humboldt Forum 2021). 'Access to art' framed as 'a universal human right' (Tate 2020). The assertion that 'the cultures of the world' [...] can be brought 'together under one roof' (British Museum n.d.). Codes of ethics which state that museums 'preserve [...] the natural and cultural inheritance of humanity' (ICOM 2017) and 'maintain and develop collections for current and future generations' (Museums Association 2016). The International Council of Museums' definition of museums as a 'permanent institution in the service of society' and 'open to the public, accessible and inclusive' (ICOM 2022b).

In articulations such as these – which are not hard to find replicated – the active ideological formula of museums is palpable. There are big claims that are *in themselves* never achievable and act as constitutive deficits that need constant effort (forever, permanent, human rights, universal surveys, transformative impact, inclusive). The claims are in tension *between themselves* to varying extents, requiring endless negotiation (e.g. between access and preservation). There are expansive constituencies that can only be imagined (humanity, everyone, future generations). Together these deficits, tensions and abstract constituencies generate a requirement for a governance relation of acting 'on behalf of' these imagined constituencies (in service of; 'for'). Museum constitution's 'loopiness' (Massumi 2015b, 241), in common with numerous other political formulations of liberal modernity, is 'quasi-causal' in Brian Massumi's terms (2015b, 216). It is through built-in everyday problematics – making things happen, trying to do things that others seem to be employed to stop you doing – that the constitutional cycle is fuelled.

The roles of learning, interpretation and access have all played a crucial role in the ongoing animation of museum constitution. It has been people doing these job roles – jobs that I have done – who kick-start the circuit every time they try to push the museum to be more inclusive of different types of visitors and to represent a greater diversity of people or experiences in the galleries or collections. These roles are not easy to inhabit (Kahn 2021; Morse and Munro 2018; Morse 2020; Munro 2014; von Oswald 2023; Zwart 2023).[4] You are constantly required to challenge the institution that employs you. A set of personal commitments is demanded of you by the institution – to have faith in the transformative effects of institutional inclusion – as a precondition for your employment. At the same time these personal commitments always position you as 'in and against' (London–Edinburgh Weekend Return Group 1980) the museum – persuading, pushing, cajoling and fighting the very institution that created that role for you to play.

The first part of the book characterises the circuit of museum constitution and the animating role of those of us who hold the access, inclusion and representation missions of museums. I have come to believe that kick-starting museum constitution is something more than just a conscious and dutiful enactment of job descriptions. Rather, it is something closer to a reflex. 'Reflex' draws attention to the ways in which political reactions are habituated, formed in repetition and in our bodies as much as our minds. Gayatri Chakravorty Spivak uses 'reflex' across a number of publications, but in particular in the 2004 article 'Righting wrongs'. In this article Spivak describes the following 'conviction' – one she associates with her students at Columbia University:

> I am necessarily better, I am necessarily indispensable, I am necessarily the one to right wrongs, I am necessarily the end product for which history happened. (2004, 532)

Reflex, here, holds the sense of an in-the-moment reaction, but one that is conditioned in various ways. This somewhat righteous reflex, following Spivak, contains a strong impulse towards a certain type of agency – one characterised by responsibility-taking, ethical certainty and urgency. When I am in a meeting and someone asks a question such as 'who is not here?' or 'how can this exhibition, museum, project be more diverse?' my pulse rises, calling me to respond and to take up the challenge as my own. In the past, responding in this way has felt right, good and necessary. Even once the flash of righteousness died and all I was left with was the hard work, taking on such a role still felt purposeful, romantically hard, like fighting a good fight if very slowly. But this has changed.

What changed was that I shifted from facilitating access to facilitating participation – by which I mean working with groups of people not employed by the museum to make exhibitions, to add to collections or design events (Crooke 2008; Golding and Modest 2013; Watson 2007; Witcomb 2003, 86). When I first started working in museums in the mid-2000s it was still the case that 'access', 'inclusion' and 'representation' primarily meant things such as doing oral histories, testing exhibits with user groups, running workshops, touch tours or BSL tours – all somewhat 'arm's length' activities, emotionally speaking. The activities were scaled to support the broadcast one-to-many function of the museum or to be limited in contact time (such as a workshop or tour) so they could be delivered as a standard offering to lots of different people. Even while you were embroiled in the drama of museum constitution internally, your relationships with those outside were kept within boundaries, always held in check by the balancing abstractions of public, visitor, everyone or future generations.

With the rise of participation, museum workers became required to sustain relationships with individuals and groups over many weeks, months or years. And with this the nature of the joining point between museums and those it was seeking to engage was also transformed (Onciul 2015; McCarthy 2018). The type of activities I described above – oral histories, contemporary collecting or access tours – were compatible with museum constitution. They were logical ways of addressing the intrinsic deficit contained in museum ideals to be accessible to all or to represent all. There was a legitimacy to internal arguments over the line between access and conservation – which was the issue that provoked the corridor realisation with which I opened. It was institutionally consistent – whatever part of the conflictual mission your job role had to steward – to believe that the museum needed to strike a balance in the best interests of all between the public who might want access now and those not yet born. However, the Introduction of participation meant that those facilitators came to have increasingly deep and committed personal relationships with individuals and groups situated outside the museum which required 'to-ing and fro-ing' (Ames 1999, 48) and 'maintenance work' (Zwart 2023, 238–40). Crucially – and this is core to the argument of the book – participation also introduced different logics of political legitimacy, drawing on a distinctly different political genealogy.

Museum constitution is based on a liberal and representational political tradition – one that has come to characterise public institutions in postcolonial contexts since the 1980s. This is a political tradition that Elizabeth Povinelli has termed 'late liberalism', which she defines in terms of the 'governance of social difference in the wake of the anticolonial movements and the emergence of new social movements' (Povinelli 2011, ix). Povinelli suggests social difference has become governed through the 'cunning of recognition' (2002). Late liberalism's 'cunning' arises from a perpetual activation of 'horizon' ideals that treat 'radical critiques of liberal colonial capitalism as if they were a desire by the dominated to be recognized by the dominant state and its normative publics' (Povinelli 2021, 8). In practical terms in museums, a late liberal politics of access, inclusion and representation was enacted through the type of practices I have already mentioned, such as access tours and including people's personal testimony and objects in exhibitions.

Initially this move to greater inclusion and representation was possible to do without any expectation that the people included or interviewed would have any control over the nature of their access or representation. The higher justification was the production of quality events or content for visitors in the name of social justice or social validation. Increasing access, inclusion and representation was in itself seen as a legitimate means of mobilising museum expertise for the benefit of the greatest number. It has been political intentions of these types that have been used in justification of 'on behalf of' professional and trustee governance.

In contrast, participation is rooted in anarchist and direct democratic traditions. Participation's central tenet is for decisions to be made by those they affect. It is about relationships, mutual aid and accountability, and being together differently. It is about means, not ends. It works when small is considered beautiful (Schumacher 1972). Its approach to scale is not to scale up, but to scale out. Its future is lived in the present, prefiguratively, and not deferred. It is drawn to epistemic singularity rather than epistemic representativeness. Participation makes its own realities; it 'induces the creation of its own field', in Orlando Fals Borda's terms (1991, 6).

I am aware that different voices in this debate have drawn attention to the sheer variety of ways in which the word 'participation' is used (Carpentier 2011) and to how its enrolment in liberal governance can act as 'tyranny' (Cooke and Kothari 2001). Certain voices have preferred to jettison participation because other terms – for example, co-production, co-creation (Jubb 2018) or 'constituent' (Hudson 2017; Morgan et al. 2018) – seem to offer greater transformative potential.[5] However, it is my contention that tying the meaning of participation strongly to its genealogy in horizontal political practices is useful, precisely because it indicates why adding participation to museum constitution has been so difficult.

To put it straightforwardly, the reason why power has not been ceded to participatory museum projects (Fouseki 2010; Kassim 2017; Lynch 2011a; 2011b; Lynch 2019; Lynch 2020; Morse 2020; von Oswald 2023) is because in retaining power senior museum leaders have believed – often in good faith – that they are acting on behalf of the visitor, the public and in the name of being accessible to all (Strauss 2023).[6] In short, facilitators of museum participation have been forging not only long-term inter-personal relationships, but also an accommodation with incompatible political logics.

In their extensive work on participation and power, John Gaventa and Andrea Cornwall have made a distinction between 'claimed' and 'invited' spaces of participation (Gaventa 2021). Claimed spaces or 'sites of resistance' (Cornwall 2002) are 'where less powerful actors [...] can shape their own agenda or express their own voices more autonomously' (Gaventa 2021, 119) and 'invited' spaces refers to the way in which institutional participatory spaces are 'framed' by institutions 'who create them' (Cornwall, Schattan and Coelho 2007, 11). There has perhaps been an implicit working assumption that participation in museums could remain contained as an 'invitation' (Lynch 2011a; 2011b; Lynch 2020). A museum invitation that frames participation as a mode of engagement and is focused on channelling people into the roles of 'beneficiaries' (Lynch 2011a, 7; Lynch 2020, 6) and 'contributors' (Morse 2020, 30).

However, this book's argument is that participation never really remains an invitation. While it is often said with a sigh that participatory projects leave little or no institutional legacy, I want to suggest that participation always 'claims'. What participation claims is you. The doing of participation gets under the skin; it calls to account, opens things up and generates possibilities otherwise unglimpsed. It is in recognition of the ways in which participation's political ideas – how to be present, to share in decision-making, to be mutually accountable – are often more *felt* than theorised that this book's subtitle is 'participation's affective work'. Through doing participation you find your desire to service museum constitution and to kick-start its late liberal circuit falters and slackens, leaving you wanting something else.

It is not, therefore, that every participatory project in museums has predigested anarchist and direct democratic theory – and there is evidence to suggest that, on the contrary, thriving groups are often proud that they worked it out together without reference to precedent (Preservative Party and Harrison-Moore 2024). The central argument of Part III of this book is rather that the sheer act of doing participation generates realities based on variant political ontologies; it makes different ideas thinkable and changes who you are and understand yourself to be. Participation – through the ways it changes what the world is – ultimately makes engaging with its political genealogy both necessary and desirable, prompting new modes of organising and reimagining notions of governance. It is the ways in which living participation creates new realities and experimental modes of organising that this book terms 'participatory worlding'. Even when participation begins as an invitation its arc of affects takes over, always disclosing something else – that participation is not a mode of engagement, as it is often institutionally thought to be. It is an alternative mode not only of governance, but also of world-making.

If this all sounds a bit abstract, it is not. How many times have you been sucked into the magic of it all, in love with the group and yourself in the group? Or been wracked with doubt over something you said, because the ground of commonsense had suddenly shifted? Or, in the midst of facilitating a workshop, realising, like a belly clunk, that you can never run a meeting like this again, sending you off to read and to try and learn from others?[7] Or, on the way home, knowing you are losing your reformist religion and that you want to find a way not to get caught up again and again in the constitutional circuit, pulse rising and hand raising? All of this and many other moments are the affective work of participation.

It is not coincidental that participation got added to museums and other public organisations only slowly over the 1980s and 1990s, but with increasing rapidity in the late 2000s and 2010s. While there were a number of innovative precedents in the ecomuseum and community museum movements of the late 1970s and 1980s – seeped as they were in anarchist, direct democracy or Freirean theory (Bellaigue Scalbert 1985;

Gomez de Blavia 1985; Kinard 1985; Mayrand 1985; Querrien 1985; Rivard 1985; Rivière 1985; Hauenschild 2022 [1988]) and which we will explore in the International Museology interludes – by the late 2000s and early 2010s museums found themselves colliding with a more widespread sense of democratic deficit and lack of trust in public intuitions. Perceptions of institutional inertia were heightened by the utopian moment of web 2.0, which was inflected with ideas of self-expression, self-publishing and self-organising (Turner 2006). Participation became widely written about using the web as a reference point (Benkler 2006; Simon 2006, 2010; Carpentier 2011) and became increasingly required in museum and cultural funding guidance. The everydayness of web 2.0 meant that 'participation' could become mainstream without any need to reckon with the actual political lineage of participation or with the inevitable tensions it would produce in institutions that were themselves founded on liberal values.

It is also not coincidental that the tensions generated by adding participation to late liberalism became more clearly problematic in the 2020s. The utopian hopes for a participatory web have turned into an increasingly dystopian nightmare of algorithmic data extraction and exploitation by companies that seem beyond the regulatory powers of liberal democracies. The impact of Black Lives Matter on the US and UK cultural sectors means that now languages of inclusion and diversity are being jostled by decolonisation, racial justice and abolition.[8] With greater understandings of climate emergency and the need for significant adaption, there is the loss of a continuity future and therefore of the horizon on which late liberalism relies. The newly resonating insight that coloniality and climate change are intimately linked is only serving to pluralise the ideas, practices and affects at play when the late liberal loop of museum constitution is activated (Harrison and Sterling 2021, 9).[9]

Late liberalism is not proving equal to this 2020s landscape. More than that, its arrogant good intentions have been easy to memeify in culture wars. A strand of argument often made is that we need strong liberal institutions to counter this new right politics.[10] The question is how can we be so sure that this late liberal political infrastructure – of which museum constitution is one iteration – is not part of this problem? It depersonalises, deals with you at arm's length, assert its expertise, knows better, decides what parts of you are acceptable and expects you to be grateful. It uses your involvement as salve to its own constitutive deficits while requiring you to be in deficit whether of recognition, of inclusion, of skills or of wellbeing. Participation promised a way to mitigate the extremes of these liberal patrician tendencies. Yet what it has actually done is to make them sharper, more painful and more intolerable.

There is nothing about participation that is liberal. Participation has never been a short cut to get the ideological outcomes that liberal institutions want – an issue that often becomes materialised in museums through content and text editing in co-produced exhibitions (Kassim 2017; Lynch and Alberti 2010, 23; Lynch 2020, 5; Morgan 2013, 165, Ramamurthy 2021). Crucially, participation is not inclusive in the sense of being 'open to all'. Groups – in order to be groups – have boundaries, which inevitably create both inclusions and exclusions. What those enacting participation decide to be and do will vary wildly (e.g. Kassim 2017). Institutions are, not surprisingly, wary of this. But asserting an overarching framework of values and rights that liberal institutions guard – the hope of the post-war consensus – is on the cusp of total failure. It no longer seems possible for museums – or any other liberal institution – 'to bracket' its 'violence' as 'the result of the unintended, accidental, and unfortunate unfolding of liberalism's own dialectic' (Povinelli 2018, n.p.). Or to say that while it is a shame that it was in museums' name that hurt and harm happened, that nevertheless museums and their ideals remain the solution. If only we try hard enough, once again.

To affect and be affected: action and writing

The driving motivation for writing this book is to retrain my own reflexes (Bourdieu 2000 [1997]; Spivak 2004). The ways in which museum constitution is reflexively kick-started mean – as Pierre Bourdieu has argued – that there can be no expectation that 'political liberation' will 'come from the "raising of consciousness"'. This is because what is at play is not simply ideology as ideas or 'a simple mental representation', but rather 'a tacit and practical belief made possible by […] habituation'. Therefore, Bourdieu goes on, 'only a thoroughgoing process of countertraining, involving repeated exercises, can, like an athlete's training, durably transform habitus' (2000 [1997], 172). I have turned to theories of affect to illuminate the nature of the late liberal reflex. Theories of affect also point to the types of training needed to enable other responses and reaction.

Affect is most often defined in terms of capacities 'for affecting and being affected' (Massumi 2015a, 3) or 'capacities to act and be acted upon' (Seigworth and Gregg 2010, 1). Affect is, therefore, often differentiated from emotion. Emotion tends to be characterised as 'the way the depth of that ongoing experience is registered at any given moment' (Massumi 2015a, 4): that is, as subjective and personal and as carrying meaning. Affect, in contrast, is used to enable a sensitisation to the 'intensities' that 'pass body to body'; 'vital forces [...] that can serve to drive us towards movement' (Seigworth and Gregg 2010, 1). It is about *how* things matter, their qualities and tones, and *how much*; the type of invigoration and energy at play (Grossberg 1992, 82). Theories of affect offer a means of understanding the reflexes at work when museum constitution is enacted – how museum constitution is a political form made possible through people being enrolled and being energised in certain ways. Theories of affect also orientate attention to how disinvestment might create other political and affective possibilities.

Throughout the book I draw upon two tendencies that have emerged within affect theory. The first is the relationship between affect and attachment, as developed by Lauren Berlant. The second trajectory explores affect and intensities, as taken up in different ways through Lawrence Grossberg and Brian Massumi's engagements with the work of Gilles Deleuze and Felix Guattari.

For Berlant attachment is 'what draws you out into the world' (Berlant 2022, 6), with attachment being a 'cluster of promises' (2011, 16). Such promises are a mixture of 'projection [...] and speculation that hold up a world that we need to sustain' (2022, 27) and investment 'in one's own or the world's continuity' (2011, 13). Attachment, in the context of museums, speaks to how certain people are positioned and position themselves in relation to the 'governance of social difference' (Povinelli 2011, ix). Attachment illuminates the ways in which certain people become susceptible to animating the access, inclusion and representation side of museum constitution.

Museum constitution draws you out into the world in certain ways because it promises you something. The nature of this promise is not simple. Berlant suggests that attachment is always ambivalent; 'all attachment opens defences against the receptivity one also wants to cultivate' (2022, 76). Ambivalence, for Berlant, is 'strongly mixed'; it is 'drawn in many directions, positively and negatively charged' (2022, 27). What is being promised in the complexity of museum constitution attachment is not only the redemption of the institution but also your own, in relation to the institution as the contested site of liberal ideals. The in-ness and against-ness is how you calibrate your sense of self. It is the reflex – pulses rising – to *say something* and to call into the meeting access, inclusion or representation which *draws you out*, attached and attaching to the hope for reform, to those horizon ideals and to your own sense you need both an alibi (it wasn't me) and redemption (I can make a difference). Even as you wonder how you came to put your hand up in the same way, once more.

Affect thought of as intensities aids in exploring the overwhelming sense of urgency in museum constitution reflexes; it also sensitises us to how this may now be changing and disintensifying. Lawrence Grossberg suggests that 'affective relations always involve a quantitatively variable level of energy (activation, enervation) that binds an articulation or that binds an individual to a particular practice' (1992, 82). This means affect can illuminate both 'the strength of the investment which anchors people in particular experiences, practices, identities, meanings and pleasures' as well as 'how invigorated people feel at any moment of their lives, their level of energy or passion' (1992, 82). As such, Grossberg argues, 'affect produces systems of *difference*' (1997, 160, italics original). I take from Grossberg's point that if you repeat the same activity – such as raising the issue of access, inclusion or representation in a museum meeting – but do so with different qualities and intensities then it becomes a different thing, and different things then become possible.

For Massumi affect and its intensities indicate not only how we experience, but also how we might activate, a politics of the present (2015a, vii). If 'reflex' is a habit that has 'lost its adaptive power, its powers of variation, its force of futurity, that has ceased to be the slightest bit surprised by the world' (2015a, 66), Massumi's alternative is to 'take little, practical, experimental, strategic measures' so that we can 'access more of our potential at each step' (2015a, 5). Massumi also identifies this – in common with Spivak and Bourdieu – as a question of 'training' (2015a, 96). He suggests that we might develop a repertoire of 'affect modulation techniques', 'automaticities operating with as much dynamic immediacy as the event, directly as part of the event' (2015a, 96). The politics offered by affect lie, for Massumi, in the ways that 'affect modulation techniques' (2015b, 96) can respond to a situation's openness, its 'margin of manoeuvrability' (2015a, 3) and the ability to activate potential in any given moment.

This resonates with Kathleen Stewart's definition of affect as 'the commonplace, labor-intensive process of sensing modes of living as they come into being' (2010, 340). Or, as Massumi puts it, 'intuition' may be considered 'a political art' (2015c, 93) – one that is enacted through developing different and responsive ways of being in the present. Attending to affect might help us find ways no longer to reflex predictably – kick-starting museum constitution with pulses rising and hands raising. Instead we might develop, through experimentation and then through repetition, the affective habits for reflexing differently.

Whiteness and museum constitution

Not all of us habituated to activate museum constitution are white, straight, middle class and able bodied. Nevertheless, part of what is at work in the late liberalism of museum constitution is normativity, not least whiteness.[11] Museum constitution is a making of space which is 'ready for certain kinds of bodies' and puts certain ideas and practices – such as those that make up museum constitution – 'within reach', for some (Ahmed 2007, 154). Dan Hicks names museums as 'white infrastructure' (2021, xiii). He does this in recognition of the ways in which museums are 'a technology for performing white supremacy used to try to justify ultraviolence, democide, the destruction of cultural property, and the casting of sacred and royal objects to the open market' (2021, 233), meaning that any 'knowledge that Europeans can make with African objects in the anthropology museum will be coterminous with knowledge of European colonialism, wholly dependent upon anti-black violence and dispossession' (2021, xiii).

Hicks's focus is the theft of the Benin Bronzes, and this being ongoing, unfinished violence. Yet the term 'white infrastructure' can also be applied to the late liberal museum constitution, which is most definitely what Vron Ware and Les Back referred to as 'white-friendly systems' (2002, 5; see also Bunning 2020). Museum constitution's 'cunning' (Povinelli 2002) is that it can be seen to be a means of responding precisely to the colonial violence Hicks describes through enrolling those contesting and critiquing into the reform of institutions that have done – and continue to do – harm.

Museum constitution is a means by which institutional whiteness and class hierarchies, as well as other normativities of sexuality, gender and ability, are challenged by logics of access, inclusion, representation and – more recently – diversity; and also maintained, by the same means. The nature of challenge is also the means of negotiating political continuity. Museum constitution facilitates racialisation through a focus on inclusion, representation and diversity. This in turn sorts people into different kinds of roles with different types of agency, such as those of the includer and included (Brown 2000; Paur 2012; Wynter 2013). As Sara Ahmed puts it, 'reification is not then something we do to whiteness, but something whiteness does, or to be more precise, what allows whiteness to be done' (2007, 150).

Logics of representation and inclusion create whiteness as a norm – the '"unmarked marker"' (Frankenburg 1986, 1) – that stands above and outside diversity as a means of producing and managing difference (Scott 2003; Hage 2012). It is a political ontology based in separability, rather than recognising our 'difference without separability' (Ferreira da Silva 2016) and 'entanglements' (Barad 2007, 2010). It is a political ontology that sees race as an institutional 'problem' to be solved by means of management and representational curation rather than as a technology of domination that is 'killing' us all (Harney and Moten 2013, 140–1). Although it is certainly the case that race is killing the white people who make up the bulk of museum employees in postcolonial contexts (O'Brien, Laurison, Miles and Friedman 2016, 121) 'much more softly', to invoke Fred Moten (Harney and Moten 2013, 140–1).[12]

If you are asking yourself why this book focuses on museum facilitators of participation rather than on participants themselves, it is because – the book's argument goes – our bodies and minds are a site where tectonic political shifts have been happening precisely *because of* the incompatibility of late liberalism and participation. To be the institutional includer has become an uncomfortable position to hold. Even to contemplate retraining our reflexes is now possible because something in our habituation has already shifted, caught up in the rippling forces and contradictions of our present moment, this 'conjuncture' (Hall 2021 [1988]). This book's contention is that it is worth trying to articulate such a shift and its consequences. The fraught livedness of facilitating participation institutionally has also gifted a chance to reflex differently and to be in the world, and to make worlds, differently. It seems timely to develop techniques (Spatz 2015)[13] that might make this more possible.

As already noted, everything written here comes from 20 years working in and, latterly, with museums through a number of projects framed as research.[14] Where it is appropriate I cite this work, especially where other people have written about our collective work in ways that have shaped what I thought and could think. But this book is not based in ethnographic or autoethnographic verity. There is an ethics to this, as my participatory research is co-produced and co-written and I have no right and no desire to write 'about' anyone I've collaborated with. I am hopeful this mix of abstraction and citational acknowledgement manages these two different ethical concerns.[15] It is an ethical commitment not to write about anyone or on their behalf, together with a commitment to find modes of attention that aid in the retraining of reflexes, that has led this book – as I will have explained by the end of this Introduction – to unfold in three registers: those of critical abstraction, affective proximity and speculative trajectory.

Participation as world-making: museum studies and heritage studies

I hope this book can make contributions to two ongoing clusters of work in museum studies and heritage studies. The first relates to descriptions of museum and heritage political infrastructure that have been foundational to museum studies and critical heritage studies. There are a number to which I want to draw attention. Tony Bennett's insight – in his work on nineteenth-century museums – that museums' claims to be accessible and representative are 'insatiable', and that there are 'mismatches' between ideas of access and museums' political rational of differentiating people for the purpose of reform (1995, 90–1). Authorised Heritage Discourse developed by Laurajane Smith, and especially her concept of dissonant heritage as 'a constitutive social process that on the one hand is about regulating and legitimizing, and on the other hand is about working out, contesting and challenging' (2006, 82).

Barbara Kirshenblatt-Gimblett's argument that 'world heritage is predicated on the idea that those who produce culture do so by dint of their "diversity," while those who come to own those cultural assets as world heritage do so by dint of their "humanity"' (2006, 183). The concern expressed by Ben Dibley that museum studies is locked in a redemptive cycle of critique and then hopes for reform, seeking instead 'refusal' (2005, 22–3). Bernadette Lynch's diagnosis of how participation in museums remains stuck in a beneficiaries mode, proposing instead ideas of solidarity (2011a; 2020). The observation that participation in museums requires people to act as contributors, as if offering an institutional tribute, made by Nuala Morse – leading her, in contrast, to advocate for ideas of care (2020). The framing of 'museum constitution' is in debt to this now long-standing diagnosis of a circular or looped tendency in museum and heritage.

The second cluster is related to the recent turn towards plural heritage ontologies (DeSilvey 2017; DeSilvey and Harrison 2020; Harrison and Sterling 2020; Whitehead, Schofield and Bozoğlu 2021), including considering affect in museums and heritage (Crang and Tolia-Kelly 2010; Tolia-Kelly, Waterton and Watson 2016; Farrell-Banks 2023). This cluster of theorising has drawn attention to the processual and emergent nature of heritage. It has also challenged the idea of linear time with a continuity future (Harrison and Sterling 2021, 9) and drawn attention to loss over preservation.

Part of what I want to contribute is to elaborate further the political work done by the ways in which museums and heritage are made up of constitutive deficits, tensions and abstractions. The purpose of naming this late liberal circuit 'museum constitution' is to characterise its efficacy as a political formation which lies in combining an ideological structure with habitual affective dynamics, kick-started through reflex. Forming up museum constitution into a 'thing' is, to reiterate, not to make an evidential claim; rather, it is a means of retraining reflexes in order to avoid falling again and again into the redemptive trap, always renewing the hope for reform, as diagnosed by Dibley (2005). Naming museum constitution in turn also works to illuminate the status of participation in current museum and heritage practice. My hope is that characterising museum constitution in terms of representational logics of legitimacy – and in combining, developing, condensing and heightening the formulations identified by others before me – indicates more clearly why participation has been so difficult, subject to so much institutional resistance and experienced as painful and disappointing by so many participants.

A related contribution arises through experimenting with how we attend to the dynamics at work in everyday museum work. While museum studies has been well served by a mixture of critical case studies and ethnography, this book's methods ask whether a self-conscious mix of greater critical abstraction, affective proximity and speculative flights might help to illuminate and open up both the politics of museums and the lived experience of museum practice. Academic prose is often calm, conducted at a certain distance – but I have always experienced museums as an existential panic attack. My hope is to articulate the ways in which museums are sites of political drama, locales of desire and urgencies and of disengagement and slackening. In essence, while I am in debt to a museum studies that has been about establishing what museums have been, are or should be, this book contributes to a museum studies which is more about approaching museums as predicaments of our present moment:[16] sedimented, always restless and swarming with potential for becoming something else.

Finally, in framing 'participatory worlding' I connect with the recent work in museum and heritage studies while drawing on wider theorisations of emergent and relational ontologies – in particular via Karen Barad, Donna Haraway, Brian Massumi, Kathleen Stewart and, from participatory research and action research, Orlando Fals Borda, John Heron and Peter Reason. The contribution here is to elaborate the dynamics of participation as a practice that 'induces the creation of its own field', in Orlando Fals Borda's terms (1991, 6). In other words, it is to position participation as generating its own political ontologies – its own realities – precisely through the affective exposure of seeking to be mutually accountable. The lived experience of participation and its complexities generates a desire – I'd like to suggest – for experimenting in modes of organising and of governance which, in turn, scaffold and extend the world-making potential of participation.

In doing so I foreground the importance of the participatory reimagination of governance. The argument I develop is that the relational is a politics (whether expressed as participation, solidarity or care) that requires – and is only possible through – actively chosen forms of organising, so it can both 'go where the energy is' – as the phrase goes – and surface and mediate power.

The concepts of hybrid forums (Callon, Lascoumes and Barthe 2011; Harrison 2013, 223) and of assembling (Latour 2004, 22–3) have indicated how an emergent and relational ontological shift might be organised politically. Yet what I hope this book can offer to this debate is greater engagement with the praxis of emergent and relational organising developed in participatory research and action research, and in political theory.

This book tries to take up where the baton is generally passed back to practitioners.[17] This book starts in the mess of practising participation. It tries to show how participation can indeed offer ways out of museum constitution loop – if participation's ontological and organisational implications are embraced.

Practice and the status of knowledge in this book

Writing the book has been, in itself, an act of retraining my reflexes. This could be true of reading it too, should you find that any of this resonates. The status of the 'knowledge' in this book is not that I am claiming to represent what has happened or is happening 'out there' in an accurate and rigorous way. To be explicit, I am not claiming 'museum constitution' as a factual and universal description of all museums, nor indeed of any specific museum – this is why it is not referred to either as 'the' museum constitution or 'a' museum constitution.[18] Rather, I am using museum constitution as a tactical naming of a political tendency in order to create greater critical friction and to slow down the (my) reflex to 'right wrongs' (Spivak 2004). In taking this approach I am enacting the same ethical responsibility I argued is at play in participation – that what I am doing through writing is playing a small part in world-making, in worlding. This book is writing *as* participatory worlding – that through writing we take part in generating what there is in the world, 'call[ing it] into being' (Gibson-Graham 2008, 620).

There is, of course, an experiential basis for the book. Its impetus arises from the confusion of working in and with museums in dialogue with the reading I have done, seeking insights from others that might help me make sense of what I do and continue to do in spite of myself. But the purpose of this book as a form of practice research and action research is not to account faithfully for what I have done in an evidential way. It is to use this process of writing actively to reform that experience in useful ways, and to change how I am as I continue to be caught up in participatory processes.

Part I – Museum constitution – uses Chapter 1 to develop an abstracted political map. It does so using a critical register to identify how the inbuilt deficits, tensions and contradictions of museum constitution animate and organise *as if* it was possible to see this ideological framework without endless contingencies. But, of course, these contingencies are constitutive: the ideals of museum constitution sustain not only in how they are taken up or the ways they are done in everyday work, but also in the energetic desire to realise their promise – and so Chapter 2 introduces affective poetics. Chapter 2 seeks to evoke being caught up in the cycles of museum constitution, including how the reflex is triggered and the complexities of its after-effects. Moments when you stick your hand up and assert the need for greater inclusion. Or when you are having meetings outside of the museum, suddenly finding that you are not quite sure why you are there. Or getting a consent form signed, but awkwardly, disrupting the flow of conversation and relationship. Chapter 2 concludes by introducing the first meaning of *participation's affective work*: that to do participation in relation to museum constitution creates a slackening of desire to carry on fuelling the constitutional circuit.

Part I draws to a close with the first of the International museology interludes, focused on the ICOM museum definition. It argues that in spite of the furore around a proposed new draft in 2019 – and the feeling that it was a break with previous iterations of museum definition – the basic ideology structure of museum constitution was still at work. What was different, crucially, was the way that it felt. Its tone, texture and atmosphere seemed to require different attachments and intensities that some clearly wanted to reject.

In Part II – Detaching – we explore how to use stirrings of disinvestment in detaching from museum constitution. Berlant suggests that 'when an ordinary form of life is radically disturbed such that a subject's or people's sense of continuity is broken, what results is the release of affective enmeshment from its normative habits' (Berlant 2022, 124). Through Chapter 3 and Chapter 4 we explore different orientations to detaching. Chapter 3 explores de-intensification. It investigates what happens when similar activities are repeated, but where the nature and quantity of the investments has shifted. Experimenting using affective poetics, the chapter successively speeds up the circuit of museum constitution, slows down and carries on without any righteous flash.

Chapter 4 uses a speculative register, 'following out' (Berlant and Stewart 2019, ix) dynamics identified in Chapter 3. Detaching is indeed about letting go, but to detach is also to attach to something else (Anderson 2023). It imagines detaching from institutional demands to report on participation, whether via supplying demographic data, pictures of 'diverse' participants or claiming projects as 'best practice'. Then the speculative narrative attends to the political desire latent in the present, seeking new attachments and new ways of being with each other, becoming wilder in the process (Halberstam 2013).

In Part III – Participatory worlding – the second resonance of participation's affective work is elaborated through an exploration of the political ontology participation generates. In Chapter 5 participation is elaborated as world-making, rather than world-reflecting or representing. Drawing on both participatory action research and materialist theorisations – in particular on the work of Karen Barad, Orlando Fals Borda, Peter Reason, Brian Massumi and Kathleen Stewart – *to world* is to understand everyday actions as making realities, creating time, space, people and things. Participatory worlding is enabled by the affective work of being 'with' other people and the more-than-human, where 'with' is made up of 'entanglements' (Barad 2007, 2010) and 'difference without separability' (Ferreira da Silva 2016).

Wherever possible, participatory worlding is concerned to generate abundance and reduce instances of scarcity and competition. Where conflict is unavoidable, participatory worlding is enabled through direct democratic approaches in order to activate minds and bodies in thinking-feeling. If detaching is the response to the ways in which museum constitution generates attachments, enabling us to be drawn into the world – and to world – differently, *modulating* is the response to intensities of urgency and agency generated by the loopiness of the constitutional circuit. Modulating – explored in Chapter 6 – draws from Brian Massumi's elaborations across a number of books, introduced above. If museum constitution is kick-started by an intense urgency to right wrongs, Massumi has elaborated ways of being present differently that can support 'the tweaking of an arc of unfolding, on the fly' (2015a, 96).

In Chapter 7 we explore participatory worlding as organising. This connects us with participation genealogy as a political practice, emphasising direct and participatory modes instead of delegated authority or 'on behalf of' governance. The first part of the chapter reworks the political problems at the core of museum constitution – of the abstracted constituencies of 'all affected', of the fragile and rival object and of the valued space of recognition. This is done in ways that de-intensify the need for formal 'big D' decision-making and the need to balance out interests. In the second we meet the newly rescaled political problems with a variety of theories and practices of self-organising that are decisively direct and participatory. Among them are theories and practices of *commoning*, *divergence and democracy as attractor*, *consensus decision-making*, *restorative justice circles* for dealing with harm and *self-constitution* to enable all types of political endeavour including agonistic interactions. None of these offer a holistic solution, but their very variety indicates the range of ways in which people can be directly involved in shaping the conditions of their own participation.

Part III is bookended by two International museology interludes. The first – International museology II – draws out connections between 1970s community museum and ecomuseum innovators and participatory research and action research to amplify approaches to participatory governance and worlding making. The second – International museology III – uses the exciting approaches to ontology and governance of early community museums and ecomuseums to ask whether the concept, or indeed the word 'museum', can be deconstituted.

Experimenting, enacting

This book's experimentation is a response to Patricia Clough's specifying of mechanisms offered by experimental academic writing:

> [Experimental writing offers] methods [...] for cutting out an apparatus of knowing and observation from a single plane or for differently composing elements of an apparatus with the aim of eliciting exposure or escaping it, intensifying engagement or lessening it, speeding up the timing of willed influencing or slowing it down, enjoying pleasure and suffering pain or eluding them. (2000, 286)

Taking from Clough's set of possibilities, I am interested in naming museum constitution as 'cutting out an apparatus [...] from a single plane' to enable a process of loosening (Berlant 2022, 27). Through oscillating between hyper-clarity and something more evocative. Through varying the intensities of museum constitutions' different elements – 'intensifying engagement or lessening it' (Clough 2000, 286) – as a way of changing the nature of its loopiness. Through adding the elements together differently or 'recombining' in Berlant's terms (2022, 28) in order to create different political logics. Through 'speeding up' and 'slowing' down in order to practise over-'exposure' or 'escape' (Clough 2000, 286). In all cases the experiments through writing are a trying-out – where 'out' is both an emergent unfolding and a hope for enough velocity to resist, even if momentarily, the centripetal and habitual force of the constitutional loop.

Methodologically 'cutting out an apparatus' (Clough 2000, 286) and, in Michel Foucault's terms, 'multiply[ing] not judgments but signs of existence' (1997 [1994], 323) led me to enact different registers – critical, affective and speculative. Each is introduced in the preface to each section. The critical register seeks the benefits of abstraction, clear arguments and clarity, yet it is enacted in a way that is a little bit too hyper – over the top and too much – to avoid drawing attention to its own occlusions. The affective engages with the complexity of how ideas and political forms are lived, seeking poetics that can deal with attachments and intensities, and with their fraying and slackening. The speculative creates trajectories for political desires that might otherwise only be fleeting in the present of institutional participation. Playing with these three registers – with their abstractions, proximities and trajectories – is not, it is worth repeating, for describing what has happened, but rather for making it possible for other things to happen.

A note on endnotes. There are more than a few endnotes offered in this book. This is primarily because I accept that experimental academic writing needs to show its workings – especially when you are trying to make specific arguments, as I am. I also want to make visible as many of my debts as I am currently able to fathom, which won't in any way be all of the debts incurred by the life I live. It is also to make very tiny steps in trying actively to reshape my worlds by who I read (Ahmed 2017; McKittrick 2021, 37). I hope it doesn't really need saying, but please do not feel you need to read all the endnotes to get what you need from this book. Follow an endnote when your interest is piqued, you want further discussion around an idea or you feel that something is unsubstantiated and seek more by way of justification. I really enjoy reading other people's footnotes or endnotes. They take you down a side street where the best bar can be found. They let one idea have a room of its own so it can breathe. Endnotes are intriguing asides that draw you into a different kind of intimacy.

Towards the conclusions

While the object I am seeking to loosen is the cultivated, ideological-affective structure of museum constitution rather than museums in their lived variety, the implications for the everyday working of museums do need to be drawn out. In particular, deconstituting museums raises questions such as – can museums be deconstituted and still be museums? What does it mean if we remain attached to the word 'museum' while seeking a different political worlding?

These are questions I take up in the close of Part III and in the conclusions, which also mobilise the book's three registers of critical, affective and speculative. Whether through addressing what this means for museums in terms of their political and democratic design, considering how deconstitution relates to abolition, charting the extent to which my retrained pulse is calmed, the conclusions move towards constitutional unwinding, spinning off and leaning in as momentum gathers.

Notes

1 The pithiest quotes that set up the tensions include Corinne A. Kratz and Ivan Karp: '[Museums] have different and often multiple mandates and complex and contradictory goals' (Kratz and Karp 2006, 1); Robert Janes and Richard Sandell: 'Museums are one of the most complex organizations in contemporary society' (Janes and Sandell 2019, 1); Sharon Macdonald: 'Museums shouldn't forget the great collections of objects that they have accumulated over the years, neither should they forget their public cultural status. Museums are invested with a rather unique and special complex of cultural authority, property and expertise. Perhaps more

than anything, they need to protect this against attempts to cut this down to more limited and culturally impoverished size' (Macdonald 2020 [2002], 259).

2 The existential issue has been noticed by a number of writers. Hilda Hein: 'Today's museums are reflexive and wracked with the anguish of self-interrogation' (Hein 2011, 114); Robert Janes and Richard Sandell: 'Considering these opportunities and challenges, it would be salutary for museum workers to suspend their professional and conventional opinions about what meaningful museum work *is* and, instead, consider what the work of museums *should be* in the early 21st century' (Janes and Sandell 2019, italics original); Sharon Macdonald: 'One of my own most lasting impressions from behind the scenes is of the dynamism, passion and commitment of many Museum staff. This may make them "stubborn buggers" and lead to "factional warfare", as I was warned at the beginning. But it also creates an energy in the place and makes it sufficiently complex and diverse to resist attempts to frame it too narrowly. This excess is its magic' (Macdonald 2020 [2002], 260).

3 I want to make an early mention of Stacy Douglas's *Curating Community: Museums, constitutionalism and the taming of the political* (2017). Given we both use the term constitution, it is useful to set out the differences in our projects. Douglas's focus is to suggest that the museum can be a place that constantly 'disrupts' the 'proclivities' within state constitutions to tell smooth stories about the national community (2017, especially 57). Therefore the core of Douglas's argument is both to see the benefit in the state constitution's role of maintaining shared political norms and to see the benefit in museums' undermining any simplicity at work in the state's constitutional story.

The use I make of the term constitution is therefore quite different as I intend it to describe a political formation at work in museums themselves powered by a deficit to its own ideals.

A deconstituted heritage would offer something that would certainly be an ongoing counter to any desire to tell one national story. So it might be the focus developed here offers something in support of Douglas's overarching argument.

4 Nuala Morse argues '[Museum] [o]utreach workers described the experience of doing community engagement work as often being faced with "black lines", "where things stop flowing". Such black lines express the institutional resistance to community engagement work' (2020, 106). Margareta von Oswald reflects on her ethnographic research at the Ethnology Museum of Berlin: 'being affected helped me to understand curators' difficult position: how emotionally draining it was to engage critically with an organisation while having to defend it, especially one so complex and hierarchical, and the resultant lack of control over the final results, authorship and public communication' (2023, 87).

5 Some people have sought to make a big distinction between participation, co-creation or ideas such as constituent museum. For example, Alistair Hudson argues: 'I have a problem with the idea of being "participatory" because in the art world we often talk about "participatory art", but for me that's "museum 2.0", where you get people to participate in someone else's agenda' (2017). I wonder if this desire to treat participation as if it only describes 'invited', participation in John Gaventa and Andrea Cornwall's terms rather misses why participation has been explosive for museums; such participation can be 'invited', but it comes from a direct democratic genealogy incompatible with the types of representational legitimacy of those institutions doing the inviting. I engage with the idea of self-constituting in Chapter 7.

6 For example, while they recognise that this might be 'an excuse for evading responsibility for responsiveness', Anne Marie Goetz and John Gaventa note a 'tension' between participation and 'impartiality', suggesting the desire to resist 'special interests' might explain the 'enthusiasm of public servants for creating distance and boundaries between themselves and the public they ostensibly serve' (2001, 6). Marian Barnes, Janet Newman and Helen Sullivan argue, based on their work observing various public engagement initiatives, that participatory work tends to 'open up important issues about how a diversity of social groups in a plural polity can be "represented" […] The importance of this question is highlighted by the way in which notions of representation and representativeness pervaded the discourse of both officials and lay members' (Barnes, Newman and Sullivan 2007, 196). An ongoing debate in the literature concerns whether self-interest, or the interest of specific groups or identities, is to be embraced or avoided in participatory process, and whether there is a danger of losing the wider scale offered by representational/public structure which consciously works 'on behalf of' all and for some idea of 'common good' (Phillips 1993, 136).

7 David Bollier and Silke Helfrich – in their treatise on commons and how they might be organised – argue that governance must be freed from its association with government and its characteristics of 'something that a group of people vested with power does to and for another group of people, perhaps with their participation and consent, perhaps not' (2019, 121). Instead they want to recuperate governance as a term to describe an 'ongoing process of dialogue, coordination and self-organization' (2019, 121). To underline the difference between government and the governance they are elucidating they term it 'peer governance'. We will return to the question of participatory self-constitution in Chapter 7.

8 In 2020, after the murder of George Floyd, a number of museums released statements (see Twitter archive curated by @JohannaZS https://twitter.com/i/events/12724883 27984427008). Since then there has been a strong sense of these statements being 'performative' (Dalal-Clayton and Puri Purini 2021, 11). Yet Marquis Bey captures something of what happened to some of us who are white since 2020 and the agenda of Black Lives Matter came into our everyday working relationships: 'I refuse to believe that those white folks or those cis folks or any of those hopelessly normative-identificatory folks who began experiencing tremors in the austerity of (their) whiteness and cisness and identificatory normativity just disappeared. They are still there, thinking and feeling and experiencing the subtle and not-so-subtle tugs of radicality. In other words, they cannot fully put themselves back together after having been fractured. [...] even though the ground has in many ways re-congealed, at the very least, it has not congealed in the same way, and that difference is consequential. That difference means that something else, something new is now possible that was not before [...]' (Bey 2021, n.p.).

9 As Rodney Harrison and Colin Sterling argue: 'it should be noted that many museums would not be innocent victims of [... climate] collapse. The emergence and spread of museums around the world is closely bound up with many of the forces that have led the planet to the brink of climate breakdown, including the separation of human and non-human life; the marginalisation and oppression of Black, Indigenous and minority ethnic peoples; and the celebration of progress narratives dependent on unlimited economic growth. Recent years have witnessed a profound shift in the way museums engage with such legacies, but their underlying logics of preservation, interpretation, curating, education and research remain largely unchallenged' (2021, 9).

10 This played out very strongly in the 2024 US presidential elections and the discussion that has opened up after Trump's victory. The 'threat to democracy' line used in the Democrats' campaign tried to assert the organs of the liberal state as a mitigator and guarantor of democracy. However this, it has been argued, forced the Democratic candidate into defending a status quo that is not experienced positively (e.g. Berman and Rosenburg 2024). For an early account of the UK Labour Party's attempt to learn from this, see Peter Hyman (2024).

11 Throughout the book I have chosen not to capitalise white. This was a difficult decision as the debate on the politics of this choice is still very live. The argument in favour of capitalisation often turns on the need to draw attention to 'white' as intrinsic to all processes of racialisation and racism. I remain very mindful of the argument made by Kwame Anthony Appiah that 'white people don't deserve a lowercase *w* and shouldn't be allowed to claim it [...] Racial identities were not discovered but created [...] and we must all take responsibility for them' (2020). Yet, as racial identities were 'created', our aim – one shared by all those engaged in this debate – is to ultimately undo them and disintensify their power. In mulling this over I often went back to this phrase of James Baldwin's: 'the people who think they are White have the choice of becoming human or becoming irrelevant' (2017 [1984], xviii). To become human – no longer White – I wonder if I have to know myself as *white* in order to stop thinking I am White. My hope is the lower case white makes whiteness visible – after all as the 'unmarked marker' (Frankenburg 1986, 1) whiteness is often not mentioned at all – but without stabilising it as a fixed identity. To extend this argument, the capitalisation of Black relates to the creation of an anti-racist political identity that precisely has enabled whiteness to become more visible as constitutively linked in the process of racialisation. If read in this way, Black needs to be capitalised so 'White' can stop being the dominant unmarked marker. This is why a critical approach to whiteness benefits from both an insistence on the existence of whiteness and its active political effects, while not reproducing 'White' as an identity available either to be overtly taken up by the far right or to fall back into an invisibility that

has been afford by liberal institutionalism. The debate will continue and may come down in favour of capitalisation but this is my thinking as of publication.

12 A term that is getting attention in the conversation about museums and participation is 'solidarity' (Lynch 2020), not least through an international network – of which I am part – called Solidarity in Action, facilitated by Bernadette Lynch and Salma Jreige (Lynch 2023). I don't activate the term 'solidarity' as a political concept in this book, but just would like to add here that solidarity for me means this type of intervention from Moten. That being in anti-racist solidarity as a white person is to understand that race – racialisation – is white people's 'problem' and deep loss, although this is always experienced in much, much softer ways. In other words, solidarity is a relation of how every difference, boundary, cut (an issue, an identity) creates entanglement in the sense elaborated by Barad (2007; 2010). In these terms 'solidarity' is a politics of addressing entanglement – but, I suggest, also one that requires grounding in participatory modes of organising.

13 Ben Spatz draws a strong distinction between practice as a specific instance of something being done and 'technique': 'Technique is precisely repeatable and moreover is not bound to a particular moment, place, or person. Technique is not ahistorical but transhistorical: It travels across time and space, "spreading" from society to society' (Spatz 2015, 41). He makes this case as part of dismissing the idea that 'practice research' is unexplainable and undocumentable. Spatz argues that, on the contrary, technique is a form of transmissible knowledge created through dialogue with a scholarly archive. I might then conceive of what I am doing in this book as developing technique for deconstituting museums through connecting detaching, modulating, organising and participatory wording to their archives (in the form of different academic and practice literatures) – and, of course, through their further elaboration throughout this book.

14 I have worked on a series of collaborative museum and heritage research projects that are being drawn on here. The appendix sets out all these projects.

15 The firm intention not to write 'about' anyone is also reflected in a decision not to use case studies of museum practice, or to gesture towards practice as a way of making points I want to make. I have cited practice where it is published, in whatever way, but what I have not done is to develop my own characterisations of practice based on visits.

16 With my use of 'predicament', I am lightly evoking James Clifford's definition of what he calls the 'predicament of culture' – that is, 'a state of being in culture while looking at culture, a form of personal and collective self-fashioning' (1988, 10). In this case of this book it is a state of being in museums while looking at museums as a process of self- and re-fashioning.

17 It is not uncommon in museum and heritage studies to return both critique and ethnographic complexity to practice. Tony Bennett believes that politics happens in the tinkering (1998, 195) or adjustments (2006, 622). For Laurajane Smith heritage is about the everyday negotiation of these conflicts (2006, 83). Sharon Macdonald is always attentive to the ways in which otherwise 'intractable' political debates can 'within the specific institution of the exhibition [...] be accommodated or even brought productively together' (2023b, 174), encouraging practitioners to see every day wrangling as producing an 'excess' which is museums' 'magic' (2020 [2002], 260).

18 Fiona Candlin and Jamie Larkin report on their attempt to define a museum (2020). Having beautifully worked through the difficulty of definition, they decide museums are 'difference all the way down' (2020, 124). Candlin and Larkin identify three propensities: of 'conservation', 'a change in pace and style from surroundings' and 'public orientation' (2020, 124–5). The three identified propensities both reflect dynamics in museum constitution – perhaps suggesting how connected museum constitution is to museums in their lived realities. However, Candlin and Larkin's focus on treating these propensities as 'difference all the way down' also indicates how each might also offer sites for deconstitution and participatory worlding, as explored here in Part III.

Part I
Museum constitution

Part I – Chapter 1 and Chapter 2 – elaborates the ways in which museum constitution is an entanglement of ideas, principles, political logics of various kinds, everyday practices, attachments and intensities.

Chapter 1 is in critical mode. Chapter 2 is in the mode of affective poetics. The purpose of these two registers is not to make a grand statement which says ta da! 'this is what museums are' as a type of 'instant sociology' (Latour 2005, 50). Rather the aim of the combination of registers is to name and characterise a political formation in ways sharp enough and resonant enough to act as grit to its workings. Grit that slows and stutters reflexes that would otherwise kick in.

Chapter 1 develops an abstracted political map of museum constitution. It does so using a critical register to identify how the inbuilt deficits, tensions and contradictions of museum constitution animate and organise, *as if* it was possible to see this ideological framework outside of its everyday affective life. Influenced by theoretical currents that have sought to describe critique's 'limits' (Felski 2015), the register is somewhat hyper – tonally it is hoped it will feel a bit too much. Striking this tone is a way of drawing attention to the chapter's occlusions, the complexity it has to ignore in order to gain its abstractions. This critical map is *both* too simple, reductive, forced *and* a necessary heuristic in 'loosening the object' (Berlant 2022, 27). It offers satisfactions, but makes visible its own failures. It is not where we start or end. It is a pause, a mode, a mood. Indeed, the main current of this book is that museum constitution cannot be seen without attending to its everyday activation.[1]

Chapter 2 uses affective poetics to explore museum constitution in dynamic movement and to consider the ways in which its 'insatiable' nature (Bennett 1995, 90–2) is powered by *how* it is lived. To know complex dynamics of affecting and being affected and acting and being acted upon (Massumi 2015a, 3; Seigworth and Gregg 2010, 1) is to try and be 'in the middle' (Massumi 2015a, 48, 91), to be in the 'varied, surging capacities to affect and be affected that give everyday life the quality of a continual motion of relations, scenes, contingencies, and emergences' (Stewart 2007, 1–2). Museum constitution is enabled through the urgency and energy at play – the intensities of how the work happens and is done.

The third piece in Part I is International museology I, which explores the changing dynamics of the ICOM Museum Definition. The 2019 draft definition was very controversial. It ended up being scrapped, with a new definition being adopted in 2022. Far from accepting the arguments made against it at the time that it offered a breach from previous definitions, I argue that the 2019 version contained the same late liberal ideological structure, perhaps even more tightly drawn. The difference seemed to lie in how it felt, its tones and textures. In other words, it was affect that made a difference.

Along with the explicit refusal to see my coining of the term 'museum constitution' as a claim to what is 'really going on', I have not used either the definite article 'the' (for it is not stable) or 'a' (for it is never entirely singular). For the purposes of retraining reflexes I hope it is useful to think about the ways in which the ideological structure of museum constitution is always there to be called on, aided by the ways in which it has been given written form in mission statements, codes of ethics and memorable slogans and in the separation and naming of different types of museum work in job descriptions. Crucially, however, I hope it is also helpful to consider the ways in which the conceptual dynamics of museum constitution always need to be energised in order for it to become an 'operative logic', an 'apparatus of capture' (Deleuze and Guattari cited Massumi 2015b, 213). For museum constitution as an 'operative logic' (Massumi 2015b, 209) to exist, it has to 'presentify' itself in every new moment (Massumi 2015a, 147) – and this is something habitual, something beyond conscious and deliberate choice-making (Massumi 2015c, 19–20; see also Chapter 5). In Brian Massumi's terms 'structures of power […] emerge, self-structuring, surfing the crest of outside energies, and they can only perpetuate themselves by diving in and catching the wave again. They have no motive force of their own' (Massumi 2015a, 102). Appreciating museum constitution as ideological structure and affective attachments and intensities is to make it possible to conduct exercises in retraining, working different muscles for greater resistance.

Attending to 'energies', Chapter 2 begins in the 'middle' of things. So – as you turn to Chapter 2 – prepare yourself to find yourself in a museum meeting room, pulse rising, and to end Chapter 2 with the beginnings of participation's affective work, a certain de-intensification and the first stirrings of detachment.

1
Museum constitution, critically

Of course this is too simple. Too clean. Too sharp. Too bright. Simplifications always carry dangers. But there are also dangers in not giving form to the political dynamic of museums: of not appreciating within the complexity, the embroilment and the ambivalences of practice the ideological loops at work in museums, seeking their legitimacy. We need to wrestle from the mess of practice something like an 'operative logic'; to draw onto the page the 'conceptual formula' enlivening, and enlivened by, everyday tensions and conflicts (Massumi 2015b, 212). While museum constitution may be at work in many museums for at least some of the time, museum constitution is not identical to museums, given their lived variety. Therefore, the process of describing and naming museum constitution is – as with this book as a whole – not a simple knowledge claim that museums are *this*. Rather this chapter's purpose is to characterise the political formation in which my reflexes have been trained as an act of retraining, with the aim of throwing grit into the machinery of museum constitution.

Simplifications tend to generate excesses, things left out, things occluded and shadowed by the sorting, the scalpel and the spotlight. Excesses will certainly be one consequence of this tack – and we will tease out some of the 'elusive and chaotic complexity expelled, produced, or suppressed' (Law and Mol 2002, 11) by this chapter's simplification in Chapter 2. Together the first two chapters of Part I evoke museum constitution through two different modes – critical and affective. Each mode is partial and each produces excesses whose weight cannot be entirely picked up and borne by the others' contribution.

Below – in critical mode – is a constitutional mapping relevant to the 'European idea of the museum' (Preziosi and Farago 2004, 1) and especially to those museums that have collections. It can be objected that not all museums have collections, but those that do not are freer of this constitution (Marstine 2017).[2] It is through the production of things as objects, of objects as both singular and representative and of objects as requiring both protection and accessibility, that museum constitution, and indeed a world, has been 'raised' (Latour 1983).

Museum constitution I

Let's start with two specific claims.

> Museums conserve objects for future generations.[3]
> Museums make objects accessible for everyone now.[4]

Each of these constitutional claims has a constituency. 'Future generations' is generally understood as the not-yet born to whom we owe some kind of duty (Burke 2008 [1790], 82; Ruskin 1849, 171). 'Everyone' is sometimes defined very widely and characterised as the public (Duncan 2004, 252; Ashley 2019, 103),[5] nation, society or humanity (Kirshenblatt-Gimblett 2006); sometimes 'everyone' may be all those who live in a specific locality. In contemporary museum practice 'everyone' is often broken down into demographics, but demographics that remain equally abstract.[6] Both 'future generations' and 'everyone' are expansive constituencies, acting as an 'undifferentiated mass' (Hooper-Greenhill 2000, 125) impossible to know and too abstract to be real or specific people. *Therefore 'future generations' and 'everyone' always need to be conjured.*[7]

Museum constitution produces things as objects. It is crucial that these objects are singular. It is also crucial that they are fragile (Holtorf 2015; DeSilvey 2017). In economic terms they have to be 'rival', meaning that use by one needs to affect use by another. The objects must be in need of care and protection. Being both singular and fragile means objects become a non-renewable resource. When paired, these constitutional claims enshrine tensions. A tension between conservation and access and a tension, a conflict of interest even, between future generations and everyone now, as well as between all of us who are here now. *Therefore balances always have to be negotiated.*

To this basic structure we need to add another element.

> Museums represent the world.[8]

A particular contradiction is crucial to museum constitution. While objects are singular they also, and at the same time, have to be able to be used in representational ways. An object has to be able to stand in for other objects, people or ideas – objects have to stand in for the world. Like 'everyone', what is meant by the 'world' also varies. For some museums this is their local area or a specific topic. For other museums it is precisely the 'world' which is evoked. Across these different articulations, however, shared is the sense of something outside the museum that can be usefully understood through a series of techniques of representation on the inside.[9] *Therefore decisions always have to be made about who and what is in the world and how the world should be represented.*

A final element of museum constitution now needs to be added:

Museums shape the world.[10]

The idea that museums shape the world is expressed through claims around education or supporting wellbeing and health as well as claims around democracy, intercultural exchange, combating prejudice (Sandell 2007; 2016) or social or planetary justice (ICOM 2019, cited in Kendall Adams 2019). The nature of these types of claim, their logics of causality and their underpinning political ontologies vary significantly. For some it is through convening an archive that ongoing research can influence the present. For others it is through representing issues or perspectives that people's minds are changed. For others it is through interacting with the museum as an institution that people and society are changed. *Therefore the question of political ontology – between conserving the world, representing the world or reforming the world – is a live, conflictual problematic.*

Museum constitution is animated through claims of this type – claims which are very easy to find in museum definitions, mission statements and codes of ethics, as the footnotes to each claim attest. Crucially, museum constitution is perpetually open to challenge by its own mechanisms, this comprises its 'insatiable' nature (Bennett 1995, 91). Tony Bennett identified museums' insatiability through a focus on the nineteenth-century museum – but the core argument is still relevant to museums in the 2010s and 2020s (Bennett 2006). It remains the case that it is always possible to say that museums are not yet accessible and are not yet representative – but far from claims like these quaking the institution's foundations, it is the ongoing task of dealing with its own failures that powers museum constitution's self-authorisation.

In particular these claims generate three mutually enabling loops forged in deficits, tensions and contradictions. *Deficits* are created through museum constitution being cleverly populated with a fixed, non-renewable resource and 'impossible to realise' intentions and entities so big they can only be imagined. Museum constitution is a political form based in *tensions* that sets up conflicts of interest between constituencies so they have to be endlessly negotiated. Museum constitution is based in a political ontology which sorts and differentiates. It is a political ontology that separates people and objects, distinguishes certain people from other people, solidifies a linear passage from the past via the present to the future and strongly polices the boundary between inside and outside. Museum constitution is also a political ontology in which objects need to be singular, rival and in need of protection while also needing to be able to be put to work representationally. Ontological differentiation and *contradictions* are generated, and then managed, in ways that secure agency for the museum.

On behalf of

It is precisely through the elements of insatiable deficits, irresolvable tensions and ontological sorting and contradictions that the key political structure of museums is secured – that of working and making decisions 'on behalf of' others. The circuits of museum constitution self-authorise the claim that museums make decisions 'on behalf of'.

If there were no ideals that always needed to be redeemed, if the institution was not characterised by a fixed and non-renewable resource of collections and representational space, if there were no competing abstract consistencies whose interests were placed in tension, if there was no contradiction between singularity and representativeness then there would be no need for museums' trustee and professional governance.

Museum constitution is, therefore, representational in both political and epistemic senses. Museum staff work 'on behalf of' abstract entities and ideals, just as objects 'stand in for' other people, places and events (Lynch 2020, 6). Museum constitution is a political form that thrives on abstraction and self-generated political contest, which always circles political attention and energy back centripetally towards museums' reform. Constant inabilities to fulfil the deficits created by its own objects and ideals or to resolve its intrinsic tensions and contradictions are the motor of museum constitution's continuity.

Museum constitution II

In order to unfold the mechanisms at play in museum constitution's constitutive dissonance, let us now connect the sketch above to allied circuits identified by theorists of modernity and late liberalism. In particular: Elizabeth Povinelli's 'cunning of recognition' (2002), which sensitises us to the transactions bound up in the deficits created by institutional representation and inclusion; Brian Massumi's unfolding of the tensions that abstract political constituencies create between representational and direct democratic logics; Bruno Latour's 'modern Constitution' (1991) that underlines the contradictions at play in the ontological work of modernity's political forms. Each describes 'loopy' political logics (Massumi 2015b, 241), energised by their inbuilt deficits, tensions or contradictions.

Deficits

Povinelli's 'cunning of recognition' at work in 'late liberalism' (Povinelli 2002; 2016; 2021) sensitises us to the spatial logics of inclusion. Inclusion creates a centre and, through defining a centre, defines what is important. Museum constitution does this both through creating collection objects and the space and time of representation in exhibitions as fixed and non-renewable resources – making inclusion both in theory endlessly expansive and welcoming and in practice a competition. The other aspect of late liberalism's spatial imagination is the way in which universal ideals and norms such as inclusion, human rights and equality operate as a 'horizon'. These ideals are so ideal that they are not achievable as such, and so always require renewed effort. The effect of the 'horizon' nature of these ideals is, Povinelli argues (and as noted in the Introduction), 'to bracket all forms of violence as the result of the unintended, accidental, and unfortunate unfolding of liberalism's own dialectic' (Povinelli 2018, n.p.).

The bracketing Povinelli describes helps us locate museum constitution as a particular expression of late liberal logics. Museum constitution is a never finished – or finishable – task. Whatever museums have done (in terms of colonial violence) or have not yet done (in terms of addressing colonial violence or achieving inclusion) is suspended in the present through the horizon of that-which-is-always-being-worked-towards. The horizon of late liberalism allows museums both to acknowledge past exclusions and institutional violence and yet nevertheless to see the institution, precisely through our labour of recognition and inclusion, as a vehicle of and for transformation. The idea of a centred, valued and fixed non-renewable resource, and of insatiable horizon ideals, enshrines the sense of 'never enough'. There will never be enough resource to go around freely – whether in terms of access to collections or space in the galleries. Resources conceived as being fixed and non-renewable will always be used to conjure up a need for institutional management to make decisions 'on behalf of' abstract constituencies. There will never be enough access, representation or inclusion. Its ideals will always invite endless demands and will always produce institutional mediators to take up the task.

Tensions

In his exploration of Abraham Lincoln's Gettysburg phrase 'of the people, by the people, for the people' (2015b, 209), Brian Massumi shows how its formulation activates different, expansive and conflicting political tendencies within its 'part-concepts' (2015b, 214).[11] At play is not only an abstract ideal of unity, '*of* the people', but also a mechanism by which some of 'the people' become separated from that unity so they can act '*for* the people' on their behalf *as if* it is done '*by*' them' (2015b, 209–10). Each part-concept constantly questions and unsettles the legitimacy of the other, where 'by' implies 'a direct democracy without organs of representation' (2015b, 210); and where 'for' firmly evokes the 'on behalf of' logic of representational democracy and therefore always raises the question of how some people become able to act on other's behalf. The effect of this is endlessly to require political labour:

> The conceptual formula is 'problematic' precisely in this sense: as an abstract matrix for the practical production of problems on an ongoing basis. This is the actual 'continuity' that will become an unfolding riven with tension, driven by the tension's working out, cut into by conflict every step of the way. (2015b, 211)

The 'practical production of problems on an ongoing basis' is the basis of museum constitution. Its insatiability, its unresolvedness, is museum constitution's motor as it 'agitates abstractly in the interval, for a return to unity' (Massumi 2015b, 209–10). The ongoing production of problems is there in the enshrinement of conflict between the claims of conservation and access and their abstract constituencies. It is also there in logics of inclusion which appear generous while also creating conflict over resource (collections; time and space). The tensions have only become greater as participation and its direct democracy ethos are added to museum constitution's representational logics, constantly producing conflictual questioning over the issue of who should decide.

Contradictions

Bruno Latour coined the term 'modern Constitution' to describe a rigorous separation between nature and culture, between things and people, between non-humans and humans and between knowledge (science) and power (politics):

> a way of organizing the division [...] between appearances and reality, subjectivity and objectivity, history and immutability. (2010, 447)

Through this political ontology, the modern Constitution creates a flexible political ontological structure where two positions are in paradoxical contradiction. On one side 'nature' is '*a res extensa* devoid of any meaning'; it is there to be used, exploited and constructed. Museum-wise, this side of the modern Constitution enables objects to be raised up out of life and used to stand in for and to represent other issues, people or places (see Peter Vergo's 'contextual' exhibitions (1997, 48)). Yet, on the other side, nature in Latour's modern Constitution – or objects in museum constitution – are also 'the ultimate reality' (2010, 477), transcendent and determining what is possible as if without the mediation of science and scientists' (or curators and interpreters in the case of museums) (Latour 2010, 477; see also Wynter 2003). It is this aspect of the modern Constitutional dynamic which creates objects as singular, enables objects to 'speak for themselves' (Hooper-Greenhill 2000, 49; see Vergo's 'aesthetic' exhibitions (1997, 49)).

When channelled through museums, it is this contradiction – and the need for it be in constant negotiation – that dictates a whole institutional structure based in trustee and professional 'on behalf of' decision-making. In these ways, Latour argues, the modern Constitution – which can easily be extended to the museum iteration and its contradictions – is 'a rather neat construction', enabling the class of people whose agency is forged in European modernity 'to do everything without being limited by anything' (1991, 32).

Museum constitutional circuit

As already cited in the Introduction, Massumi considers 'operative logics' of this loopy type as 'quasi-causal': deficits, tensions and contradictions work to 'fold back into the potentializing matrix and inflect its coming expressions. They co-operate in the energizing of the process' (2015b, 216). To map museum constitution 'loopiness' (Massumi 2015b, 241) in ways connected to other allied late liberal and modern circuits is also to notice its intended political trick. Museum constitution makes it possible for museums to try to deal with any new politics in terms which are activated and enabled by its own constitutional claims and logics.

In particular, museum constitution's deficit to its ideals produces a fixed and valued centre. It seeks to turn politics of whatever kind into a demand for greater access, inclusion or representation so that it can be managed through the constitutional circuit. The 'cunning' of museum constitution is to place different and always abstract constituencies in tension (future generations, everyone now and between everyone now) in ways that guide political energy centripetally, looping it back towards 'on behalf of' decision-making. The contradictions of the constitutional dynamic mean that objects can be seen to be put at the service of access, representation and inclusion while also – to evoke Latour – requiring museums to be structured in certain ways that hold people at a distance, through producing and mediating competition over fixed and rival resources. Museum constitution is always energised by the rough and tumble of critique and its deficit to its own ideals. It is always creating the potential for energy produced through everyday contest to be circuited back in and reincorporated.

To this critical mapping I want to add a note to myself for the ongoing retraining of my reflexes – a note that will be picked up in Chapter 2. *It is in response to these deficits, tensions and contradictions that my reflexes are triggered. It is because I/we respond that museum constitution is kick-started and renewed.*

Museum constitution III

Let's now develop further the mapping of museum constitution. In each of the sections that follow I will tether fragments related to the three domains pointed to by Povinelli, Massumi and Latour: the deficits of the inclusion ideal, the democratic tensions between representation and participatory political forms and the implications of contradictory modern political ontologies. Each fragment drawn into this mapping holds an insight that is undeniably of use, included not because any given fragment is accepted wholesale or treated as 'correct', but because they add grit of different consistencies into the machinery of museum constitution.

The deficits of the inclusion ideal

While appearing to be an endlessly welcoming value, it is through the ideal of inclusion that a centred, valued and non-renewable resource is created. It is through the need for this centred and valued resource of access and recognition to be managed fairly that different types of people are generated.

To our sketches in museum constitution I and II we now need to map in a series of fragments. All are concerned by the ways in which access, representation and inclusion can be understood as terms that create subjecthood and distribute agency.[12] Crucially, the insights we draw on help us notice that the type of subject generated for museum workers *seeking to include* co-produces through the same move a different type of subjecthood for those *being included*, based in the perception of their deficit (a deficit of empowerment; a deficit of representation) (Naidoo 2016, 511).[13] In her critique of the ways in which museum participation has operated, Bernadette Lynch refers to this as a 'beneficiaries' model' (2011a, 7; 2020, 6). In so doing Lynch highlights the ways in which participation not only creates a class of people who are 'benefiting' but also, crucially, a class of people who become the enablers of benefit.[14]

To add grit to the machinery of museum constitution we urgently need help in unseating any residual sense that the differentiated subject positions produced through practices of inclusion are benign, and to perceive their roots in the long-established and violent differentiation that has characterised modernity. Sylvia Wynter's work on 'coloniality of being' has argued that the production of certain humans as the 'political subject of the state' – the category she terms 'Man' – arose through also producing a less-than-human 'subhuman' subject in ways that generated and relied on 'race' as a political concept (2003, 263). Denise Ferreira da Silva shows how a post-Enlightenment 'knowledge arsenal' derived from 'nineteenth-century scientific projects of knowledge [...] institutes racial subjection as it presupposes and postulates that the elimination of its "others" is necessary for the realization of the subject's exclusive ethical attribute, namely, self-determination' (2007, xiii).

In terms of recent museum practice, we might reflect on the deficit thinking at work in the desire to say that 'Museums Change Lives', in the words of the UK Museums Association's Awards. In the phase 'Museums Change Lives' it is clearly 'museums' that are self-determining, their work being to influence and improve those perceived to be lacking. While in any given project so awarded we can be sure that there will be many other dynamics at play not captured by this phrase and its logics, the required differentiation in subjecthood in the phrase 'Museums Change Lives' echoes with the nineteenth-century idea that museums and other forms of cultural activity could 'act on' people in ways that enable them to self-govern better (Bennett 1995; 2006).

The dynamics of the 'cunning of recognition', Povinelli argues, require those 'being-included' (those judged otherwise to have a deficit of self-determination) to take up the burden of speaking on already fixed terms:

> *Tell us your cultural and social values. Just don't tell us anything that will actually threaten the skeleton of principle which gives the body of our law its shape and internal consistency*. This doublespeak double bind of recognition – this revised horizon of the Human – marks all others as having been let in. This mark genders and racializes the bodies of all excluded from the horizon of whiteness. (Povinelli 2018, n.p., italics original)

We might recognise in Povinelli's argument about the late liberal state in general the ways in which museums in particular invite difference to be spoken as a condition of inclusion – all the while requiring a significant tailoring of what can be legitimately said and, *through the act of inclusion itself*, solidifying the speakers' positionality as 'other' (see Fouseki 2010, 184; Waterton and Smith 2010, 11; Boast 2011, 67). Wendy Brown has noted the 'paradox' at work in assertions of rights or representation, as any such assertion 'entails some specification of our suffering, injury, or inequality' which can 'lock us into the identity defined by our subordination, while rights that eschew this specificity not only sustain the invisibility of our subordination, but potentially even enhance it' (2000, 332; see Tinius 2023, 167).[15]

In being represented in museums there is therefore a potentially risky transaction at work – that in being recognised, represented and included you might be required to tell certain stories and that these stories may come to define who you are, figured through a 'logic of contribution' (Morse 2020, 30). It is useful to keep in mind the idea that through these transactions difference is generated and managed as part of institutional continuity.

Resonant with Wynter and da Silva's insights, Barbara Kirshenblatt-Gimblett shows how differentiated forms of subjecthood are created through the UNESCO Masterpieces of Oral and Intangible Heritage where – as already cited in the Introduction:

> World heritage is predicated on the idea that those who produce culture do so by dint of their 'diversity', while those who come to own those cultural assets as world heritage do so by dint of their 'humanity'. (2006, 183)

While difference, or diversity, might be what makes you a producer of heritage, it is the subject of an *un*marked (white) humanity that will manage and govern it – precisely because it is no longer only on your behalf but everyone's and future generations (see also Naidoo 2016, 506; Smith 2006, 11, 19; Harrison 2020, 25).

Taken together, these clusters of memorable fragments map detail into the ways in which museum constitution acts as 'social triage' in Bennett's terms, 'sorting people into different groups and arranging these hierarchically – [this has] always operated along racialised as well as class lines' (2018, 186).[16] The grit these insights offer to the workings of museum constitution is an appreciation of the ways it needs continually to produce new articulations of exclusions in order to remain continually in the process of working towards inclusion, being redeemed and creating museum workers as redeeming subjects.

In recent decades exclusion and inclusion have morphed from an association with more classic modern ideals of equality and human rights via a culturally relativist twist that now includes terms such as 'diversity' and 'plurality'. Not only are continually renewed articulations of exclusion needed for museum constitution to be kick-started increasingly, as Jasbir Paur has put it; evocations of '"difference"' act to produce 'new subjects of inquiry that then infinitely multiplies exclusion in order to promote inclusion' (Paur 2012). One of the earliest articulations of difference and plurality in museum studies can be found in Eileen Hooper-Greenhill's 'post-museum', where she contrasts the modernist museum with a new type of museum where 'many voices are heard' (2000, 144) and 'histories that have been hidden away are brought to light' (2000, 145). While the hope has been that these characteristics of the post-museum offer a completely different political basis to the 'modernist museum' (Hooper-Greenhill 2000), questions have been raised concerning the means by which 'difference' and 'plurality' are produced and sustained. As David Scott argues:

> The possibility of seeing *all* difference as merely and fundamentally *relative* depends upon an omniscient epistemological vantage from which (and of course in relation to which) all difference is simultaneously available to a detached, surveying gaze which itself is *not* relative. (Scott 2003, 104–5, italics original)

Or, in Ghassan Hage's words:

> White multiculturalism requires a number of cultures. White culture is not merely one among those cultures – it is precisely the culture which provides the collection with the spirit that moves it and gives it coherence: 'peaceful coexistence'. Here again, however, for exhibitory purposes this time, left to themselves 'ethnic' cultures are imagined as unable to coexist. It is only the White effort to inject 'peaceful coexistence' into them which allows them to do so. (Hage 2012, 161)

Scott and Hage enable us to hold in mind that the newer right to govern 'difference', 'diversity' and 'plurality' may be reserved just as actively as the right to govern the interests of 'future generations' and 'everyone'. As long as there is an institution deciding on the acceptable extents and expressions of plurality and managing the fixed and non-renewable resource of exhibition space then, whatever the affordances of plurality, it is unlikely to operate much differently to inclusion.[17] A lot of hope has been placed in adding diversity or plurality to museums, but the constitutional circuit serves to produce another all too similar task of governance in which some types of people sit above plurality and organise it and others are required to produce themselves as 'diverse' and 'plural' in acceptable ways (Boast 2011; Macdonald 2023b, 187). Through these critical fragments we might usefully piece together a warning. Plurality cannot be added to a representational 'on behalf of' political structure or to a representational ontology where objects and stories 'stand in for' without in turn reproducing representational logics and looping back into inclusion.

So far this section has drawn on a variety of thinkers to suggest that inclusion produces us as differentiated subjects with differentiated types of agency. We will end this section with a small gesture towards Karen Barad's 'agential realism' (2007; 2010), with the hope it will indicate how this section's critical engagement with inclusion might open us towards the relational ontologies that are the focus of Part III of this book.

For Barad entities ('things', 'people', 'animals') do not exist prior to their interrelationship; rather, entities are produced through their intra-action. These intra-actions produce cuts, agential cuts, that in turn produce separability. Rather that this being 'separability' in the everyday sense (or, as we will see, Newtonian sense) of completely riven, Barad names this 'agential separability' which holds together both difference and entanglement – what they term a 'cutting together/apart' (2010, 244). In other words, the means by which difference is produced also produces, through the same process, entanglement. For Barad entanglement is not 'a name for the interconnectedness of all being as one, but rather specific material relations of the ongoing differentiating of the world' which 'are relations of obligation – being bound to the other – enfolded traces of othering' (2010, 265). When thinking of access, representation and inclusion in museum constitution, and exploring the differences and entanglements they produce, we might simply note for now that when the project ends, the objects are returned, the labels taken down and the consent forms filed away there is no final end to the matter – no clean cut.

A note to take forward to Chapters 2 and 5: *the desire to say you need to be included and I will be your includer produces an ongoing obligation to the 'other' that was created in the same cut that created 'you': a political and ethical task that can never just be 'finished'.*

Democratic tensions

In Massumi's activation of the phase 'of, by, for' a tension lies in how a small part of the whole ('of') comes to act on behalf of the whole ('for') as if the whole of the people are governing ('by'). Massumi's crucial point for institutional practice is that this tension between participatory and representational democratic impulses produces everyday problematics. Through the mapping of museum constitution, we can see this tension in everyday museum work into which participatory practice has been added. We perceive that there is an ongoing negotiation between – on the one side – the right of the professional and trustee to act 'on behalf of' future generations, everyone, the public and visitors, all produced through the dynamics of museum constitution, and – on the other – the idea that groups of people, deriving their authority from experience, can act in and with museum resources on their own behalf. Grit offered up to the machinery of museum constitution comes from noticing that participation adds a different set of political logics to the representational loop that defines museum constitution.

The consequences of both representational and participatory modes of legitimacy being practised in the same institution at the same time can be traced through two strands of ongoing debate – found both in the museum literature and in the wider, cross-disciplinary participatory research literature. Both point to participation's failure in museums.[18] Both serve to question any sense that participation can be the answer to greater access, representation and inclusion.

A key cluster of debate has revolved around whether the depth and extent of involvement in any given participatory endeavour is meaningful. This concern arises from the political genealogy of participation where the purpose is for people to come together in self-determining ways (Pateman 1970; 2012). Following Sherrie Arnstein's 1969 classic article on the 'ladder of participation', pursuing the question of depth has led to the proliferation of ladders and scales of participation (e.g. Simon 2010; Jubb 2018). A key issue articulated through a concern with depth is whether participation is just manipulation – the bottom rung of Arnstein's ladder – or whether significant power is handed over.[19] In museums a concern with depth has been predominant, with criticisms of 'tyranny' (drawing on Bill Cooke and Uma Kothari's edited collection in Development Studies), 'beneficiary' models and 'empowerment-lite' (Lynch 2011a), as already mentioned, as well as a growing number of case study examples of where decision-making was not in fact ceded (e.g. Fouseki 2010).

Another cluster of critique has formed through a push back to participation related to scale of impact. This concern arises from logics of representational legitimacy. This tendency has been concerned with whether participation supports 'public service' in terms of values of equality, fairness and balancing out sectional interests. It also remains anxious about whether the groups involved are just the loudest voices, often termed 'the usual suspects' and therefore not representative. The scale critique is concerned by the very small numbers of people involved and is sceptical that participation has made much impact on addressing inequalities in the demographics of who visits museums or in museums' wider role in social change (O'Brien 2019, 140). This concern arises more in everyday debates in museums than it does in the academic/policy literature, although Mark O'Neill has been consistently making this case (2006; 2012; O'Neill, Seaman and Dornan 2019).

Both these significant concerns about participation in museums – depth and scale – are often expressed in relation to museum constitution and its ideals (access, representation, impact) and constituencies (everyone). In both cases what is often being judged as lacking – whether in terms of depth or scale – is efficacy in making change. For example, failed representation in an exhibition might be attributed to a lack of shared decision-making (depth), or the persistency of the exclusive class and race profile of most museum visitors might be pointed to as proof of the failure of participation to bring about wider transformation (scale).

In the wider participatory research literature, concerns over lack of depth have led to specific work on facilitation (the skills to address inequalities and design collaborative decision-making) (Burns 2007; Dick 2021; Mackewn 2009), on power analysis (Gaventa 2021) or on means of linking individuals, communities and systems (Burns 2007). Yet while some of these techniques have been brought over to a museum context, both depth and scale remain hard to achieve because of the pervasive hold of abstract constituencies and of the 'on behalf of' representative rational of museum constitution.

Typical expressions of how the 'on behalf of' representative rational in museums prevents depth of participation include:

- not wanting to give special access/use of collections to a specific group because of the wider commitment to conserve for public and future generations (Smith and Waterton 2009, 11);[20]
- justifying editing text/controlling interpretation in participatory exhibitions in terms of the quality of visitor experience or curatorial reputation (Kassim 2017; Lynch and Alberti 2010, 23; Lynch 2020, 5; Morgan 2013, 165);[21]
- feeling greater duty to the abstract and more numerous 'visitor' over a small number of passionate volunteers;
- problematic of asking a community group to act 'on behalf' of a wider demographic group, which serves only to prompt institutional anxiety about that group's legitimacy (Fouseki 2010, 181);
- a sense that museums need to provide balanced views or offer neutrality rather than a platform for a group to self-express (Murawski 2017);
- use of projects (and especially photos of projects) to show that the museum is 'representing diversity' (over any sustained commitment to participatory governance);[22]
- turning all political issues into exhibitions and therefore into representations to be then constrained by professional interpretation standards and visitor needs.

Equally in the wider participatory literature the importance of participation and scale is well recognised. However, the logic of 'scaling up' has tended to be replaced with 'scaling out' (Burns 2007; Burns, Howard and Ospina 2021) or the need to increase 'scope' horizontally (Gustavsen 2017; Gustavsen, Hansson and Qvale 2008; Gustavsen and Qvale 2014).[23] In museums 'scaled-out' approaches are hard to achieve because of the constitutional logic of collections as fragile and scarce resources.

Typical ways in which museum constitution limits the potential of museums deploying a scaling-out logic include:

- approaches such as handling collections or school sessions with reproductions that are seen as 'not real';
- anything that happens without a collections link is questioned with 'why are we the right people to do this?';
- a strong preference for museum-to-many communication (large exhibitions, large events, public opening);
- work related to scaled-up initiatives being higher status and scaled-out workshops being lower status.

It is in these ways that participation remains stuck in relation to museum constitution because it never allows either depth of devolved power or scaling out. Another way of describing the everyday instances in the inset boxes above are as the point where participation meets the representational machinery of museum constitution. Museum constitution has come to desire participation as it appears to be a means of energising its ideals. However, museum constitution always bundles participation up in its endless looping. Having invited in participation, museum constitution then delegitimises participation through a reassertion of its own representational logics of legitimacy.

A note to take forward to Chapter 2, Chapter 5 and Chapter 7: *the catch has been that participation has brought much more with it than can be entirely reincorporated by museum constitution. This is true not least in the different logics of legitimacy, which generate its 'affective work'.*

Paradoxes of modern political ontologies

Latour's modern Constitution elaborates the political effects of single container modernity: how humans and non-humans are separated so that certain humans can claim dominion over nature while also claiming nature's transcendence, in ways that only shore up that same human agency. In museum constitution – as the mapping of fragments of Latour's modern Constitution has already shown – there is an allied productive paradox in the way objects are treated both as open to being used in representational ways and also as being singular, in peril and therefore dictating an entire governance structure.

Latour's argument is that the paradox of purification of humans and non-humans actually enable hybrids of nature and culture, directing 'our attention simultaneously to the work of purification and the work of hybridization' (1991, 11). In museum terms this suggests paying attention to the various ways in which the purifications of the political ontology of museum constitution – the separation of people and things, the past from the future and the inside from outside – enable hybrid combinations of humans and objects, as well as of spatial and temporal logics. For example, we might pay attention to how the museum constitution's conflicting requirements are navigated in hybrids such as the display case which materialises a negotiation between conservation and access (Graham 2016). As Latour puts it, 'museums have never been modern, either'. He adds that 'no one has ever been modern, so museums have always maintained an extraordinary diversity of approach, always mixing art and science and antiquity in some way' (Latour in Latour and Franke 2010, 86). The museum studies ethnographic literature abounds with examples of hybridity in excess of normative purity, offering much to our work of retraining reflexes (see Macdonald 2020 [2002]; 2023a; 2023b; 2023c; Morgan 2013; 2018; Geoghegan and Hess 2015; Candlin 2015; Candlin and Larkin 2020).

Museum constitution – and Latour's modern Constitution – can be understood as based in a Newton ontology, in the terms expressed by Karen Barad. This is the world as associated with 'metaphysical individualism': the idea 'that the world is composed of individual entities with individually determinate boundaries' and 'representationalism', the concept 'that representations and the objects (subjects, events or states of affairs) they purport to represent are independent of one another' (Barad 2007, 134, 55, 28). As set up in the first sketch of museum constitution above, museum constitution relies on the separation between people and things, the ability to separate inside and outside, the perception that time is linear and that things can represent – that is, stand in for – other things. Drawing on quantum physics, Karen Barad's 'agential realism' offers an ontology where 'primary ontological unit' is not time, space, the individual or the object, but rather phenomena which are 'constitutive of reality' (2007,

139, 140). What this means is that reality is phenomena. 'Reality is composed not of things-in-themselves or things-behind-phenomena but of things-in-phenomena' (2007, 140). Phenomena, crucially, are 'intra-actions' that are not between already existing entities (whether people, certain types of people, or things), but are the means by which subjects and objects are created, how boundaries between inside and outside are produced and how different agential possibilities are enabled. Through this process what Barad terms 'spacetimemattering' (2007, 179) happens. The grit that Barad's thinking introduces to museum constitution is to see how the intra-actions its political formation requires are not reflective of a reality but productive of it – making people and things as different, making the idea of both singularity and representation possible and generating an inside and outside.

Other grit we might throw to make museum constitution stutter comes from Walter Mignolo and Catherine Walsh who – in their advocating of a pluriversal world – argue that 'Western thought is part of the pluriversal. Western thought and Western civilization are in most/all of us […]' (2018, 3). They therefore advocate:

> transcending rather than dismantling Western ideas through building our own houses of thought. When enough houses are built, the hegemony of the master's house – in fact, *mastery itself* – will cease to maintain its imperial status. Shelter needn't be the rooms offered by such domination. (2018, 7, italics original)

In place of Western ontology Mignolo and Walsh draw attention to 'the resurgence and insurgence of re-existence today' that serves to 'open and engage venues and paths of decolonial conviviality, venues and paths that take us beyond, while at the same time undoing, the singularity and linearity of the West' (2018, 3).

Re-existence from Mignolo and Walsh's theories of decoloniality helps us to consider the ways in which museums have been institutions of de-existence, coloniality, extraction and white infrastructure (Hicks 2021). Povinelli has argued that the horizon of liberal ideas and of reform is implicated in the temporality in which climate change is often discussed: it is often seen as a coming catastrophe that can still (just about) be prevented. In contrast Povinelli argues that the catastrophe has already happened. It is an 'ancestral catastrophe' (2021, 18),[24] formed in the extractions of colonialism and enslavement. The aspect of museum constitution that keeps in play the idea that there is a continuity future within which objects can be conserved and accessed, representation and inclusion achieved or that catastrophe can be averted is a repetition of the constitutive deficit of the liberal horizon. In Povinelli's words: 'No liberal violence seems large enough to shatter liberals' ability to slough it off by acknowledging they had made a mistake but are now back on track, leaving in their wake endless worlds that know the eternal return of this trick' (2021, 147).

Finally, I want to nod to Mieke Bal's classic article 'Telling Objects', which indicates why, in spite of its deeply representational logics, museum constitution may still desire participation. In her engagement with James Clifford's 'On Collecting Art and Culture' (1988), Bal notes that the very ontology of modernity – creating 'the separation between subject and object […] makes it impossible for a subject, caught in the individualism characteristic of that separation, to be part of, or even fully engage with, a group' (Bal 2004, 91). This in turn produces 'an incurable loneliness' that leads to the urge to collect (2004, 91). We might perhaps add, as grit to museum constitution, the sense that after having collected, loneliness has only persisted – making us seek not only people to be with but also, as I will argue in Part III, a more participatory way of being with things and being in the world.

A note to take forward to Chapter 5: *This modern, Western, colonial ontology that renders us different from each other and from objects, that detaches the past and future from the present and creates boundaries of inside and out, creates a sense of loss – an unarticulated loneliness that doing participation only makes more palpable, sometimes painfully so*.

The critical as grit

The critical has special import in retraining reflexes as museum constitution is itself fuelled by critique. It is the deficit created by horizon ideals that requires a constantly renewed unveiling of museums' failure and hypocrisy that drives museum constitution. My use of a critical voice has been in pursuit of the looped nature of museum constitution, which is itself looped through critique. Critique tends to be driven by the belief that power can be revealed through ideas of 'exposure' (Sedgwick 2003, 138) or 'unveiling' (Latour 2010). As such it has been named 'paranoid' (Sedgwick 2003, 131), 'the hermeneutics suspicion' (Ricoeur, cited in and developed by Felski 2015) and a mode of knowing that is 'never surprised' (Latour 2010; see also Sedgwick 2003, 130). Eve Kosofsky Sedgwick draws attention to the 'reflexive and mimetic' nature of critique – the ways in which it is just as loopy as the late liberal dynamics of museum constitution: 'Paranoia seems to require being imitated to be understood, and it, in turn, seems to understand only by imitation' (2003, 131); '[critique] sets a thief [...] to catch a thief' (2003, 126–7). Critique is, Sedgwick suggests, 'anticipatory', explaining that 'paranoia requires that bad news be always already known' (2003, 130).

Yet for the purposes of this book the kind of conceptual clarity critique offers is useful, precisely because it introduces 'vigilance, detachment, and wariness' (Felski 2015, 3) into the habituated late liberal cycle described above. Indeed, having engaged with incisive explorations of the 'limits of critique' (Felski 2015), far from running from critique entirely I have come to the conclusion that I need it in certain doses and at a certain strength. Truly I do need a little paranoia when it comes museum constitution, because of my endless surprise at how I get drawn back in.

While critique might imply that it has access to what is 'really going on', in my case I use it as a temporary choice, not a final pronouncement. Its claim to 'distance' is something I only want a little of too. The 'distance' I seek is less a false and dangerous 'god trick' (Haraway 1988, 581) and more that sprinkling of grit, micro- and shifting-distances, to slow down and disturb the dynamics of museum constitution as it is lived. Sedgwick's intention in describing critique as paranoid was not to suggest it was never useful, but rather to challenge the ways in which

> paranoid inquiry comes to seem entirely coextensive with critical theoretical inquiry, rather than being viewed as one kind of cognitive/affective theoretical practice among other, alternative kinds. (2003, 139)

There are great benefits in treating critique, in Felski's terms, as *a* thought style, formed of certain kinds of 'rhetoric and form, affect and argument' (2015, 2). What I have sought to do in this chapter, and with this book's critical mode more generally, is to treat critique as just 'one kind of cognitive/affective theoretical practice' (Sedgwick 2003, 128). In this vein, critique is just one of this book's three modes. Foregrounding critique as a register or style, I deliberately play up critique's aesthetics and formal qualities. I've sought to find a tone for this which is a sort of hypercritique, taking what critique can offer but in a way that is tonally a bit too much not to draw attention to its costs, its expulsions and the excesses that have had to be pushed aside for such statements to be given written form. In this tonal choice I am very heavily indebted to Bruno Latour.

Latour has regularly drawn attention to his version of this dilemma. His stated intention – both in *We Have Never Been Modern* (1991) and a string of publications since – has been to challenge critique. Yet while doing so he also – as have I – draws, no question, on critical techniques and, notably, tone.[25] It could be said that in Latour's work the hypercritical style always points back towards the complexity at work in modernity, the 'hybrids' meshing nature-culture which enable the purifications of 'modern Constitution'. In this sense naming modern Constitution or the dynamics at work in critique shifts attention. For Latour this is a 'suspension of the critical impulse' which creates 'the transformation of debunking from a resource (the main resource of intellectual life in the last century, it would seem), to a topic to be carefully studied' (2010, 476).[26] However, there is also something in Latour's style and register that is significant. The way Latour writes feels like a sort of acceleration, a doubling down, a speeding up in the hopes of spinning the paradoxical circuit of modernity off its axis. It is a way of doing critique which bears its own occlusions.

I have done my accelerated hypercritique through a light use of the concept of mapping. Maps make claims to represent the world, of course, and to be good enough representations that they can act as guides. The most available relationship between critique and the map is linked to the idea that critique can show what is really going on and that certain modes of representation can give better, more clear-sighted access to reality. Yet if this is the 'strong theory' claim of what Sedgwick calls paranoid critique – to be 'capable of accounting for a wide spectrum of phenomena which appear to be very remote, one from the other, and from a common source' (Tomkins cited Sedgwick 2003, 134) – my version is faux-strong and deliberately weaker. It has marshalled fragments and patched them together. But it has shown its joins, undercutting itself. After all, it is only one of the mappings of museum constitution on offer in Part I of this book.

In a representational ontology there is a mapper and the world which exists in advance of the map. In a full-throttle critique, its charismatic purveyor always has clean hands. The maps I make are never just representations of a reality 'out there'; they arise from messy, implicated, dirty and uncharismatic embroilment in the world. And the process of producing them has, I can only hope, changed this mapper. I am seeking to produce myself differently through mapping and for the mapping to make this more so, to keep me changing, recursively. This chapter has been not so much a representation as a 'performative presentation'; 'rather than being simple go-betweens tasked with re-presenting some pre-existing order or force', I hope this map and the map in Chapter 2 possess 'an expressive power as active interventions in the co-fabrication of worlds' (Anderson and Harrison 2010, 14).

What we have gained through the critical is some hope now not to be caught up in the same way, but to have a nameable thing to hold at greater arm's length, making the most of slivers of distance created by critical grit. What we have lost through this chapter's use of the critical trajectory is, for the most part, how museum constitution is lived. And how it is lived is everything. It is, after all, why it has been necessary to try to name this ideological loop, because the loop never exists in abstract – even here. On the contrary: it reignites because we want it, desire it and need to be needed through animating it. The map is of, and is always returning to, the living of it.

Latour argues that critique '"ran out of steam" because it was predicated on the discovery of a true world of realities lying behind a veil of appearances' (2010, 474–5). In this chapter, while I have used a critical voice I have set this up as a form, an aesthetic choice for a purpose. This is a crucial distinction because the naming and mapping of museum constitution doesn't unveil, of course, a really 'real' reality nor any kind of privileged access. Through the process of mapping, the veil has swung up, down and around like a faulty theatre curtain. Yet all that can be glimpsed 'behind' is the excess, the close up and messy particulars, always undercutting the clarity of critical abstraction. Glimpsed there is me – and maybe you – sitting in strip-lighted meeting rooms, pulses rising, getting fired up and increasingly, in spite of ourselves, kick-starting museum constitution yet again.

Notes

1 David Scott in *Stuart Hall's Voice*, written after Hall's death in 2014, writes in an imagined letter to Stuart Hall: 'Contingency, therefore, is a way of thinking with determinacy and indeterminacy without being trapped by a reductive idea – a closed form – of *determination*. It is contingency that calls into play the strategic necessity of political action. If you take contingency seriously you are always obliged to ask yourself – and others: Where are we now? What are the questions that present themselves? Are we in a new conjuncture, a new configuration of the present? If you take the idea of contingency seriously, you will be encouraged to think and act politically, as you famously say, "without guarantees"' (2017, 60, italics original). Scott also draws out the difference between practice in Hall's work and action in his work, where Hall's 'practices' are about 'contingency attuned to openness' and Scott's action 'is contingency attuned to finitude' (2017, 60). Both orientations within contingency figure in Chapter 2 when I draw out the affective poetics of museum constitution.

2 This distinction between those museums with and without collections has been noted by many in terms of the politics of museums, but including Janet Marstine in her exploration of 'critical practice' (2017, 117). Marstine acknowledges that 'new institutionalism … developed primarily in non-collecting galleries' but adds that 'the next generation of discursive institutions … which evolved in museums with permanent collections' show the possibilities

for the 'use of collections as generative tools to reflect on institutional histories and imagine new possibilities for reconciliation in the present and future' (2017, 117). Yet – as is argued in later sections of this chapter – access, representation and inclusion as political logics do in any case produce a late liberal loop, even without additional museum constitutional elements of collections' scarcity and evocations of posterity. Almost every contemporary public institution is likely to be caught up in some way with the 'cunning of recognition' identified by Elizabeth Povinelli (2002).

3 The concept of *conserving objects for future generations* appears in various international museum codes of ethics. Museums are said to 'preserve ... the natural and cultural inheritance of humanity' (ICOM 2017). Museums 'maintain and develop collections for current and future generations' (Museums Association 2016). Other examples include: 'Once accepted into a given collection, will be maintained in optimum conditions, protected by good record-keeping and security systems and held in trust for the public and/or on behalf of iwi [a Māori term which describes a tribe or people]' (Museums Aotearoa 2013). Museums hold 'collections in custody ... serving people, both present and future generations' (Alliance for American Museums 2000) as part of 'the trust of stewardship' (Canadian Museums Association 2006 [1999]).

4 The second plank of museum constitution – *museums make objects accessible to everyone now* – is equally clearly expressed in museum codes of ethics. 'Museums ... should ... use collections for public benefit' and 'actively engage and work in partnership with existing audiences and reach out to new and diverse audiences' (Museums Association 2016). 'Museums have an important duty to ... attract wider audiences from the community, locality, or group they serve' (ICOM 2017). 'Provision is made for maximum public access to collection items' (Museums Aotearoa 2013). 'Museums serve society by advancing an understanding and appreciation of the natural and cultural common wealth through exhibitions, research, scholarship, publications and educational activities' (Alliance of American Museums 2000). 'Museums seek to be public focal points for learning, discussion and development, and to ensure equality of opportunity for access' (Canadian Museums Association 2006 [1999]).

5 Susan Ashley, in her exploration of the many dimensions of publicness in the Royal Ontario Museum, noted that there remained an idea of 'the "public"' which 'was thought of as patron or audience or client, in all cases people targeted with institutional selling more so than knowledge-building dialogue or collaboration' (2019, 102). It is the of abstract idea of public – as Ashley describes – that is core to museum constitution.

6 Hooper-Greenhill hoped that the new science of visitor demographics would shift away from treating museum constituencies and audiences as a 'undifferentiated mass' (2000, 125). Since then a range of different demographic approaches has been trialled, ranging from socio-economics to the motivation demographics of contemporary museum practice e.g. 'Metroculturals' or 'Trips and Treats' (Audience Spectrum n.d.). While I can see why this would have appeared to be a step away from the abstract totality of 'everyone' or 'the public', in practice each of these demographics is equally abstract and requires the same techniques of representation in practice. After all, each demographic is also made up of so many people it cannot be known or represent itself. Furthermore, these sub-demographics can also simply be activated as being in conflict with one another, just as future generations and everyone are in conflict in museum constitution. While conflict between demographic groups may be operating at a more refined level, it is nevertheless very much in keeping with the loop of self-authorising logics in-built in museum constitution. For example, 'enthusiasts' might be pitted against 'family day outs' as if their interests are in conflict and requiring mediation and balancing. In basic terms, it is always worth thinking who is gaining agency from claiming to speak on behalf of an abstracted grouping.

7 In Michael Warner's terms *public* is never specific people, but rather a necessarily abstract idea; it is a 'social totality' and a 'relation between strangers' (2002, 55).

8 The third dynamic I have drawn out in museum constitution – *museums represent the world* – is also very visible in museum codes of ethics in terms of questions of accuracy, bias, integrity and diversity of focus. Museums 'should [...] provide public access to, and meaningful engagement with, museums, collections and information about collections without discrimination' and 'ensure editorial integrity in programming and interpretation' (Museums Association 2016). 'As well as collecting the past, collections policies look to the future and consider the increasing plurality of Aotearoa New Zealand' (Museums Aotearoa 2013).

'Taken as a whole, museum collections and exhibition materials represent the world's natural and cultural common wealth. As stewards of that wealth, museums are compelled to advance an understanding of all natural forms and of the human experience' (Alliance of American Museums 2000). Museum 'presentations should endeavour to represent the multiple perspectives held by different groups in a fair and impartial manner; when museums do present a singular viewpoint, this bias should be made clear to the public' (Canadian Museums Association 2006 [1999], 11).

9 The interest of museum studies in the 1990s and early 2000s with museums' representativeness was noted by Donald Preziosi and Claire Farago in the introduction to *Grasping the World* (2004). They note that 'the general concern has been with teaching museums to become better representatives of a wider (multi)cultural world. Yet virtually all of the recent literature treats this concern as if it were a classic map-territory problem of representational adequacy. ... They invariably share a fundamental thesis – that a museum is primarily a representation, an artefact as "natural" as the "specimens" it preserves, rather than an institution for the construction, legitimization, and maintenance of cultural realities. A principal corollary of this assumption is that representational "adequacy" consists of a *synecdochal* (a part standing in for the whole) relationship between an exhibition's contents and a wider world of cultural objects and social practices. And, conversely, the assumption that an exhibition could represent that wider world in a meaningful way has been the prime justification for taking objects from the settings for which they were initially made and reassembling them for study and contemplation. These assumptions justify the institutional framing of objects as *specimens*' (2004, 1–2, italics original). While the conceptual challenge with the call for greater representation has now had more than 20 years of critical attention, it has not waned in policy, practice or even that much in museum studies.

10 The fourth dimension of museum constitution is the principle of impact and efficacy – *museums shape the world*. Though this aspect of museum constitution finds less clear expression in codes of ethics than it does in other policy documents, not least the ICOM museum definition debates (see International Museology I) and in individual museum missions. However, in codes of ethics it is expressed in these terms: 'Museums are public-facing, collections-based institutions that preserve and transmit knowledge, culture and history for past, present and future generations' (Museums Association 2016). 'Museums have an important duty to develop their educational role and attract wider audiences from the community, locality or group they serve' (ICOM 2017). 'Museums make their unique contribution to the public ... to advance knowledge and nourish the human spirit. ... They are organized as public trusts, holding their collections and information as a benefit for those they were established to serve' (Alliance for American Museums 2000). The idea of museums shaping values is widely expressed in the museum studies literature (e.g. Sandell 2016).

11 This is a phrase that has developed new currency in museum practice through the 'Of, By, For, All' project led by Nina Simon, author of the 'Museums 2.0' blog that brought participatory practice to a wider audience in museums (Of/By/For All n.d.).

12 'Distribution of agency' is owed to Tony Bennett, who has described his concern as being 'with the distribution of new forms of agency across the relations between museum and field, metropolis and colony, colonizer and colonized, scientist and subjects, and collector and collected' made possible by 'these entanglements' (2018, 206).

13 Roshi Naidoo draws attention to dangers of a political ontology that reinforced ideas of inside and outside: 'The inside/outside paradigm may appear to be a pragmatic means to facilitate good work in the sector, but by serving its own, mostly unspoken, agenda it can ensure that the cultural heritage of outsiders remains outside. It often prevents exploring the centrality of the politics of difference and the exclusionary "whiteness" of the cultural heritage deemed to be normal or mainstream. It also releases the inside of its obligations to interrogate the role the outside plays in the formulation of the inside' (2016, 511).

14 The question, as Craig Clunas put it in his essay on Chinese collections in British museums, 'of who gets to represent what to who' (2004, 471).

15 This form of recognition has also found compatibilities – Jasbir Paur has argued – with the adaptive operations of Western-style national states, where women's rights and gay rights have been used as rhetorical resources in the war on terror – what Paur calls 'homonationalism' (2007) – or the ways in which the disability movement's claims for (some) disabled people's

rights to self-determination have become alibis for the creation of a classed and racialised social care workforce predicated in precarity and what Paur has termed 'debility' (2017).

16 The interest in nineteenth-century museums adds an important element to making sense of the contemporary phenomenon of museum constitution. We could add to our map Tony Bennett's account of the purpose of taxonomy in nineteenth-century museums. Bennett positions the 'exhibitionary complex' as part of the 'machinery of modernity', creating a 'space of representation' which constructed a 'temporally organized order of things and peoples' which was 'totalizing … metonymically encompassing all things and all peoples in their interactions through time'. Crucially its representational economy 'organized the implied public – the white citizenries of the imperialist powers – into a unity', conceived as the 'just beneficiaries' of the 'processes of evolution and identified as a unity in opposition to the primitive otherness of conquered peoples' (1995, 80; see also Clunas 2004).

17 Richard Sandell, for example, argues for museum cultural authority to be secured precisely by curating acceptable difference. Sandell writes: 'It might be argued that the inclusion of multiple perspectives serves to strengthen the museum's authority claims especially when the opinions, however diverse, evidence a normative consensus and, in doing so, offer a more powerful endorsement of the museum's overarching messages' (2007, 193). While Sandell wants to suggest an interest in unresolved difference, he does also advocate consistently for a predetermined framework of acceptable expression within which unresolved discussions can be contained. He further argues: 'adopting and seeking to engender support for a particular vision of the good society, one that draws on concepts of justice and equal human rights, need not preclude the accommodation of different perspectives and the deployment of interpretive techniques designed to elicit and value visitors' diverse opinions. There are ways of constructing exhibitions which avoid moralising didacticism, which open up rather than close off possibilities for debate but which nevertheless offer ethical parameters within which conversations about difference can take place' (2007, 210). This obviously then requires museums to take up this authority and set 'ethical parameters', which in turn shores up professional authority.

18 Failure in cultural participation projects has been a focus for Leila Jancovich and David Stevenson (2023). Jancovich and Stevenson very usefully challenge the culture of policy and funding which leads to pointless celebratory narratives and prevents 'social learning' processes (2023, 46). In the context of my argument I would note how failure is a necessary outcome of late liberal use of participation because it continues to drive the redemptive hope that things can be different in future – this is how late liberal organisations organise political energy and are endlessly renewed. In a way *Deconstituting Museums* and the conversations I have had with all the people in the acknowledgements over the years is my own little social learning process leading me to believe the only way to change the terms of failure is to stop doing participation in relationship to late liberal frameworks of access, representation, inclusion and diversity.

19 For David Jubb the scale they were convening for the Co-Creating Change Network was not to say 'that one position on the scale is better than any another. Because work and partnerships exist for different reasons and can be successful in very different ways', but nevertheless a scale 'might ensure that when we are debating and developing practice, we can be clearer about whether that practice exists in the same territory or not' (2018). This has been a very helpful intervention.

20 Laurajane Smith and Emma Waterton have the following 'direct message' for 'professional workers in the heritage sector': 'You are a community, but just one community of interest among many others. Once we cut through the rhetoric of custodianship and stewardship and the authority accorded to expert knowledge by society in general and government and the state bodies in particular, experts in the heritage sector are just another community with an interest in the past. The different is they get paid for it, and define themselves, and their careers, by their engagement with the past, but their interest in it is no more, or less legitimate, or worthy of respect, than anyone else's' (2009, 11). Smith and Waterton's message is powerful in part because professional ethics often tend towards being sceptical of other 'special interests' (Introduction see n.6).

21 Jennie Morgan offers an example of how exhibition text becomes a focus for negotiation between teams over the museum priorities. The example isn't related to a participatory exhibition, but nevertheless reveals the back and forth around language: 'The learning and

access curator desired words that would be understood by the imagined visitors; scientific exactitude was important to the natural history curators; and the editor was concerned with issues of style and clarity' (2013, 165).

22 Nuala Morse gives an example shared by an Assistant Outreach Officer: 'In the meeting a manager exclaims "How can we get the Yemeni community involved with this?" and turns expectantly to the Assistant Outreach Officer and says: "Just run off some digital stories with the Yemeni community". And I remember saying to my line manager, I don't understand what they want us to do? There isn't a Yemeni community sitting in a room waiting for me to say "let's do some digital stories!".' Morse comments: 'This (mis)perception of communities "waiting in a room to be engaged" or be "magic-ed up" was felt by the team as a significant barrier to recognising community engagement work as it negates the practices required to build up relationships and bespoke projects with communities, not least the requirements of time' (2020, 88).

23 On 'scope', Bjørn Gustavsen argued that 'The point is to make the cases talk to each other and bring the participants to form networks that can encompass a continuously growing number of participants and networks until a general impact built on experience can be achieved' (2017, 109).

24 Povinelli described 'ancestral catastrophe' in the following way: 'The ancestral catastrophe is not the same kind of thing-event as the coming catastrophe, nor does it operate with the same temporality. When we begin with the catastrophe of colonialism and enslavement, the location of contemporary climatic, environmental and social collapse rotates and mutates into something else entirely. Ancestral catastrophes are past and present; they keep arriving out of the ground of colonialism and racism rather than emerging over the horizon of liberal progress. Ancestral catastrophes ground environmental damage in the colonial sphere rather than in the biosphere; in the not-conquered earth rather than in the whole earth; in errancies rather than in ends; in waywardness rather than in war; in maneuvers, endurance, and stubbornness rather than in domination or resistance, despair, or hope' (2021, 18). The crucial implication for museums might be that their ontology is collapsing because of their ontology.

25 Latour has a little moan about this in 'Why has critique run out of steam?': 'I have written about a dozen books to inspire respect for, some people have said to uncritically glorify, the objects of science and technology, of art, religion, and, more recently, law, showing every time in great detail the complete implausibility of their being socially explained, and yet the only noise readers hear is the snapping of the wolf's teeth' (2004, 232).

26 Or, more recently, Latour has pointed to acts of 'composition', to assembly, to compose, to construct rather than deconstruct: 'compos[ing] the common world from disjointed pieces instead of taking for granted that the unity, continuity, agreement is already there' (2010, 485).

2
Museum constitution, affectively

In the museum meeting room pulses start to rise, knowing something must be said.[1] What needs to be said is expected. It is factored in. It is required by job descriptions saved in shared HR files. It is required by the specification of skills and commitments that were responded to in the job application, and already evidenced by the examples of how the job might be done that were given in the interview.[2]

Yet to say something still feels like something.[3] To know that you need to ask *variously*, who isn't here? How is this going to work for? Should we work with? How will decisions be made?

Or it is to say *variously* … that can't work; they can't touch that; that's not in the conservation plan; it can only be on display for …; it's getting too late, we need these forms to be filled in now.

To say these things can come with a flicker of righteousness, a gathering of intensity. Like the belly uptick of half-reading a news article on the train about a government policy on refugees. Like listening over breakfast to a government spokesperson reciting a list of what they have done to alleviate food poverty, tonally provoking an already embedded suspicion that they don't care. Like the cauldron-habit of reading your bubble of social media.[4] A flicker that has colour, texture and depth, articulating with films where what is good is certain, known and triumphs, and when, without intention, tears roll in the cinema dark, brushed away before anyone sees. Or else owned up to, shuffling along the aisle towards the exit, with embarrassed irony. Genre: Romantic, in its own way.[5]

Factored in and mapped in though it is, something does still need to be said. It still needs to be made something in the present of the meeting.[6] Sometimes it can feel good, desirable, as though it is the right thing, 'righting wrongs', your 'alibi' for all the museum has done and still does (Spivak 2004, 523). It can feel better afterwards because it is done.

Sometimes the eye contact in the room can be warm. What is said can be acknowledged, even received well – it was expected, after all, and, after all, it did need to be said. Sometimes eye contact is avoided and a memory of past disagreements in a similar vein balloon, then recede.

Then, after the meeting, what happens tips over. Huddled in the corner spots in open plan offices. In the kitchen, if no-one else is there. On the corridor back stairs, if that's the only option. Coalescing. They didn't say that, did they?[7] A moment is spent pondering motivations or perhaps a shared meta-analysis of why a person or team does-what-they-do and says-what-they-say is tweaked. Then someone adds a note of *trying to be constructive* and energy wanes. Fed if not nourished, meeting rooms are returned to, to try again.

***

Hanging there somehow always ready to be grasped and enrolled at any moment is what might be thought of as museum constitution:[8]

- Museums conserve material culture for future generations
- Museums make material culture accessible to everyone now
- Museums represent everyone and the world
- Museums shape society and the world

Never making an appearance coherently or as a whole, it is always fragmentary, sutured in the sociality of the moment, always a 'creature of affect' (Massumi 2015a, 102). Yet it is there ready in part because it has been written down, it has been read, the connection between ideas has been formalised and rehearsed, it has been enshrined in codes of ethics, it is expressed in museum mission statements, it has been sloganised in straplines.

The claims can come in, capturing, channelling and organising the trajectory of a conversation, and it is renewed through being so enrolled. Museum constitution is that mix of pulse, language and format, surfing the meeting. It appears as something is forming, as something familiar is becoming at stake. Where the roles people had agreed to play on their 'conscription' (Scott 2004) become activated, with some fighting for access, for representation, for a social role for the museum, and others concerned with the impact on objects and what is needed to show care for them, and therefore for future generations.

It offers those caught up a moment of clarity, a major chord that can be played out of the messy minor.[9]

It draws everyone together in contest, organises attention, structures focus in ways that mean that tension is sustained and distributed. Different people are employed to do different roles, pulling hard at each end in ways that absorb energy, leaving little for any other 'vector' (Grossberg 1992, 196).[10]

Tumbling are excesses of different kinds. Excess that legitimises the quantity of the investment, that through *how much* you care the commitment is justified (Grossberg 1992, 397). And excess that can't quite be circuited back into the constitutional loop, but defines it just the same, marking its boundaries, cohering what it is by what it can't contain (Massumi 2015a, 103).

But museum constitution, coming in as it does, makes the endless tension – museums' seemingly split mission – into a shared song.[11] Like any song sung out loud, different parts are taken. There is always someone forgetting the words, someone who is out of tune, someone rushing through heading for a middle eight and someone wishing they weren't there (Gregg and Seigworth 2010, 11).[12]

***

Sometimes it has been agreed that you go out and develop a community project. That is your job, after all, and you had said that it should be done, you said it was needed and you had said that you wanted to do it.

Bumping into another member of staff, you tell them where you are going and feel that motive righteousness flicker once more. All the while knowing righteousness never burns as cleanly on the outside, in the doing.

On the bus – or maybe you cycled – something circulates as background positivity, a rhythm, a beat. Like what you want here, what has brought you here, is freedom to just be with, a becoming-with. Like you always want dancing in packed dark to be, and sometimes is. Like dancing sometimes is in films and on television, *in it*, no narrative, no plot, no characters. Potential.

You want that, *to just be with*, but know it will not only be you there. The museum is coming with you. Having sought to use this very encounter to make yourself an alibi for the museum's culpability, you know now you don't have any kind of alibi as you knock on the door – it is your knuckle landing on hard wood.

The door to someone's home is opened, and you try and work out whether to take your shoes off.

Or you are ushered into the ongoingness of a day centre.

Or it's after hours in a community café, quiet and spent.

In some past you might have felt like the museum professional codes of ethics you read and signed up to would offer you protection in moments like these – *if the rules are followed (if you find yourself able to follow the rules)*. The impossible ethics of the public service ideal in the time of the participatory turn – to build relationships free of personal obligation.

Even now, it might be that as you irritate every interaction with subtle modes of *being professional* that separate you from those not so bound that, without entirely meaning to, you accept the promise of this protection. Yet all the time you know *that this protection against personal obligation will always fail*.

First there's small talk. Though at some point your body gives off some signal you've been trying to conceal. That slight change in energy, leaning out of the chat and towards, as you know you need to take responsibility for moving the conversation on to the matter at hand, on to the reason you walked through those doors. Sometimes you do this well. The flow is maintained, it can feel OK, good even. Sometimes it clunks, heavy, and you catch and have to carry that weight. But not only you. Power manifests tangibly in clearly uneven ways. You need something from them which you want to take back. You are offering something which they may want, though *what* is often hard to define, even when you both try. And even in the flow of the good iteration, a lurking thought – maybe it shouldn't feel good.[13]

Another time, awkwardly, you slip out the consent form. Kind of casual and knowing it can't be as it needs to be a performative moment so the 'partnership' can be passed back through the museum gate. The slightly staged fumbling over pens, slipping in a micro-personal failure in disavowal of the moment. Have you got a pen? (though of course you have brought one and know exactly where it is). All that is, has been and will be relationally turned into a line in the sand.

Sometimes, going back through the door of the museum or as you go back into the strip-lighted meeting rooms, you know you 'will have been wrong' (Povinelli 2002, 33). Always not on the right side of ethics, while always claiming that you are. Always taking responsibility for others in relation to others, without ever quite knowing if this is being responsible or patronising. Always saying we're not therapists or social workers, while never quite saying, 'no, but never just equals either'.

Always motored by your need to be needed – by the institution, by your collaborators. The insertion of yourself in this political tension, a career built on managing this need, this contradiction, by owning it, taking it up as your own, wearing it as well as possible.

Sometimes you have found something almost pleasurable in this. Your implication can almost be enjoyed, tapping into genre-tragedy.[14] That you will never have anything but grubby hands. The sense 'that well-intended human purposes often have unintended consequences' (Scott 2014, 800). That you are caught in 'a maelstrom of perpetual disintegration and renewal, of struggle and contradiction, of ambiguity and anguish' (Berman 1982, 15). Like walking home in the November dusk, songs about loss and *keeping going* playing on your headphones. Like the structure of feeling of the closing scenes of much-missed television programmes from the 1990s. A tragic not-righteousness that draws things together.

***

Righteousness died on your lips once, as you were in the moment of channelling, of becoming captured and conscripted. Gone from sweet fuel to the kind of bad taste that lingering longer at first can be forgotten but that returns unbidden, familiar, as the energetic constitutional pull fires up and as those same words, structured in that way, appear again. Yet differently now.

You are out again. Taking with you a string of terms, jostling. Each on any given use flooding the scene with memories, books, people, policy. The words are: Access. Inclusion. In recent times also Plurality. Diversity.

You put plurality into play, the idea of lots of different people's stories. Lots of different cultures. It feels OK to say. Other people maybe come back with 'representation' or 'recognition', but your newer word hangs too. You've let it drag in an aura of relativism, or you hope it has.

Conversations unfold.

Sometimes all discussed is possible. It feels strong, the right thing. No contradictions seem to appear. Then what is discussed feels not-right. Anxiety rises, wondering how to move from here back to there. Reasoning and affect 'are out of joint' (Povinelli 2002, 5).[15] Tolerance's limits have been touched.

You stutter in your grafting of plurality onto the liberal horizon. Your role outside or above this plurality suddenly spatialised concretely. Your public duty to govern acceptable difference now far too palpably achieved through 'a detached, surveying gaze which itself is not relative' (Scott 2003, 105).

Things start to rhyme with phrases recently heard as you now find yourself not editing but policing (Saad 2020).[16]

You bristle as someone makes a claim on you personally – and you notice yourself bristling; the kind of interference that creates the tarnished comfort of re-established distance.

Sometimes you can still see the good, the power of recognition in a public sphere. But sometimes the burden of self-representation is too clear, the consequences of this public act definitely personal.

... And someone avoids the form filling.

... And personal objects coming in for the exhibition, supposed to be parcelled up in acid-free paper, paperwork signed in advance, are defiantly dropped in reception. The phone rings. Come down, I am here now.

Perhaps what we are doing is not that important.
Perhaps it is not pleasant to think about.
Perhaps there is too much at stake to look at it straight.

Your whiteness has started to vibrate in every encounter, disclosed to you in real time as it was not before as words and phrases rewrite parts of you in the living (Hafeez 2021; Sarah 2021; Shaffi 2021; Zahoor 2021). Holding enlightenment in your gut newly in-digests as a bad feeling, telling you something is wrong. Drawn in Different D.

Sometimes this figures as ambivalence. Mixed. 'Drawn in many directions, positively and negatively charged' (Berlant 2022, 27). Calibrating the different intensities, combining and hybridising with other forms, doing different things, never under control.

Exceeding tumbles desires and ideas over the edge of the constitutional loop, leaving a political-affective remainder.

Slackening happens. You find yourself playing the same roles, but less intensely. You say your lines with conviction, but less. You care, but less so; you are less likely to be caught up in the drama, dialling back the melodramatic to some other genre form. A bit flatter.[17] Certain things become harder to say. You might find yourself in a meeting where you know what you should say but can't. Or a word once said confidently can't be any more. Or you try, but you stumble over the familiar script, adding a texture to your role-playing others can't fail to notice. Or maybe they don't.

Sometimes there is *accelerating*, a certain recklessness cultivated by the distance now in the relation. A doubling down on your preferred side of the constitutional equation, spinning the looping off its axis.

You feel it first tipsy, not paying attention. A making eventfulness. But it can become something else more considered, with a deliberate foot down, seeking escape velocity.

Trying happens if an impasse is felt. Some mode that hasn't given up, but can't be fired up. Just hard; definitely no romance and not even in a tragic way, neither righteous nor not-righteous. A keeping going after-belief has waned. More endurance than event (Povinelli 2011). Not committed to reform, nor revolution. No goal. But neither any sense of joyous emergence. Uncertain if this can take us anywhere but stolidity in keeping going.

Turning uses the distance in relation differently to reorientate – neither the bristly gap created by professionalism nor the righteousness of needing-to. 'In-difference' (Gordon 2018, v). Turning tries to vibrate the caughtness to expand the 'elbow' room **not** *for* 'against' but *for* 'for' (Harney and Moten 2013, 147–8). A holding open for something else.

Even in those too-bright, airless museum rooms, something else can sometimes happen, until.

Deeply desired, although you can't plan for it or will it into being. In some interval uncaptured and not-channelled. An opening up where a future emerges colourful. Ideas feel new and fluidly change shape in the back and forth of shared, joyful making. Feels like life while it's happening. Whole political designs in potential are conjured and crumble in those intervals.

And it can tip, becoming looped back, just like that. Channelled, re-conscripted upticking righteous for a moment as something else is left over. The sort of relief that never satisfies.

Affective as grit

This was the earliest writing that I did that made its way into the final version of this book. The writing process was methodological. It started with a desire to make sense of why my pulse rose as it did, and still does, even as I also felt a slackening in my desire. The first sentence acted as a prompt and became a way of re-entering all of those meeting rooms where I felt, and made, responsibility flow towards me as I took the museum's accessibility and representativeness on as my own, again and again. The writing form that arose from these experiments – this sense of being caught up and circling round and around – allowed me, as I read more widely (Povinelli 2002, 2021;

Massumi 2015b; Latour 1991), to conceptualise museum constitution as a loop or a circuit.

The section that has knuckles landing on hard wood is a return back again and again to those moments in participatory projects which are existential and tinged with shame. You don't know why you are there or exactly what you want or what you are asking of people. Seeds that can become heeded and can grow into a different way of being in the world, as will be proposed in Part III.

The second person – the use of 'you' – just happened in the experimentation phase, but it stuck. It now offers a way for me to give myself a talking to and as a way of creating a dialogically bound type of distance, a type of distance that is not 'outside' or 'above'. If you find the text interpolating your 'you', then so much the better.

It was after some early attempts at poetics that I became able to connect what I was doing more deeply with affect theory and could then discern Berlant's notion of attachment at play – which I then amplified in redrafting. How calling myself to answer requirements of access, representation and inclusion had given me purpose and fire, drawing me out into the world in a certain way, righteous and panicky. Drawing me out in ways which produce differentiated agency. A reflex through which I have positioned myself as *doing the right thing*, taking responsibility for the institution and its reform.

As I tried to pay attention to how my pulse continued to rise, even when I did not actively want that righteous role any more, it took me to theorisations of habit and reflex. Being called by museum constitution was not a conscious choice. Somehow, I came to think, my body-mind has been trained and, over time and 20 years of different job roles, trained itself to respond. A reflex through which, before we even quite realise what we have done, we become characters in a familiar modern story, styling ourselves as protagonists. It is this reflex that kick-starts museum constitution. It is a righteous reflex, an individualising sugar rush.

I've long had Grossberg's definition of affect in terms of *how* and *how much* in mind, and had felt the variability of quality and quantity in those marginal places: kitchens, stairs, toilets, on the way home. The sense that there was an urgency that then lessened, and with it activated different textures. As I generated text, which was then edited to create what you have read above, I also came to notice the other affects of tragedy, of *going on*, the affective structure that romanticises the perpetual ups and downs of life, dark nights, rain and sad songs. It became possible to think that there might be an affective phasing within museum constitution that organises modern genres, in the senses of David Scott (2014) and Lauren Berlant (2011). It became useful to the process of retraining reflexes to consider the ways in which museum constitution loopiness not only produces the righteous hit of starter fuel, but also kicks over through romantic tragedy of fighting the good fight and, inevitably, of never quite succeeding.

Of course, the impetus for writing this partly came through the slackening I felt, a disintensification that slowed the circuit or at least stuttered it. It was through writing and reading that I can now think of moments of slackening as offering an affective basis for techniques; techniques of detaching and modulating. Both detachment and modulating as techniques are explored in greater depth in Parts II and III. But the roots of detachment and modulating were in this chapter's writing, which helped make more palpable what it might mean if you tried to stutter the way you call yourself into being and experience intensities differently.

Editing the writing drafts to be more condensed and stylised acted as affective grit to museum constitution, to complement the critical grit of Chapter 1. My pulse can't rise in the same way now I've written about it like this and read it aloud in public – and found it was possible to meet people's eyes during and afterwards.

The hope is to generate a strong enough form – just as with the critical in Chapter 1 – so I might recall phrases and formulations, and take a breath as pulses rise, then to try out detaching and modulating as techniques rather than as passing moods.

Notes

1 This opening is to enact the classic definition of 'affect' as 'to affect and the ability to be affected' which are, Brian Massumi argues, 'two facets of the same event ... There is an affectation, and it is happening in-between. You start with the in-betweenness. ... You start in the middle, as Deleuze always taught, with the dynamic unity of the event' (Massumi 2015a, 48).

2 I am interested here in the institutional histories of how we are sutured affectively in any present moment – how technologies of governance (such as job descriptions or performance management objectives) make you expected to do and say certain things. In this I have in mind Ben Anderson's characterisation of 'a body's "charge of affect"' being 'a function of both a series of immediate encounters and the geo-historicity of the body – the manner in which capacities have been formed through past encounters that repeat, with variation, in the habits, repertories and dispositions of bodies' (Anderson 2014, 85).

3 Perhaps you might hear in this phrase Sara Ahmed's dinner table: 'Someone says something you find problematic. You respond, quietly, perhaps. You might be speaking quietly, or you might be getting wound up, recognizing with frustration that you are being wound up by someone who is winding you up. However she speaks, the one who speaks as a feminist is usually heard as causing the argument. Another dinner ruined' (Ahmed 2012, 62).

The odd thing about the institutional tables of late liberalism is how this is both expected, even required, and yet there is still so much at stake personally for those who take up this task.

4 The reference of cauldron calls in Elizabeth Povinelli: 'National subjects find that no matter the heroic rhetoric of enlightenment understanding, "their ways" cannot cease to make "us" sick. And this sickness scatters the self (I, us) across contrasting obligations to public reason and moral sensibility. It is this cauldron of competing social impulses that interests me, because of the way it generates new ethics and metaethics of national and international social life' (Povinelli 2002, 5).

5 In Hayden White's account of the narrative tropes through which history came to be written in the nineteenth century, romance played a significance role. Romance for White celebrates the 'triumph of the good after trials and tribulations' (White 1973, 9). David Scott – drawing on and extending White's arguments – has noted the significance of romance to post-colonial imaginations: 'They have tended to be narratives of overcoming, often narratives of vindication; they have tended to enact a distinctive rhythm and pacing, a distinctive direction and to tell stories of salvation and redemption. They have largely depended upon a certain (utopian) horizon towards which emancipationist history is imagined to be moving' (Scott 2004, 7–8). The romance lies in the task not being easy, in the encountering of resistance, in the need to conjure up energy and determination, but with an expectation of a happy ending. That the good and the righteous will prevail.

6 For Massumi: 'The term "immediation" is a way of drawing attention to the event as the primary unit of the real. The idea is that whatever is real makes itself felt in some way, and whatever makes itself felt has done so as part of an event. It has entered in some way into the immediacy of the moment as a factor in the event now taking place. This means, paradoxically, that whatever of the past is going to count in this event has to presentify itself' (Massumi 2015a, 147). I wanted to enact this process of 'presentifying', this work of making something 'real'.

7 Lauren Berlant talks about tracking 'the waning of genre, and in particular older realist genres (in which I include melodrama) whose conventions of relating fantasy to ordinary life and whose depictions of the good life now appear to mark archaic expectations about having and building a life' (Berlant 2011, 6). There remains something very melodramatic about institutional life. To be prepared to be caught up in some ways in the melodrama is part of being invested in the social dynamics of the institution. Museum melodrama (given all the built-in tensions) is a necessary dimension of museum constitution. Once we start to care less why another team in the museum does this or that, we might be able to have care for other people and things – and in different, less melodramatic ways.

8 A number of endnotes in Chapter 1 situate these four museum constitutional claims in a variety of texts, ranging from museum definitions to museum mission statements and codes of ethics.

9 For Erin Manning: 'The major is a structural tendency that organizes itself according to predetermined definitions of value. The minor is a force that courses through it, unmooring its structural integrity, problematizing its normative standards' (Manning 2016, 1). So to evoke the minor here is to draw on Manning's attentive interest in that which organizes in predetermined ways (major) and in that which unmoors (minor).

10 With 'vector', I am leaning on Lawrence Grossberg: 'The affective individual always moves along different vectors. Its mobilities are neither random nor subjective; like the nomad, it carries its historical maps (and its places) with it; its course is determined by social, cultural and historical knowledges, but its particular mobilities and stabilities are never entirely directed or guaranteed. The affective individual is both an articulated site and a site of ongoing articulation within its own history' (Grossberg 1992, 126). The evocation of vector here is to signal the very strong map offered by museum constitution.

11 I am thinking here of Lauren Berlant: 'Nor is the overdetermination of feeling that we call ambivalence only a relation between antithetical tones; to the contrary, the tones belong together like vocal cords in disharmony with themselves' (Berlant 2022, 10).

12 I want to find a mode which might capture this multiplicity. I had in mind Melissa Gregg and Gregory Seigworth: 'Affect is persistent proof of a body's never less than ongoing immersion in and among the world's obstinances and rhythms, its refusals as much as its invitations' (Gregg and Seigworth 2010, 1).

13 Or. as Stefano Harney and Fred Moten put it, 'There are lots of people who are angry and who don't feel good, but it seems hard for people to ask, collectively, "why doesn't this feel good?"' (Harney and Moten 2013, 117).

14 David Scott's target in exploring the capacities of tragedy for the post-colonial moment was the romantic, as introduced above, as the 'predominant mode of emplotment of the anticolonial and radical postcolonial imaginaries' (Scott 2014, 799). The tragedy arises from the 'dramatic confrontation between contingency and freedom, between human will and its conditioning limits' (Scott 2004, 135).

15 Elizabeth Povinelli draws attention to the lived contradictions of liberalism: 'In moments like this, persons face most starkly the fact that following one law means violating another. They discover that their reasoning and their affect are out of joint: I should be tolerant but you make me sick; I understand your reasoning but I am deeply offended by your presence' (Povinelli 2002, 5).

16 In *Me and White Supremacy* Layla F. Saad frames 'Day 3' as 'You and Tone Policing' (Saad 2020).

17 In the reference to 'flatter' I am thinking about Lauren Berlant: 'But underperformativity, like passive aggression and other problematically evental modes of relating, sneaks around the codes of sincerity and intelligibility that make possible normative social trust and trust in the social' (Berlant 2015, 195).

International museology I: ICOM museum definition

Given its stated intention to create international professional consensus around what museums are, the International Council of Museums (ICOM) museum definition is an exemplary site to explore museum constitution as well as the ongoing deconstituting tendencies exacerbated by the affective work of participatory approaches.

1974 definition: museum constitution organising urgency and ideological variation

The first ICOM museum definition came in 1946 with the establishment of ICOM. It was very slightly modified in 1951 and 1968 (Lehmannová 2020). These early definitions did include ideas of being 'open to the public' and of permanence, but the more complex dynamics of late liberalism kicked in more clearly in the 1974 definition.

The 1974 ICOM museum definition arose from a period of challenge, both within ICOM and beyond (de Varine 2017; Mairesse 2020a; 2020b). The 1971 ICOM Conference held in Grenoble had three keynote speakers – Robert Poujade, Mario Vázquez and Stanislas Adotevi. Taken together, these three contributions have been understood as being the international inception point for '*la nouvelle muséologie*' (Desvallées 1992).

Robert Poujade – previously Mayor of Dijon and then the French Minister of the Environment and following discussions with Hugues de Varine and Georges Henri Rivière – framed a new model of museum practice 'designed to build heritage awareness, not for a public but for and by a community'. In his speech the concept of 'ecomuseum' – to which we will return in International museology II and III – was instantiated (*Museum International* 1985, fn.2, 184).

Mario Vázquez, who had been involved in the National Museum of Anthropology and who had set up Casa del Museo in the barrios of Mexico City (Sánchez-Juárez 2015), used his speech to challenge traditional notions of the museum. In it he called for 'museums to be made first and foremost for the people and to free themselves from the constraints imposed by the European tradition' (Mairesse 2020a, fn.4, 34).[1]

Stanislas Adotevi called for the de-Europeanisation of museums in Africa. He noted (in a published version of his speech):

> The museum [...] is theoretically and practically tied to a world (the European world), of a class (the cultivated bourgeoisie), and to a particular view of culture [...]. This world is, no doubt, disappearing [...] nevertheless the museum remains [...] the outdated obsession of a class that still believes in expanding its power. (Adotevi 2022 [1971], 41)

Adotevi sounded a call of a 'new generation' and 'grasping things by the root'. He ended by declaring: 'we will see then if museology is to be radical or not' (2022 [1971], 42, 51).

As de Varine has reflected in an account of the 1971 conference:

> This succession of non-conformist points of view encouraged a group of young participants from many countries, especially from Europe and North and South America, to ask, sometimes vehemently, for a modernization of the museum, its missions and its practices, and also a modernization of ICOM, its structures and the status of its members. (de Varine in Mairesse 2020a, fn.4, 76; see also Mairesse 2020b)

A series of agitations then led to the reworking of the museum definition in 1974. The full 1974 definition reads as:

> A museum is a non-profit making, permanent institution in the service of society and its development, and open to the public, which acquires, conserves, researches, communicates and exhibits, for purposes of study, education and enjoyment, material evidence of man and his environment. (ICOM 1974, in Lehmannová 2020)

The 1974 definition was, then, informed by the establishment of ecomuseums and US community museums and the elaboration of the 'integral museum' via the 1972 Round Table of Santiago on 'Role of Museums in Today's Latin America' (Round Table of Santiago 2014 [1972]), which centrally involved Mario Vázquez.

The most notable contribution to the 1974 definition from the Round Table of Santiago is the phrase 'in [the] service of society' (Round Table of Santiago 2014 [1972]). This was certainly seen as significant at the time – a sign of the desire to respond to some of the criticism levelled by Vázquez and Adotevi in 1971 (Hauenschild 2022 [1988], fn.3, 74).[2] In the Round Table of Santiago resolutions the phrase 'in the service of society' was connected to a highly politicised sense of 'a profound crisis', visible through the 'imbalance between the countries which have achieved great material development and others which remain on the periphery of development and are still enslaved as a result of their history'. Crucially, the Round Table of Santiago notes 'that most of the problems, revealed by contemporary society, have their roots in situations of injustice and cannot be solved until those injustices are rectified' (Round Table of Santiago 2014 [1972], 175).

In the light of a statement like this, the desire for museums to be 'in the service of society' has particular resonance. The intention was for a museum to

> stimulate those communities to action by projecting forward its historical activities so that they culminate in the presentation of contemporary problems; that is to say, by linking together past and present, identifying itself with indispensable structural changes and calling forth others appropriate to its particular national context. (Round Table of Santiago 2014 [1972], 175)

Yet that phase – 'in service of society' – also contains a particular type of relation between museums and the imagined abstraction of society. In the idea of 'service', while appearing modest, lies the difficulty of establishing what society might need, locating museum agency in its ability to respond and requiring museum staff to make those determinations and decisions. With 'open to the public' another abstraction is evoked, raising the endless question of precisely who that 'public' might be. The word 'permanent' embeds the central purpose of institutional maintenance: that the intention is, as much as anything else, for museums to continue to exist. 'Conserve' raises the question of what this means and modifies its relationship to being 'open to the public'.

In other words, the different elements of museum constitution are there in the 1974 definition. It is crucial to note that these museum constitutional elements – based on abstract constituencies, deficits of expansive claims, tensions and contradictions – are not in any simple sense reactionary tendencies. The different museum constitution elements are there precisely in response to the 1971 conference and its aftermath, influenced by the radical experiments of ecomuseums and calls to challenge museums' European roots. Nevertheless, the response offered by the 1974 definition is a clear expression of the late liberal circuit diagnosed in Chapter 1, creating grand ideals, constitutive deficits and tensions and calling into being an endless requirement for reform.

2019 draft definition: the limits of museum constitution's ability to organise ideological variation

Between 1974 and 2016 a number of relatively small additions and subtractions were made to the museum definition, most notably 'tangible and intangible heritage' in 2007. This addition was significant as it had the effect of definitionally enshrining complex questions of what it means to conserve, exhibit and communicate heritage, which is often embodied, lived and practised. Nevertheless, the 1974 iteration succeeded for over four decades in offering a relatively stable conceptual architecture for the museum definition.

In 2016 a committee was established to begin the process of creating a new definition. By 2019 the committee was ready to propose a new definition after a significant period of engagement (Sandahl 2019; Bonilla-Merchav 2019). The draft 2019 definition read:

> Museums are democratising, inclusive and polyphonic spaces for critical dialogue about the pasts and the futures [*sic*]. Acknowledging and addressing the conflicts and challenges of the present, they hold artefacts and specimens in trust for society, safeguard diverse memories for future generations and guarantee equal rights and equal access to heritage for all people.
>
> Museums are not for profit. They are participatory and transparent, and work in active partnership with and for diverse communities to collect, preserve, research, interpret, exhibit and enhance understandings of the world, aiming to contribute to human dignity and social justice, global equality and planetary wellbeing. (ICOM 2019, cited in Kendall Adams 2019)

The new draft definition caused a furore (Brulon Soares 2020, 23–4; Weiser 2020). Due to be confirmed at an ICOM conference in Kyoto in 2019, the new definition provoked such controversy that the vote was postponed and led to the initiation of a new process to resolve the issues (ICOM 2022a).[3]

The reasons for the postponement and the development of a new process and a new definition seem various from the reports. There were some process objections, though the process used to determine the draft had been passed by the relevant ICOM committee (Abungu et al. 2020). There was clearly a sense that too many additional ideas had been added, making it, in the views of some, less a functional definition and more of a mission statement based on identity and values (Mairesse 2020a, 38; Mairesse and Guiragossian 2020; Girard 2020). It was also accused of being 'ideological' (Juliette Raoul-Duval, cited in Noce 2019) and as being characterised by 'over inflated verbiage' (Hugues de Varine, cited in Noce 2019).

Yet if you look carefully at the structure of the 2019 draft definition it might be noted that, far from being a revolutionary break with the previous iterations, the 1974 ideological architecture is still present.

In the 2019 draft definition conservation is reflected in the use of the word 'preserve' – a word with less conceptual flexibility than 'conserve'. It is linked to the requirement for museums to hold 'artefacts and specimens' and to be involved in 'safeguarding diverse memories' for 'future generations'. Access is present, and given a specific liberal form, through 'equal rights and equal access'. The updated yet still recognisable idea of representation is also here in the terms 'inclusive' and 'polyvocal'. Museums impactfully shaping the world is there through 'critical dialogue' and a requirement to contribute to 'human dignity and social justice'. The institutional and professional role to make decisions 'on behalf of' is also there in the phrase 'in trust for'.

The only specific articulated ideological fault line that can really be drawn is between the implied universal in earlier definitions and the 2019 claim to the polyvocal. However, to return to David Scott, as cited in Chapter 1, if you ever try to curate or manage polyvocality you are likely, in any case, to slip into 'a detached, surveying gaze which itself is not relative' (Scott 2003, 105). Indeed, in the 2019 draft definition plurality was safely contained within the insatiabilities and tensions of liberalism. Counterintuitively, there are ways in which the draft 2019 definition is even closer to what I have named museum constitution than its predecessors. The ambitions and ideals are greater, the part-concept tensions are even more striking, and therefore the constitutive deficits created are deeper and more urgent.

Yet while the same basic museum constitution ideological structure is present, some of the vocabulary clearly *felt* to some both different to the 1974 legacy and wrong. The terms that seemed to have this affect were those such as human dignity and social justice, global equality and planetary wellbeing.

This is odd in one way, given very similar type of debates were happening around the time of the 1971 conference and indeed led to the 1974 definition. Yet we should recall Lawrence Grossberg's intervention that 'affect produces systems of *difference*' (Grossberg 1997, 160). Terms such as these create different qualities and quantities of investment and disinvestment.

The point I want to draw out is that museum constitution did not fail in its job of organising ideological variation in the 2019 draft definition because museum constitutional structure had been jettisoned – in fact it was very much still present, even more so – but because of how a very familiar ideological framework was affectively activated.

2022 definition: participation constitutionally incorporated

After a long, fraught debate in the wake of Kyoto in 2019, in 2022 the Extraordinary General Assembly of ICOM approved the proposal for the new museum definition:

> A museum is a not-for-profit, permanent institution in the service of society that researches, collects, conserves, interprets and exhibits tangible and intangible heritage. Open to the public, accessible and inclusive, museums foster diversity and sustainability. They operate and communicate ethically, professionally and with the participation of communities, offering varied experiences for education, enjoyment, reflection and knowledge sharing. (ICOM 2022b)

The 1974 language, itself drawing on 1971 Santiago 'Integral Museum', is present – 'in service of', 'conserves', 'open to the public' – yet is now given greater museum constitutional sharpness through the terms 'accessible and inclusive' and the conflictual need to prosecute the in-practice meaning of 'diversity'.

The approved 2022 definition also adds – reflecting the concept of 'partnership' in the 2019 draft – 'with the participation of communities'. In doing so, the 2022 definition indicates the ways in which participation has come to be seen as a mainstream method for making museums 'accessible and inclusive' and for managing 'diversity'.

However, by adding 'participation' the 2022 definition also brings into the fold an ideological-affective force which, this book argues, will ultimately unwind the museum constitutional structure that is so consistent (and even tightening) within the evolving ICOM museum definitions.

Notes

1 Andrea Hauenschild says of Vazquez's contribution to the 1971 conference, 'He believed that the museum as an institution would either have to change radically or lose its right to exist and sooner or later disappear' (Hauenschild 2022 [1988], 73).

2 François Mairesse, reflecting in 2020 on his interview with de Varine, notes that the 1971 debates that led to the 1974 definition 'were, in many ways, the same issues to those being discussed today, [and] which were pushing several members to ask for a new definition' (Mairesse 2020b, 75). Additionally the 1974 definition retains from earlier ICOM definitions 'open to the public' (from 1949) and 'conserves' (from 1951).

3 The furore was partly over process and whether the statement really reflected the consultative engagement (Mairesse 2020a) and partly over whether it was a statement that could hold globally (Mairesse and Guiragossian 2020; Girard 2020); but it also included renewed debate over the definition of 'definition' (Davis 2020). A number of those involved suggest that the new definition was more like a mission for a specific museum than a description that could hold for museums of all types (Mairesse 2020a, 38). The debate prompted others to question the premise and whether there really was value in seeking a universal definition (Maranda 2020). The legitimacy of the process was defended by those involved in developing the 2019 draft definition, arguing that the methods used were officially approved (Abungu et al. 2020).

Part II
Detaching

Part II's Chapter 3 and Chapter 4 explore what it might mean to detach from the reflex to animate museum constitution. If Part I sought to throw grit into the workings of museum constitution's machinery to aid in the retraining of reflexes, Part II supports the trajectory of not being caught up in museum constitution in the same way. It gives technique to enhance the affective work that participation does in making late liberal museum constitution feel wrong and unsustainable.

Chapter 3 explores the modes of detaching through a variety of techniques of affective de-intensification. It asks what changes when the same – or similar – activities are performed but where the nature and quantity of the investments has shifted. As in Chapter 2, Chapter 3 uses affective poetics as a means of animating a variety of ways in which to engage with a structure such as museum constitution. What happens if you speed up or slow down? Or if you carry on without enthusiasm or spirit?

Detaching is certainly a letting go – but it is also a process of making room for attaching to something else. Chapter 4 uses a speculative register, 'following out' (Berlant and Stewart 2019, ix) dynamics identified and named through Chapter 3's affective poetics. The speculative narratives arose as a way of paying attention to the political desire latent in the present: the political fantasies that arise when facilitating institutional participation.

This move to diagnose, to expand potential speculatively while being committed to the fullness of the present, is allied to Haraway's 'figuring' of her 'speculative fabulations'. Through 'speculative fabulations', Haraway advocates 'promiscuously plucking out fibers in clotted and dense events and practices' before seeking to:

follow the threads where they lead in order to track them and find their tangles and patterns crucial for staying with the trouble in real and particular places and times. (2016, 3)

Haraway offers a means of being attentive to the 'dislocal' (Latour 2005, 60) of this present moment, of grasping the conjunctural (Hall 2021 [1988]).[1] The here and now (Clarke 2019, 136) where we are tangled up, yet the tangle forming in discernible patterns, 'dishevelled but [...] predictable' (Berlant 2011, 53). Using the diagnostic affective poetics as an analytical mode I've sought to dwell in those moments and then, through speculative narratives, move to 'plucking out fibers' (Haraway 2016, 3) and 'following out' (Berlant and Stewart 2019, ix; see also Anderson 2021). The speculative narratives act as a noticing, an enacting and a passing back.[2] Through giving form and trajectory, the speculative narratives take up an energy already in the present to be ever iteratively adapted, re-figured, passed back and passed on.

The speculative narratives are resolutely focused on means not arrivals, and on how we do what we do. They are, as I hope is clear, certainly not utopian blueprints. There is no intention here to have worked everything out. The speculative narratives are motivated more by a desire to 'attend to and elaborate a loose assemblage of emergent lifeworlds' (Berlant 2022, 14). Or by 'the many real and imaginary strivings for a livable and humane social existence' that happen in what Avery Gordon calls 'the utopian margins' (Gordon 2018, vii), where 'things are other than they are' (2018, 286).

The intention is that the different registers of the book – critique, affective poetics and speculative narrative – can vibrate new types of resonance between realities and the imagined, in ways that can be amplified to enrich our abilities to hold what Gordon calls 'in-difference' (2018) to institutional forms of liberalism: 'to stop loving that which you claim to despise ... to practice freedom in preparation for collective self-governance' (2018, 48).

3
Detaching, affectively

It felt right until it didn't.

Museums contained your contradictions too, as you were containing theirs.

Institutional liberalism infuses. The most common of common senses. Warm and safe when inside, softening the path of expect resistance, which is also least resistance. Illuminating, softly, the promise that you can both challenge and gain approval. A cluster of promises made in institutional love, conditional-unconditional, ever-anxious, the double-binded filigrees of attachment. Still, then, thinking that you would be thanked.

Detaching begins not in those meetings, pulses rising. It begins as you walk away from those strip-lighted rooms. Maybe in the toilet, finally alone for a moment, and something is replayed freshly cut with shavings of unease. Or on the walk to the train station, bland realism the only genre available.

Slackening chooses you. Slight at first. Like a small crest of everyday low mood. Just a bit less. Not detached yet, still attached, still being drawn out into the world by its dominant common sense. But less. With less trajectory, with less momentum and with less spirit towards the liberal circuit. Other things start to appear, unformed at first. Generating unbidden fliting uncertainties, still for now easily filed away.

Now slackened, detaching grows in conversations. Starting in the kitchen, if no-one else is there, or in the back corridors as you pass, half-way up the stairs. In basements, if available. Then it develops, gathering as you decide to meet somewhere else, slightly further away. Or you start to meet outside, walking through the city. Varying the distance between, keeping moving if you can, taut at times then less so, still circling something but deliberately putting it out of focus.

Trying is tough. Impassed. Trying is slackening taken hold. Like the final five miles on a long walk, but without any hope of a destination or ever taking your boots off. Hard work. Stolid grafting. Detaching simply through trying with the wrong spirit, without the old intentions that made it all work. Representation in this mode is still worked towards, but with a hollowness, like the awkwardness of a photoshoot or filming session where everyone knows their soul is being chipped. Or when the word 'story' is alighted upon too casually, settled on as if it can be mutually agreed but drops like a dead weight, now knowingly over-determined, straining at its packaging. A dull working of contradiction. Atmospherics, always now a giveaway.

Recklessness offers a relief from trying, *accelerating*. Doubling down on the endless loop, spinning it fast. As if you are just really committed. It is ethically imperative only to try this at home, inside the institution. The *how* of your ideological attachments hyper-forced, a crash test. The safety features that are crafted to manage contradictions often kick in. Sometimes relieved by this and sometimes frustrated, with greater force you push that peddle down. Escape velocity still out of reach, but now feelable, imaginable, fuelling something else that might become later a more responsible, a less carbon-intensive unwinding.

Exceeding, you expand your political fantasy life by living now. Structures of feeling you encountered in books when you were still too young to know what to do with them resurface as half-memories, offering themselves now to be roughly stitched together with ideas, phrases and cadences newly discovered. Making fertile this interregnum through moving your attention closer, a rich dark soil in which much more can be seen and is already there. And what is there is utterly singular and utterly resonant, where new proximities foster a richer political vocabulary.

You exceed inclusion, appreciating beneath the boxed headline an 'everything'. Exceeding inclusion is a dwelling in its undeniability and impossible. Entirely agreed upon in those meetings, though nodding can be anything between impassioned, earnest or vague, and in practice is always utterly contested all the way down. Detaching is aided by fully appreciating inclusion's workings. An always failing promise. A promise whose redemption is never quite now. An idea that confirms a centre and periphery. An idea that generates exclusion as fuel.

The alternative is not to do nothing. Instead we make a thousand tactics to replace one kept-on-the-shelf strategy that no one can disagree with and no one can love. Exceeding detaches through an explosion of light and particularity. The multiplicity of inclusion-in-practice might have already been happening, already underway, but much is gained by not allowing it to be reincorporated, repackaged, flattened by a word that means nothing and everything. Indexed out of utility. Occupying to transform an idea forged too neatly in only one political tradition. Instead, many.

Turning comes slowly, aided by the page and the word, first that of others and then your own. The beginnings of an opening up to something else. A cultivating of indifference blossoming (Gordon 2018). Moving out from the basement and those half-lit corridors to those other places of light and air further away, even if you return to the dark places to tend your wounds. Wanting a different mode of life, of not being caught up, at least not in precisely the same way.

A turning which is also a letting go more decisively, a choice of orientation away. Cultivating with care a '*for*' (Harney and Moten 2013, 147–8). Organising differently. Starting meetings differently, more slowly, seeking mutual convening. Trying out different political forms, decisively direct as representation wanes. Picking up the trails left by others, sometimes breadcrumbs, sometimes well marked, and thinking through different modes of organising while working them into being.

Detaching through different intensities

This chapter arises – as all the chapters do – from Chapter 2, but in a very obvious way. The experiments that led to this chapter generated a sense, following Lawrence Grossberg, that different intensities might offer a way of deconstituting, of not being caught up in the same way over and over again. This writing came from trying to give form to ways in which you might still be doing what you do – there is no easy escape – but with different qualities and in different quantities.

Lauren Berlant famously describes a type of attachment as 'cruel optimism'. Optimism is cruel 'when the object/scene of desire is itself an obstacle to fulfilling the very wants that bring people to it' *and* when 'its life-organizing status can trump interfering with the damage it provokes' (Berlant 2011, 227).[3] Berlant argues that its 'life-organizing status' means that no matter how clear its nature as an obstacle becomes, 'you can't simply lose your object if it's providing a foundational world infrastructure for you'. While you can't lose it, Berlant argues, you can 'use the contradictions the object prompts to loosen and reconfigure it, exploiting the elasticity of its contradictions, the incoherence of the forces that overdetermine it [...]' (Berlant 2022, 28).[4] Or, in the terms used by Stefano Harney and Fred Moten citing Cedric Robinson, you can recognise contradictions and 'heighten' their intensity (Moten, Harney and Shukaitis 2021, n.p.).

Detaching is aided by the varying distances leveraged by certain forms of thinking-feeling, to 'unlearn its objectness' (Berlant 2022, 28), to unlearn 'museum' and to unlearn the parts we have been playing in museum constitution. As suggested in the Introduction, detaching is enabled through a 'loosening' which works to 'slow the object's movement, to describe its internal dynamics [...] to consider its parts' (Berlant 2022, 13). To loosen, in Berlant's terms, 'is not to increase spaciousness but to make different [recombinations] available from within the scene of attachment' (2022, fn.25, 181), through what might be thought of as acts of variation in space and speed, 'ongoing expansion, contraction, looping, shredding' (2022, 13).

The writing experiments which then became this chapter tried out Berlant's 'expansion, contraction, looping, shredding' (2022, 13), as well as Clough's suggestion – introduced in the Introduction – towards 'differently composing elements of an apparatus with the aim of eliciting exposure or escaping it, intensifying engagement or lessening it, speeding up the timing of willed influencing or slowing it down, enjoying pleasure and suffering pain or eluding them' (Clough 2000, 286).

Different orientations presented themselves through the writing experiments. One might be to increase 'in-difference' (Gordon 2018, 48).[5] For Avery Gordon, 'in-difference' is to find ways of no longer being defined by that you are seeking to change. In-difference to 'existential liberalism' (2018, 146), that sense of your whole being becoming defined by being in and against that you believe (however explicitly) you can reform. To accept no longer the premise that museums are the centre and are where the power is and that you just have to keep banging against the same wall over and over again – a wall you only strengthen with every attempt to breach. Ben Anderson draws attention to the ways in which you are always both attaching and detaching; any detachment comes with emergent attachments and processes of attaching might mean other things fading (Anderson 2023, 217). Detaching is therefore a generative process. It is also a making room for something else.

There is a way in which form here is more condensed than in Chapter 2. It is informed by Chapter 1's critical map, but tries to hold those ideas in affective structures that illuminate how thinking of an idea differently – such as inclusion – also needs affective retuning.

This chapter thus acts as a transition. It begins to cultivate a trajectory, starting from wherever you happen to be. Even if this is in the bowels of a museum.

Notes

1 Conjuncture is a term associated with Stuart Hall in his work on diagnosing Thatcherism (Hall 2021 [1988]) and later the politics of New Labour (Hall 2003) and the period post-financial crisis (with Doreen Massey and Michael Rustin [2015]). It has been given specific critical life in the last 10 years by those working with Hall's legacy to make sense of recent political shifts in the US and UK, whether related to Brexit, Trump, Extinction Rebellion or Black Lives Matter. Conjuncture – or 'present-as-a-conjuncture' (Hall, cited in Scott 2017, 56) – involves 'the coming together of often distinct though related contradictions, moving according to different tempos, but condensed in the same historical moment' (Hall 2021 [1988], 41). Or, as Jeremy Gilbert has put it, conjuncture is 'the analysis of convergent and divergent tendencies shaping the totality of power relations within a given social field during a particular period of time [...] with particular attention to the ways in which those relations are changing at a given moment' (Gilbert 2019, 6). Conjuncture, therefore, is about attending to the distinctiveness of political dynamics in any given now, a present 'overdetermined [...] by the constitutive co-presence of multiple forces, tendencies, contradictions and antagonisms', while also being 'underdetermined in its multiple lines of possibility' (Clarke 2019, 136). In other words, conjuncture draws attention to the ways in which a now – and also, crucially, a 'here' (Clarke 2019, 136) – holds a certain type of political shape and yet is nevertheless open to a variety of potentials.

2 This sense of making space through reciprocal movement is fundamental to Haraway's 'sf': 'string figures can be played by many, on all sorts of limbs, as long as the rhythm of accepting and giving is sustained. Scholarship and politics are like that too – passing on in twists and skeins that require passion and action, holding still and moving, anchoring and launching' (Haraway 2016, 3, 20).

3 Cassie Kill works directly with Berlant's idea of 'cruel optimism' to explore the complexities of co-production in the context of a gallery youth collective (2022).

4 Stefano Harney puts it in this way: 'Rather than worry about governance or the sharpness of our critique of the university or our complicity with it. The university has to go, and until the day it goes I want some money out of it' (Moten, Harney and Shukaitis 2021, n.p.).

5 Avery Gordon's 'in-difference' is a poetic conceptual response to the question asked by Toni Cada Bambara via Minnie Ransom, 'healer of the district', a character in *The Salt-Eaters*. Ransom asks of Velma Henry, an activist, 'Are you sure, sweetheart, that you want to be well? ... "Take away the miseries and you take away some folks' reason for living. Their conversation piece anyway".' Gordon reflects: 'These are profound, difficult, and delicate questions that get to the heart of any radically emancipatory enterprise. What do you really want? What is involved in achieving what you want? What's the cost of taking away the miseries? What's the cost of holding on to them?' To be 'in-difference' is to be 'in-difference to the lure and the pull of the sacrificial goods and promises ubiquitously on offer and also in-difference to the familiarity of being sick of it all' (2018, 40, 43, 48).

4

Detaching, speculatively

We meet in the bowels of the museum in a room off a corridor, off a corridor, off a wider goods entrance corridor which is marked to guide two streams of traffic in opposite directions. The lighting flickers here as if we have found ourselves at the unreliable end of a system, all energy being directed elsewhere.

We'd talked about convening elsewhere: a pub, a café, anywhere else with light and air. When we talked about where to meet some of us, unbidden, glimpsed yurts in fields. Or walking up hills. Or views from mountain tops or from a beach over the sea, depending. But we decided any sense of away or outside would have been to nourish an unhelpful illusion. We were trying to no longer be dreamers.[1] We are here.

We are here (down and across, but still here) because in the other rooms in which we usually meet (the ones with windows and closer in) we have been good workers, ready to compromise to get a little of what we have been employed to do recognised. Or we've been just angry, frustrated, ready to explode. Or resigned, desiring escape. Vibrating between us have been a thousand small wedges – riven, if never totally.

We know we don't trust each other. How could we yet? We are double binds caught in double binds.

> We work with people – but never enough of them.
> We want them to be themselves – but a little bit less so.
> We ask them to be authentic – just not too much.
> We build relationships – but elide any reciprocity.
> We ask for their voice – but always edit it.
> We value them in particular – but claim the right to balance this with the visitor in general.

We invite demands for greater access – but know that soon after access is taken up it will be policed.

We do the same work but always by splitting and endlessly projecting, judging ourselves but also each other. Never ethical enough or efficient enough.

Double-binded within and between ourselves runs the endless dialogue.

We have a responsibility to renew this institution – that agency here is an illusion.
That worse could happen if we stopped – that the worst has already happened.
Make it better – tear it down.
Work harder – resist – run away.
Make a difference – refuse complicity – achieve purity.
Duty – freedom.

We now want to unwind differently.

We sit in a circle. We begin by trying to find ways of talking about our jobs in terms of what we do. We try to find words for the consistency of doing 'access', 'outreach', 'community development' or 'participation' – for the work has gone by many names. The words we try to find are instead of the words usually used. We try to be specific and notice when we circuit something particular via the abstractions of inclusion, representation, democracy, empowerment or wellbeing – all words that come too easily to be useful, arriving ready charged.

Every attempt to say what it is that we do without ideological recourse trips us up. We try:

We move culture from one place to another – *hiding the rationale that moving people, culture, knowledges and practices into the museum is in the name of recognition.*
We expand what counts as history – *concealing the idea that we, via the museum, add the validation and the institutionalisation of knowledge.*
We create community – *laughing as this one was said, striking too hard, too true with its misplaced agency, ridiculous when said aloud.*
We get people together so they feel happier – *not possible to say without sadness in what is being shaped in us and others by being so called.*

The more we try to find a simple everyday sentence focused on practice, the more impossible it becomes to keep our talk on a plane of practice only. The existence of every small act is dependent on being circuited back through constitutional contradictions.

We make the constitutional contradictions our fault lines.[2] We push the fault lines into crevices and throw stones down to see how deep they run and to hear the ricochet of resonance. Or we treat the fault lines as thread, woven so we can wrap the contradictions around us, letting different parts touch and touch our skin.

By making ourselves useful, we've been making the enlightenment useful. Activating its enablements as if its violations could be bracketed or renegotiated.[3] Putting ourselves between. Making ourselves relevant just as we are put to work in service of the museum's continued relevance. Governed through our freedom, as we've sought to govern others through theirs.

Sometimes our sadness overwhelms us. Mourning, yes, for all that inflicted in our name but, yes, also for who we used to be able to be. The time when we could hold good life fantasies (Berlant 2011) of being in service to shared ideals and viable public institutions, in which people like us were supposed to debate and decide on the right thing to do. We try out letting go of this false future, paid for by others a long time ago and still now.[4] We don't inflict this sadness on anyone else; we keep it in the room. We sometimes try but know we can't get to anger, sounding like a lie, hollow before it even gets started.

We know this is not a matter of being ourselves. How can we continue to be ourselves given who we have been raised to be? In the uncertain strip lighting we trace out the lines of edifice still visible beneath our skin. Still killing us too and still much more softly (Moten in Harney and Moten 2013, 140–1). The small cuts, the mundane, devastating micro-betrayals, the awkwardness, fluttering (Du Bois 2015 [1897]) that are always at play in our being. We try to imagine ourselves othered (Spivak 2003, 52), though it still feels impossible. We feel out reflexing differently.

We perform our conscription differently by not denying that all we do is on the ground of enlightenment-colonialism. The mean generosity of late liberalism's use of culture that we'd been expected to carry in our gut and sustain in many small ways. Not believing we can be at the limits precisely (Foucault 1984, 45), we instead just start to widen the gap, to make more elbow room, vary the tone, multiply the differences in the repetitions, look in different directions, notice different things. Always intensively, intensively, as it is in who we are (Lash 2007).

Not wanting to concede to the old pattern. Not wanting to be defined by being against. Wanting to figure it out. Wanting to rearrange our desires (Spivak 2004, 526).[5] We try to look hard at what it is we 'cannot not want' (Spivak 2013, 453).

> creating shared space for understanding who we are and how we might live together in this world
> being with other people in all the ways they live, feel and think and with all that might be possible if we all were more open to each other
> working together to think, to do things and to make things.

We start to feel the varying difference between asking: What interests you in this collection? What is your interpretation of this object? Tell me your story. What questions urgently affect your life?

If we ask the collections questions we feel the self-validation of it, the centring of this already validated, legitimised culture as collections, the demand and expectation of others' interest, our own personal status secured and growing with every question responded to with kindness. We crawl back to our basement room and share these stories, stories that might pass for a celebratory case study in the past but now are freighted. We try not to turn away. Instead we try to look at it, us, what we do, head on.

If we ask about people's stories we can feel it as generosity, showing sustained interest, but lurking is the non-relational. It cannot simply be a story told from you to us. A story shared. The story will need to pass through the constitutional process of sorting relevance to the institution's themes, validation of authenticity, policing the extent of authenticity, the mediations of being reworked for public consumption. Our work often being precisely this process of translation.

If we ask about questions they have, people either shrug or hundreds of questions flow. Questions of rent costs or why we need food banks, or why the river floods or why the government wants to stop refugees; why we have the idea of gender or why there's wasteland in the neighbourhood.[6] We find that maybe a few things the museum has support the inquiry, but thousands of other things, archives, books, film, poetry, television as well as groups, organisations and people, can help. We look outwards, make connections.

Those that shrug leave. 'Refusing', getting us out of their heads.[7] Off to do other things we hear about on the grapevine much later, beautiful and without relation to us.

Some ask us that question back – and we say, 'This is it. Being otherwise.'

And as we play all this out we also try out what it is like not being motivated in conversations, not having to shift from small talk to formal talk. What it is like not to be orientated towards *delivery*. But it's hard. It's hard for people like us truly to believe that no talk is small.

Alongside this we start to practise non-cooperation. We heighten the contradiction we've been asked to carry – sharing the load upwards instead of outwards as is expected.[8]

> They ask for numbers. We send poetry. A different type of counting.
> They ask for photos of our diverse groups. We send a painting. Representation comes in different forms.
> They ask for demographics. We send back self-descriptions that never deny race, disability, sexuality and gender but irreducibly.
> They ask for best practice. We don't respond. It's too late for all of that.

Sometimes they become frustrated, issuing threats. Just as often the paintings and poems get used in funding bids. We switch tactics.

We know it is us, all of us. We are the fuel, energising and circuiting the constitution. Out/reach has always been a problem, implying a positionality of inside-out, a hand laying on, a gathering up. We try and make the old team name a new virtue, of *out*. We're a shifting Out. Not in. Not against. Not in and against. Not exited. Still defined in relation but determinedly outwards in orientation. We starve the constitution of our part. Destituting.[9] Deconstituting.

> We let the museum be irrelevant; *as late liberalism fades the museum must too*. As it fades, other politics will bloom.
> We let the museum be unrepresentative, *after all it always was*. As attention centrifugally spreads beyond we suddenly see all those already-existing other places that have always been there, but are not by or for the likes of us.
> We let the museum be empty as things cared about by those they were taken from are returned, *after all wasn't there always an emptiness at the heart of every display?* A fullness becomes possible as the void becomes new fertile ground.
> We let the museum be inaccessible, *as if access wasn't only ever offered to be foreclosed*. If the centre is not over-valued, there is no need for access.

Withering. Circuited loops constricting, spinning fast and harder to do the same work, the axis no longer stable.

Our labour, never patient enough (Foucault 1984, 45). Guts still twisted, but less. Sutured, but more loosely. The edifice fading. Whiteness less. Our 'we' changing shape, desedimented, becoming singularities and forming collectivity. Our ground shifting as fault lines deepen, as we crack and rip them wider; it is always 'without guarantees' (Hall 1986), but sometimes, and more and more often, something springs up.

And we are stopping being museum workers. And museums are stopping being museums. And our now is expanding. And we create and continue to create. And the biggest part of life is no longer short-circuited and channelled centripetally, but is wild (Halberstam 2013), spreading, pulsing.

Detaching, speculatively

The writing experiments that led here included trying to grasp the paradoxes of everyday facilitation of participation in museums, the odd contradiction of requirements and of there always being a constitutional counterbalance. The experiments also came to be about this as a condition, as a way of life, and of trying no longer to accept this.

This speculative narrative offers a 'plucking out fibres' in Haraway's sense (Haraway 2016, 3) and a 'following out' in Berlant and Stewart's terms (Berland and Stewart 2019, ix). It is also a working through of two ideas I've been compelled by and have also found difficult: Spivak's double binds (Spivak 2013) and Michel Foucault's sense of working at the limits of the enlightenment, what he calls a 'limit-attitude' (Foucault 1984). For me these ideas provoke a certain tussling with whether politics means being a bit in love with your own implication or – and maybe *and* – being a bit in love with the idea of escape. This chapter is a step on from trying to stutter the reflex that kick-starts museum constitution, or just doing it but with different intensities, as in Chapter 3. Instead it follows out, seeking a trajectory.

To say more about how 'double binds' and 'limit-attitude' have been working me, we need a little of the kind of space for a non-critical academic practice that has been created by Kathleen Stewart and Karen Barad in their work. Stewart speaks of reading theory at the level of a sentence (Stewart 2023). For her, this means deciding to read theory not as a fixed and stable intellectual structure but instead to see in its form suggestive generative potential. For Barad, any 'critical practice' is ‘inseparable from and of the very materials one is engaging’ (Barad in Barad and Gandorfer 2021, 39). What this suggests ontologically is that ‘none of the concepts are referring. This is not the work concepts do.’ Rather, ‘there is always an iterative performative engagement with concepts’ (Barad in Barad and Gandorfer 2021, 42). Barad continues:

> It is not that I am trying to represent the theory in language per se; rather, I am trying to be in touch with the theory in the way it inhabits me and that I am inhabiting it – the way in which we inhabit each other in this strange topology, this material, embodied sense of sense-making. (Barad in Barad and Gandorfer 2021, 42)[10]

There is a way in which, since reading about both concepts, I have inhabited double binds and limit-attitudes as they have inhabited me. None of this mutual inhabitation may chime with what either author intended; what I want to enact here is rather how ideas morph as they are lived, always imperfectly.

In general parlance a double bind is being confronted by two irreconcilable demands or two equally undesirable decisions or actions. In Gayatri Chakravorty Spivak’s work double binds recur. They are a special focus in the preface and Introduction of *An Aesthetic Education in the Era of Globalization* (Spivak 2013). Spivak situates the double bind as a particular legacy of the enlightenment and colonialism, suggesting that we might benefit from ‘learning the double bind – not just learning about it’ (2013, 1) as part of a wider ‘ab-use’ (use from below) of the enlightenment (2013, 3). The writing experiments that led to this chapter are informed by Spivak’s more directional prose, as well as with her own reflections on these directions.

There is a way in which I experience Spivak in straightening ways, calling a certain kind of well-educated Western or elite subjectivity to account for its monolingualism, its lack of ability to engage in idiom, its ‘impassioned’ activism (Spivak 2003, 37), its sense of its right to ‘right wrongs’ (Spivak 2004) without any ‘democratic procedure’ (Spivak 2013, 318). I feel seen, let’s just say. Readers are then called on to ‘suture the habits of democracy onto the earlier cultural formation’ (2004, 548), work hard, learn idiom (2003) or use the enablements of human rights while renegotiating violations (2004, 524). It should be said that Spivak has become increasingly sceptical that double binds can be played following how her ‘strategic use of essentialism’ (2013, ix) was picked up and used, but she still wants us to learn ‘to live with contradictory instructions’ (2013, 3). I have sat with the possibility of, for example, using rights as 'enabling violations' (2013, 511). But my experience of trying to 'ab-use' the enlightenment does something to me, and produces me in a certain way that I can't think tends anywhere good.

I have wondered – reflecting techniques of modulating which are explored more explicitly in Chapter 6 – whether varying the intensities of ideological-affective dis/investment towards double binds offers some scope (*how* and *how much*, to evoke Lawrence Grossberg, not just what). This may perhaps only be the case if added to by no longer thinking the only repertoire available is that offered by the enabling violations of enlightenment norms. This chapter feels out – drawing on anarchist and horizontalist thought – other political modes that might take us to a different point, producing me/us/we in varying ways less accepting that we are always caught between double binds, at least not always in the same way. I do also wonder whether this type of variation within constitution norms or double binds might (through pausing the reflex to right wrongs) act as an enabler of imagining yourself 'othered' (2004, 568) – another of Spivak's firm suggestions.

In 'What is Enlightenment?' Michel Foucault advocates for 'a limit-attitude' (Foucault 1984, 45). This is not, he writes, a 'gesture of rejection' of the enlightenment, but rather an awareness that 'we have to move beyond the outside-inside alternative; we have to be at the frontiers'. This 'ethos' is enacted through two methods: 'archaeological', seeking 'to treat the instances of discourse that articulate what we think, say, and do as so many historical events' (1984, 46), and 'genealogical', in the sense that 'it will not deduce from the form of what we are, what it is impossible for us to do and to know; but it will separate out from the contingency that has made us what we are, the possibility of no longer being, doing, or thinking what we are, do, or think' (1984, 46). Significantly, the last line of Foucault's 'What is Enlightenment?' reads:

> I do not know whether it must be said today that the critical task still entails faith in Enlightenment; I continue to think that this task requires work on our limits, that is, a patient labor giving form to our impatience for liberty. (Foucault 1984, 50)

This chapter's response is to wonder whether a modest orientation to limits (a de-romantisation of the limit-attitude) and a varying orientation to outside-inside (as patterning, vibrating, differencing, repetition) can be linked to a version of 'liberty' or 'wild' or 'gaga', in Jack Halberstam's terms. For Halberstam 'the wild' is not what 'lies outside of the bounded here and now, it is something that we already conjure from within the here and now – we constantly call it into being' (Halberstam 2013, 126). In this here and now

> the wild as a set of alternatives that we are in the process of making, imagining, and inhabiting – alternatives to political discourse, to identity politics, to the set pieces of protest culture, and alternatives to how we want to think about being – both being together and being apart. (2013, 127)

The writing that generated this speculative narrative is also an experiment with the detaching 'de' of destitution and deconstituting; the 'de' (though it is not contained in the word) of Avery Gordon's 'in-difference'. There is a trajectory at work here that holds withering together with what is created, if energy is redirected.

Finally, this chapter is obviously about whiteness. In particular it is about how being less the servant of institutional liberalism might be a small step on the way to 'abolish[ing] whiteness' (Ware and Back 2002, 8). Some might see institutional liberalism as the bulwark against the other type of far-right white supremacy. However, it seems beyond time to consider that the types of liberal structures that produce exclusions, and then thrive through always partial and unredeemed redress, create the competition between groups that, in turn, makes the exploitation of this competition possible.

A final thought on form. The form of this speculative narrative has a brittleness of white women trying not to cry; there is a sort of injured stolidity, trying to face up to stuff we've done very well ignoring. There is no longer any easy righteousness, anger, certainty or any idea that you know what right is, never mind that you could know what it means to 'right wrongs' (Spivak 2004). The final paragraph signals a now. Another present that lives within our own, 'call[ed] into being' (Halberstam 2013, 126).

Notes

1 Ta-Nehisi Coates used the term Dreamers – as in 'the American Dream' – to describe white Americans. In doing so he also uses the phrase, echoing James Baldwin, 'the people who think of themselves as White', who, Baldwin says 'have the choice of being human or irrelevant' (Baldwin 2017 [1984], xvi). Coates, again following Baldwin, encapsulates the way 'whiteness' is a creation: 'The new people were something else before they were white – Catholic, Corsican, Welsh, Mennonite, Jewish – and if all our national hopes have any fulfilment, then they will have to be something else again.' His bigger point, powerfully phrased: 'race is the child of racism, not the father' (Coates 2015, 7). This chapter is concerned with people who think they are White no longer thinking of themselves as White, or trying to. It is, of course, about me

doing that along the way. It is engaged with work on the abolition of whiteness (Ware and Back 2002), but also evokes and plays through the lived difficulties and the dangerous temptation in thinking you've arrived there too easily or soon.

2 Fault lines is a reference to this suggestion from Spivak: 'Productive undoing is a difficult task. It must look carefully at the fault lines of the doing, without accusation, without excuse, with a view to use' (Spivak 2013, 1).

3 Spivak's sense is that human rights is an 'enabling violation': 'The idea of human rights, in other words, may carry within itself the agenda of a kind of social Darwinism – the fittest must shoulder the burden of righting the wrongs of the unfit – and the possibility of an alibi. [...] Having arrived here, the usual thing is to complain about the Eurocentrism of human rights. I have no such intention. I am of course troubled by the use of human rights as an alibi for interventions of various sorts. But its so-called European provenance is for me in the same category as the "enabling violation" of the production of the colonial subject. One cannot write off the righting of wrongs. The enablement must be used even as the violation is renegotiated' (Spivak 2004, 524).

4 I am thinking here of work which shows how only a certain 'genre of being human' (Wynter 2003, 269), those raced white, are given a future in common with the futurity association with the liberal horizon. Dylan Rodríguez calls this 'White Being [which] composes the foundational grammars for white modernity's symbolic, cultural, economic, and epistemic coherence under the teleologies of Civilization and progress' (Rodríguez 2021, 5).

5 Spivak writes: 'Education in the Humanities attempts to be an uncoercive rearrangement of desires. If you are not persuaded by this simple description, nothing I say about the Humanities will move you' (Spivak 2004, 526). Spivak reflected later, 'There is always coercion in education, "uncoercive" does not refer to some sort of willing suspension of coercion. It signals the future anterior: whatever you do, even if it looks like your plan succeeded completely, in the end something (else) will have happened' (2013, 80).

6 This is a reference to Sweet Water Foundation in south side Chicago: 'Sweet Water Foundation utilizes a blend of urban agriculture, art and education to transform vacant spaces and abandoned buildings into economically and ecologically productive and sustainable community assets that produce engaged youth, skilled workers, art, locally-grown food, and affordable housing'. I visited in 2019; it is incredible work. https://www.sweetwaterfoundation.com/.

7 In *Ordinary Notes* Christina Sharpe visits museums and memorials in the US, including the National Memorial for Peace and Justice which 'is dedicated to the more than four thousand four hundred known victims of lynching in twelve states in the US' (Sharpe 2023, 51). Sharpe draws attention to a participatory invitation: 'Each county in which a lynching took place is invited to research lynching in their communities and then enter into a process with the EJI in order to place the corresponding monolith in their community'. Sharpe goes on: 'As far as I know, only one community has claimed a marker' (2023, 54), leaving the significance of that open for the reader to interpret.

8 I am thinking here of Michael Lipsky. In *Street-level Bureaucracy: Dilemmas of the individual in public services* (1980) Lipsky argued that: 'a typical mechanism for legislative conflict resolution is to pass on intractable conflicts for resolution (or continued irresolution) at the administrative level' (Lipsky 1980, 41).

9 Destituting comes from the Invisible Committee's *Now* and a section title 'Let's destitute the world': 'Thus, where the "constituents" place themselves in a dialectical relation of struggle with the ruling authority in order to take possession of it, destituent logic obeys the vital need to *disengage from it*. It doesn't abandon the struggle; it *fastens on to the struggles' positivity*. It doesn't adjust itself to the movements of the adversary, but to what is required for the increase of its own potential' (Invisible Committee 2017).

10 To do this means seeing that 'theory *is* a material articulation of the world that has embedded within it specific entanglements of colonialism, capitalism, racism, but also possibilities of disrupting and undoing these forces [...] Nothing can be presumed as the already familiar and old, but at the same time, nothing can be seen as producing the "new" as if the new is a function of a discontinuous moment from the old' (Barad in Barad and Gandorfer 2021, 42, italics original).

Part III
Participatory worlding

Part I characterises museum constitution as a way of preventing the smooth running of reflexes that motor its loop. Part II develops affective techniques and a speculative trajectory for the stirrings of detaching. In Parts I and II 'participation's affective work' was used to describe how undertaking participation in institutional contexts – the lived experience of becoming mutually accountable – creates a slackening in desire to kick-start the late liberal loop of access, inclusion and representation. In Part III 'participation's affective work' takes on a more overtly creative and generative meaning. Collectively the chapters in Part III argue that participation is not, as it is often thought to be, a mode of institutional engagement. Rather, it is more productive to recognise that participation is a mode of governance – it proposes distinct and different ways of acting and making decisions together. More than that – although this is enabled precisely through innovations in how we organise our relationships and ways of being together – participation is also ontologically generative. It changes what is present and what is real; it is world-making. Participation is a way of being in the world that makes alternative worlds.

Part III opens and ends with two international museology interludes. International museology II seeks out, and in some cases generates, connections between the 1970s community museum and ecomuseum innovators and innovators in action research and participatory research. I see this as a way of acknowledging the long history of what I am doing – a history that signals a hope for further resonances now. International museology III draws out the innovative governance models and modes of world-making at play in early community museums and ecomuseums. It also questions whether the concept, or even the word ‘museum’, can be deconsituted sufficiently to enable participatory worlding.

Chapter 5 develops conceptual trajectories for thinking of participation as worlding. It asks how ‘participation’s affective work’ – which has been disrupting applications to late liberal ideas of access, representation and inclusion – can be actively turned towards responsive and relational ways of being in the world through which realities and worlds are made. Chapter 6 identifies ways of being present that activate potential through ‘modulating’, in Brian Massumi’s terms (2015a, 96), elaborating ‘modulating’ as a technique for participatory worlding. Chapter 7 characterises the ways in which participatory worlding both leads to, and is supported by, participatory approaches to organising – ways of acting, making decisions and negotiating disagreement and harm that do not rely on ‘on behalf of’ governance.

In terms of form, each chapter splices registers kept separate in previous chapters. Chapter 5 uses aspects of the critical voice, but it is inflected – in keeping with its focus – with the speculative. Chapter 6 begins in dialogue with Chapters 2 and 3 through the use of affective attachments and intensities. It then evolves into a speculative mode, imagining what might happen if you respond to the question of inclusion by not taking it on as your own. Chapter 7 initially uses a critical register to try and clarify the logics of legitimacy at work in museum constitution, and in so doing to identify what alternative logics of legitimacy are required for deconstituted approaches to heritage. However, it ends in speculative mode, drawing out instances of alternative modes of governance and therefore of worlding.

International museology II: participatory museology, participatory research and action research

I offer here a series of 'vibrating' connections. The connections I am seeking are those between the early innovators in community museums and ecomuseums and the innovators in the varied traditions of action research and participatory research. Some of the connections are tighter and documented, others looser and more circumstantial. The connections are 'vibrating' in that different lines sometimes touch temporarily and sometimes do not (or perhaps touch only on this page). The possible links are offered in the hope they might generate potential for connecting museum practice with participatory research and action research.

Although he was unable to take up the invitation (Velázquez 2019, 262), Paulo Freire – the influential creator of radical pedagogy – was invited to chair the 1972 Round Table of Santiago on the 'Role of Museums in Today's Latin America' (2014 [1972]). The Round Table went onto articulate the concept of an 'Integral Museum' and centrally involved Mario Vázquez, who created the Casa del Museo programme in the *barrios* of Mexico City (Sánchez-Juárez 2015). The invitation to Freire was issued by ICOM President Hugues de Varine (Alves and Gomes de Souza Reis 2013, abstract; Velázquez 2019, 262). De Varine had himself been jointly responsibly for coining the term 'ecomuseum' through discussions with Georges Henri Rivière and Robert Poujade, and the term gave shape to the opening speech at the 1971 ICOM Conference discussed in International museology I. Some ecomuseums, in particular the Canadian Ecomusée de la Haute-Beauce, explicitly used Freirean ideas of a 'pedagogy of liberation' (Hauenschild 2022 [1988], 104).

Early Action Research in the US is associated with Kurt Lewin (Lewin 1946), often credited in both the action research origin story and the pre-history of the 1960s 'urban renewal' investment of federal money in the '150 model cities' programme (Moynihan 1969, cited in Fals Borda 1999, 5). The same contexts of federal urban renewal in the US gave rise to Sherrie Arnstein's Ladder of Participation (Arnstein 2019 [1969], 216) and Elinor Ostrom's work (with others) in Chicago, which evolved the term 'co-production' (Ostrom, Parks, Whitaker and Percy 1978), as well as to the Anacostia Neighbourhood Museum (Hauenschild 2022 [1988], 168).

Orlando Fals Borda had access to a manuscript version of Freire's *Pedagogy of the Oppressed* (2015 [1970]; see Schugurensky 2014, 370) when he was developing his participatory action research with coastal communities in Columbia. Freire's concern with placing deep value on everyday knowledge influenced Fals Borda's emphasis on memory and folk traditions as part of the 'critical recovery of history' (Fals Borda 1991, 8). While I can't find any direct connection, Fals Borda's 'critical recovery of history' developed during the same decade as the 'Dig Where You Stand' movement in Sweden. This movement, which encouraged workers to research their own workplaces, was linked with the 'Museum of Working Life' in Norrköping, part of an international network of local working life museums (Lindqvist 2014, 265–6), as well as the then growing international oral history movement.

Although – and even more oddly – I have failed to find any direct connection here either, the 'Dig Where You Stand' movement arose in the same context as the Norwegian Industrial Democracy Movement. This movement, underpinned by an action research method influenced by Kurt Lewin, was taken up by the UK-based Tavistock Institute for Human Relations. This led in turn to a comprehensive challenge to ideas of scaling up, and to the linear notion of the application or replication of research insights in new contexts (Gustavsen 2008, 432).[1]

In the majority world, the 1970s were defined by 'the decade-long search for alternative models of development wherein the recipients of development become drivers of the process' (Jaitli 2014). Seeking a grassroots approach to development led to action research and participatory research experiments facilitated, among others, by Budd Hall and Maria Liisa Swantz in Tanzania and Rajesh Tandon in India, as well as by Fals Borda in Columbia and Muhammed Rahman in Bangladesh and internationally via the International Labour Office (Fals Borda 1987, 331). The shared motivation to intervene in development policy led to growing international co-operation via the International Council for Adult Education (Tuckett 2014, 452–3; Hall and Tandon 2017, 369) and the International Participatory Research Network (Hall 2014, 453–5; Hall and Tandon 2017, 369) – to the extent that by the 1990s

> the idea of participation and empowerment began to trigger policymaking in the international arena and national government programmes, so much so that the World Bank came up with a policy on 'participation' in the year 1994. (Tandon in Hall and Tandon 2017, 370)

The same decade, and the same context of post-colonial 'development', also shaped critiques of colonial legacies in ways that found international expression in ICOM in the early 1970s. These derived not least from the interventions of Stanislas Adotevi (2022 [1971]) and Mario Vázquez – to come full circle – at the 1971 ICOM conference.[2]

There certainly is scope for historical work establishing and developing these connections, and possible other connections, more fully than I can do here. However, my purpose in evoking these allied traditions of the 1970s is to suggest that participatory research and action research and participatory museology can be understood – and might usefully be understood more firmly and more actively – as allied traditions. Allied in that participatory research and action research and early participatory museology were responses to the same historical moments, drew on shared political resources and engaged with a set of shared problems concerning ways of knowing, ways of being, modes of organising and means of creating change.

Notes

1 Budd Hall refers to this as 'the two main streams' of participatory research. Hall names the stream associated with Orlando Fals Borda, Budd Hall, Rajesh Tandon and Muhammed Rahman as 'liberatory'. The second stream, generally associated with Kurt Lewin, the Tavistock, Chris Agyris (e.g. Agyris 2004) and Gustavsen (e.g. 2008; 2017), Hall names the 'Action Research, Action Learning and Process Management stream' (Hall 2005, 15; 2014).

2 As Stanislas Spero Adotevi has observed, 'The museum does not just provide technical assistance but remains the soul of the refined system of preventative charity called "development cooperation". The field of cultural heritage tries to create abroad, in the name of solidarity, a "civilization of the universal" that it is no longer has the strength to build at home' (2022 [1971], 42–3).

5
Participatory worlding

Participation has already been working us. Participation has already been stuttering reflexes and stirring detachment. Having been so worked, how might we work participation and its affects more actively in deconstituting museum constitution, and in making other realities understood in these terms? Finding ways to activate participation's affects is something that this chapter names participatory worlding.[1]

Chapter 1 and Chapter 5 form an asymmetrical pair. Chapter 1 sought to characterise the machinery of museum constitution, all the while throwing in critical grit – the hope being that Chapter 1's critical characterisation of museum constitution would be clear, yet resonant enough to support the retraining of reflexes. Chapter 5 seeks to elaborate the political ontology at work in participation. It elaborates the ways in which the political ontology generated through doing participation has already started to deconstitute museums, and how leaning into participatory worlding can develop into a more deliberate orientation towards undoing museum constitution.

Participatory worlding re-forms the political questions posed by museum constitution – and explored in Chapter 1 – of who there is and how they relate (the deficits of inclusion), of how action happens and decisions are made (tensions between representational 'on behalf of' governance and direct, participatory approaches) and of what there is in the world (contradictions of modern representational ontology). Participatory worlding re-organises the premises of these questions and, through this, offers up specific techniques – *modulating* and *organising* – for museums' deconstitution.

Drawing on 'worlding' in the work of Donna Haraway, Karen Barad and Kathleen Stewart, participatory worlding is a taking up of an ethical and political responsibility – or 'response-ability', in Haraway's terms (Haraway 2016, 2) – for how our ways of being make worlds, producing ourselves and others, things, time and space. Participatory worlding happens through the affective work of 'becoming-with' (Haraway 2016, 3, 12), in which 'with' is made up of differences and entanglements (Barad 2007; 2010) and 'differences without separability' (Ferreira da Silva 2016).[2] Through forging links between theories of materialism and affect and participatory research and action research – in particular John Heron and Peter Reason's 'participatory worldview' (Heron and Reason 1997; Reason 1998; 2005) and Orlando Fals Borda's '*vivencia*' (Fals Borda 1991) – I then elaborate participatory worlding as a mode of political being which seeks abundance and energy, rather than creating scarcity and competition, and seeks direct approaches to action, decision and the negotiation of harm, rather than appealing to the representational politics or normative frameworks of 'on behalf of'.

Worlding

As its verbing suggests, worlding activates the idea that we are not merely part of the world or 'in' the world but are 'of' the world (Barad 2007, 160), taking part in the ongoing making of what the world is. 'Worlding' has been used by Gayatri Chakravorty Spivak to describe how coloniality operates through processes of inscription, by which those who have been colonised come to see themselves in those terms (Spivak 1985, 254–5). In this sense, museums have certainly been technologies of worlding.

The significance of worlding in post-colonial theory acknowledged, the use of worlding I want to draw on more strongly is one which links an awareness of involvement in world-making with an ethical and political responsibility. As Helen Palmar and Vicky Hunter have suggested, 'worlding affords the opportunity for the cessation of habitual temporalities and modes of being' (Palmar and Hunter 2018). The sense that the concept of worlding encourages changes in our ways of being is something we will underline through linking – as we will do more fully by the end of this chapter – participation and worlding into the term 'participatory worlding'.

As explored in relationship to the ontology of museum constitution in Chapter 1, Barad argues that Western politics and ethics are based in a Newtonian ontology (Barad in Barad and Gandorfer 2021, 22). A Newtonian ontology where 'subject and object are understood as separately determinate pre-given entities, and the measurement of the object is performed at a distance, positioning the subject outside the range of analysis' (Barad in Barad and Gandorfer 2021, 21). Instead through their engagement with the quantum physics of Niels Bohr,[3] Barad elaborates a relational ontology in which reality – worlding – happens through 'intra-actions' that are not between already existing entities (whether people, certain types of people or things) but are rather the means by which subjects and objects, time and space, and the boundaries between inside and outside are produced: what Barad terms 'agential separability'. Through 'agential separability' differences are made – but at the same time, and as part of the same process, so are entanglements. As cited in Chapter 1, Barad sees this as 'cutting together/apart' (Barad 2010, 244) and notes that:

> Entanglements are not intertwinings of separate entities, but rather irreducible relations of responsibility. There is no fixed dividing line between 'self' and 'other', 'past' and 'present' and 'future', 'here' and 'now', 'cause' and 'effect'. (Barad 2010, 265)

For Barad worlding is ethics, the 'ethical call that is embodied in the very worlding of the world' (2007, 160). Ethics is within these processes of worlding in ways which make 'ethics [...] not about right response to a radically exterior/ized other, but about responsibility and accountability for the lively relationalities of becoming of which we are a part' (2007, 393). Ethics is therefore a matter of how to be in the present and to be responsive:

> We are accountable for and to not only specific patterns of marks on bodies – that is, the differential patterns of mattering of the world of which we are a part – but also the exclusions that we participate in enacting. Therefore accountability and responsibility must be thought in terms of what matters and what is excluded from mattering. (Barad 2007, 394)

Barad uses the idea of 'agential' to suggest that 'what matters is marked off from what is excluded from mattering' – but adds, 'not once and for all' (2007, 181). This means 'intra-actions enact specific boundaries, marking the domains of interiority and exteriority, differentiating the intelligible from the unintelligible, the determinate from the indeterminate' (2007, 181). However, and through the same process of mattering and separability, alternatives also become possible, as 'constitutive exclusions open a space for the agential reconfiguring of boundaries'

(2007, 181). In other words, we – humans and more-than-humans – generate the boundaries that create entities, ideas, moments and spaces. Yet these boundaries and their exclusions are not final; they are open for refiguring. Museum constitution's promise is that while the cuts – things/people, inside/outside, past/future – create constant work in the redemption of its own ideals, the ontological cuts themselves are clean and stable. Barad's thinking instead draws attention to the ways in which this is not the case. That which is excluded through museum constitution is never finally separated, while the constitutive nature of exclusions constantly poses ethical questions for our part in how those cuts are made and reality produced.

Worlding as 'cutting together/apart' (Barad 2010, 244) also allows us to return to, and extend our engagement with, the work of Denise Ferreira da Silva, who we first encountered in Chapter 1. Ferreira da Silva argues that 'racial grammar' (Ferreira da Silva 2016, 61) and 'cultural difference' sustain 'a moral discourse, which rests on the principle of *separability*':

> This principle considers the social as a whole constituted of formally separate parts. Each of these parts constitutes a social form, as well as geographically-historically separate units, and, as such, stands differentially before the ethical notion of humanity, which is identified with the particularities of white European collectives. (Ferreira da Silva 2016, 63, italics original)

As Ferreira da Silva goes on to argue, this is a type of separability that not only produces violence of different kinds, but also never succeeds in actually separating. She suggests that one of the 'most disturbing findings' of quantum physics is 'nonlocality', which 'assumes, beyond the surfaces onto which the prevailing notion of difference is inscribed, everything in the universe co-exists [...] as a singular expression of everything else in the universe' (Ferreira da Silva 2016, 64). 'That is,' she continues,

> when the social reflects The Entangled World, sociality becomes neither the cause nor the effect of relations involving separate existants, but the uncertain condition under which everything that exists is a singular expression of each and every actual-virtual other existant. (Ferreira da Silva 2016, 65)

While race and cultural difference are produced through the idea that strong differentiation and sorting of people is possible, Ferreira da Silva suggests that a politics can arise from appreciating the impossibility of separation.

For Barad, an allied ethical and political impulse arises from the ways in which 'entanglements are relations of obligation – being bound to the other – enfolded traces of othering' (2010, 265). We might think here of the identities of includer and included generated through the museum constitution paradigm of inclusion. 'Othering,' Barad argues, 'the constitution of an "Other", entails an indebtedness to the "Other", who is irreducibly and materially bound to, threaded through, the "self"– a diffraction/dispersion of identity' (2010, 265). Drawing on Jacques Derrida's concept of *différance*, which implies that the nature of difference is never settled and is endlessly deferred, Barad goes on to draw out the implications for 'oneself': '"Otherness" is an entangled relation of difference (*différance*)'. In Barad's terms, which resonate with the ethical and political implications of Ferreira da Silva's interpretation of nonlocality, 'ethicality entails noncoincidence with oneself' (2010, 265, italics original). To think of ethics in an entangled way is to understand that every differentiation made and generated in support of your sense of self and of the ontology of museum constitution generates unfulfilled and unfinishable connections.

Barad's worlding has commonalities with Donna Haraway's use of 'worlding'; both authors are clearly in dialogue, as they have both often said and shown (e.g. Haraway 2013; Barad 2014). For Haraway, worlding indicates the ways in which 'natures, cultures, subjects, and objects do not pre-exist their intertwined worldings' (Haraway 2016, 13) and that 'ontologically heterogeneous partners become who and what they are in relational material-semiotic worlding' (2016, 12–13).[4] For Haraway, worlding locates us all in a particular confluence or knot of 'trouble', localised expressions of capitalism and colonialism. Haraway describes this as 'the unasked-for pattern in one's hands' and invites us to 'stay' there in 'relay', passing 'patterns back and forth, giving and receiving' (2016, 12). This is not, Haraway suggests, 'becoming' as if it is an individuated trajectory. Instead Haraway qualifies 'becoming' by adding 'with': 'Becoming-with, not becoming, is the name of the game; becoming-with is how partners are [...] rendered capable' (2016, 12).

Worlding is, then, a 'with' – 'becoming-with' – where 'with' is an ongoing task of mattering with its differences and entanglements. It is ontologically participatory. As Haraway puts it, riffing off Marilyn Strathern's work:

> It matters what matters we use to think other matters with; it matters what stories we tell to tell other stories with; it matters what knots knot knots, what thoughts think thoughts, what descriptions describe descriptions, what ties tie ties. It matters what stories make worlds, what worlds make stories. (Haraway 2016, 12)

There can seem a heaviness to this requirement to see every thought, story, knot, description and tie as ethically and politically consequential. However, while sensitising us to the political consequences of how we are with each other, Haraway also emphasises a pragmatic everydayness: 'I am not interested in reconciliation or restoration, but I am deeply committed to the more modest possibilities of partial recuperation and getting on together' (Haraway 2016, 10). Through ideas of 'partial recuperation' and 'getting on together', Haraway always returns us to the affirming messiness at play in the ongoing processes of 'becoming-with'.

While often operating in a different register and using different theorisations, it is not hard to see productive commonalities between these theorisations of worlding and the theories and practice of participation. It is, of course, possible to think that the world is in all cases participatory in Barad's sense of 'cutting together/apart' (2010, 244). In Barad's terms it is through intra-actions and agential cuts that all realities are made regardless of intention. Yet, at the same time, theories of worlding also suggest that actively seeking to be participatory – taking an overtly participatory orientation, and so taking responsibility for the separations and entanglements – *worlds* in a way that is all the more participatory. The intention to be 'with', openness to being made and being changed by how you interact with others, carrying the weight of exclusions and dealing with your particular knotting in legacies of colonialism and capitalist extraction, opens the way to understanding that we are worlded by participation as we world.

Participatory worlding

As implied above, when tethered to the work of Barad, Ferreira da Silva and Haraway, there is a way in which the 'participatory' in the phrase 'participatory worlding' is redundant. Worlding is precisely an ontology of relation and intra-action where entities of all kinds take part and are produced through their 'becoming-with'. Yet I add participatory to ‘participatory worlding’ in order to help elaborate and enlarge a contact point between theories of worlding as described above, participatory research and action research practice and participation in museums. I do this by connecting ‘worlding’ to strands of thought that have claimed the practice of participatory research and action research as a form of ontological politics. In particular, I draw here on John Heron and Peter Reason’s participation as a ‘worldview’ and Orlando Fals Borda’s ‘*vivencia*’, characterised by Juan Mario Díaz-Arévalo as a ‘participatory ontology’ (Díaz-Arévalo 2022).

John Heron and Peter Reason have long connected action research – through ‘co-operative inquiry’ (Heron and Reason 1997; 2006; 2008) – to a ‘participatory worldview’ (Reason 1998).[5] For Heron and Reason a ‘participatory worldview’:

> allows us as human persons to know that we are part of the whole rather than separated as mind over and against matter, or placed here in the relatively separate creation of a transcendent god. It allows us to join with fellow humans in collaborative forms of inquiry. It places us back in relation with the living world – and we note that to be in relation means that we live with the rest of creation as relatives, with all the rights and obligations that implies. (Heron and Reason 1997, 275–6)

Taking a ‘participatory worldview’ is understood as means of healing the ‘alienation, the split that characterises modern experience’ (Reason 1998, 7): ‘to heal means to make whole: we can only understand our world as a whole if we are part of it; as soon as we attempt to stand outside, we divide and separate’ (1998, 7). Making the link with action research explicit, Heron and Reason argue that:

> The participative worldview necessarily leads to an action orientation [...] a reflective action, a praxis, grounded in our being in the world. So within the participative worldview the primary purpose of human inquiry is practical: our inquiry is our action in the service of human flourishing. (Heron and Reason 1997, 288)

For Fals Borda *vivencia*, as produced through his type of ‘participatory action research’, is ‘an experiential methodology, that is, a process of personal and collective behavior occurring within a satisfying and productive cycle of life and labor’ (Fals Borda 1991, 3). *Vivencia*, as Fals Borda outlines in a footnote,

> may be translated roughly as 'inner life-experience' or 'happening', but the concept implies a more ample meaning by which a person finds fulfilment for his / her being, not only in the workings of the inner self but in the osmotic otherness of nature and the wider society, and by learning not only with the brain alone but also with the heart. (Fals Borda 1991, fn.2, 11)

Vivencia happens through the 'open-ended process of life and work' generated by participatory action research and involving 'a progressive evolution towards an overall, structural transformation of sociality and culture, a process that requires ever-renewed commitment, an ethical stand, self-critique and persistence at all levels' (Rahman and Fals Borda 1991, 29).

Crucially, what Fals Borda gathers in this naming of *vivencia* is the ontological sense that

> PAR *induces the creation of its own field* in order to extend itself in time and space, both horizontally and vertically, in communities and regions. It moves from the micro to the macro as if in a spiral, and thus acquires a political dimension. (Fals Borda 1991, 6, italics added)

Instead of investigating a field that already exists out there and then seeking to understand it and represent it, Fals Borda argues that participatory research and action research makes its own field, makes its own world, or is a worlding in the terms I am using here. Participation – a 'philosophy of life as much as a method' (Fals Borda 2001, 29) – enables a responsive attunement to potential through action-reflecting and thinking-feeling, and through the differences that brings to who we are and who we are to each other. It doesn't simply try to change the world (though that is often a stated intention); rather, it changes *what the world is*: 'there is not one way but many, so we must keep on trying to understand better, change and re-enchant our plural world' (Fals Borda 2001, 31).

What I want to do now is to amplify the implications of Heron and Reason's and Fals Borda's concepts of participatory worldview and *vivencia* to then point in two directions. To underline the point, in the elaborations of both Reason and Fals Borda it is not (only) that there is a participatory ontology that is then applied – but rather that doing participation itself generates a participatory ontology. In one direction, doing participation in museums has generated a political ontology in conflict with the representational political ontology of museum constitution. Adding participation has already been deconstituting museums: that has been *participation's affective work*, often unintended and unbidden. Yet, if considered in these terms, there is scope to amplify and extend participation as an alternative political ontology – creating its own field, shifting how we are with each other and doing culture and heritage in ways where action and decision is negotiated directly between those involved. This is what I am suggesting could become *participation's affective work*.

Participatory worlding: participation's affective work

To develop the idea that the very doing of participation generates participatory worlding I return to theories of affect. Kathleen Stewart theorises affect as worlding. For Stewart, 'a worlding [is] an attunement to a singular world's texture and shine' (Stewart 2010, 341). This means that 'the body has to learn to play itself like a musical instrument in this world's compositions' (2010, 341). Stewart's work suggests how this is always the case; all aspects of life generate a requirement to attune and to learn how play this world's compositions. However, I now want to develop my earlier suggestion that participation is a particularly molten space for worlding, and that this is the case due to its constitutive uncertainty.

Participation is a doing undertaken with intention – to be with – but one that always produces unintended affects. It is a worlding that comes from putting yourself in certain situations. It is open to affecting and being affected in certain ways. It is a way of being with others which requires you to become attuned to shifts in atmosphere and mood. Participation is to have to intuit – knowing all the while that your intuition is maybe trained with the wrong sensitivities and that it is very likely you 'will have been wrong' (Povinelli 2002, 33). Stewart suggests the uncertainty and even peril at play:

> Affect matters in a world that is always promising and threatening to amount to something. Fractally complex, there is no telling what will come of it or where it will take persons attuned. (Stewart 2010, 340)

In *Pascalian Meditations*, Bourdieu frames this everyday peril in the following way:

> One might say that we are *disposed* because we are *exposed*. It is because the body is (to unequal degrees) exposed and endangered

> in the world, faced with the risk of emotion, lesion, suffering, sometimes death, and therefore obliged to take the world seriously (and nothing is more serious than emotion, which touches the depths of our organic being) that it is able to acquire dispositions that are themselves an openness to the world, that is, to the very structures of the social world of which they are the incorporated form. (Bourdieu 2000 [1997], 140, italics original)

Participation – even more than the usual perils that are contained in everyday life – it is to put yourself in the way of being affected, to have to take explicit responsibility for how you affect others and to be prepared for not knowing, for surprise and for new things arising.[6]

Massumi notes that affecting and being affected:

> are not two different capacities – they always go together. When you affect something, you are at the same time opening yourself up to being affected in turn, and in a slightly different way than you might have been the moment before. You have made a transition, however slight. (Massumi 2015a, 3–4)

In this eventfulness of affecting and being affected, 'there are any number of levels of organization and tendencies in play, in co-operation with each other or at cross-purposes. The way all the elements interrelate is so complex that it isn't necessarily comprehensible in one go' (Massumi 2015a, 2). There is, he observes, a 'virtual co-presence of potentials' (2015a, 5). It is this uncertainty, Massumi argues, that 'can actually be empowering – once you realize that it gives you a margin of manoeuvrability' (2015a, 2).

Participation is a worlding that comes from being stuck in things together, a doing and a happening where new things reach 'a point of expressivity' (Stewart 2014, 119). Participation generates a desire to be changed, to find that 'margin of manoeuvrability' while knowing you will always struggle to be enough for the occasions participation produces. Doing participation in relation to museum constitution – as explored in Chapters 2, 3 and 4 – creates a site of churn, visceral, personally implicating and political generative. Having considered participation in museums in this way, the question then becomes how to be, how to world.

Modulating for participatory worlding

Detaching was the first of our three techniques and was elaborated in Part II. The need to stutter the reflex that immediately is called into being by, and calls into being, museum constitution. Detaching threw micro grits in the museum constitution machinery by exceeding, slackening, accelerating, trying and turning. In Part III we explore two further techniques – *modulating* and *organising*. If *how you are* in 'intra-action' and 'becoming-with' is how worlds are worlded, then we need technique to adjust how we are in any given present. Together with detaching, modulating and organising are techniques for participatory worlding. We will work closely, both here and in Chapter 6, with Brian Massumi's theorisation of modulating, which aims to support the micro-differences we can make in the present through a practised retraining of our intuitions. If worlding happens in every environment and context, it is nevertheless significant to consider – as we will do in Chapter 7 – how we might actively create modes of organising that centre 'becoming-with' and, in particular, do not create requirements for 'on behalf of' decision-making.

Modulation, Massumi argues, is not done by a conscious, choice-making individual. Rather, 'at the decisive moment', we are 'absorbed in a readiness potential that is intensely *overdetermined*' in a present where a 'whole range of potentials are in it together, in their difference'. The different potentials 'are in a state of mutual inclusion, on the verge, poised toward the collapse destined to resolve the over-determination of the and-both into this-not-that determinate effect' (Massumi 2015c, 20). The 'nonconscious "sub-threshold latency"' – what Massumi calls 'bare activity' – is 'churning with the intensity of a mutually inclusive range of potentials, in co-motional intensity' (2015c, 20). This means that far from the person being autonomous, '*It is the act of choice that is autonomous*, in the dissociative dimension of the dividual: that of the individual, absorbed in its relation to itself, plied by superpositions of contrasting states in a mutual immanence of functional indistinction' (2015c, 19, italics original).

Bearing Massumi's words in mind, if we think of those museum strip-lighted meeting rooms where pulses rise – which we first explored in Chapter 2 and will return to in Chapter 6 – it becomes possible no longer to think of individual people consciously choosing to stick their hands up, making a clear judgement then acting on it, fully cognisant of what they are doing. Those 'choices' to reactivate museum constitution definitely do happen and those moments are, in Massumi's terms, a 'creative: an ontopowerful act', 'tantamount to an existential decision'

(2015c, 19). However, it is perhaps not straightforward to know *who* decides. The answer, Massumi argues, is:

> no one – as in the French *personne*, which can mean both 'someone' and 'no one'. Decision happens: affectively-systemically, in the nonconscious processual autonomous zone where mutually exclusive states come together. The event decides, as it happens. (Massumi 2015c, 19–20, italics original)

Those museum meetings when someone says 'who is not here?' or 'are they the usual suspects?' or 'what about the visitor?' are where the 'event decides' to reanimate the late liberal loop 'as it happens'.

Massumi understands these moments as a way of countering the kind of critique which will always ask of politics which operates at a micro-level questions such as 'where does this go?' or 'what does this add up to?' Massumi challenges the idea of some judge hanging over every event to decide whether it is politically worthy. He places value instead on 'modulations of becoming that produce self-justifying surplus values of life: pulses of life experienced as worth the living by virtue of the event they are, immanent to the event, as a function of its immediate experiential quality [...]' (Massumi 2015c, 35). Relocating politics into the present and for its own energetic intensity articulates the difference of a participatory worlding – a worlding uncoupled from linear time, a determinant and predicable causality and a politics where ends justify means.

While always committed to the present as the real, Massumi uses this to reimagine the meaning of strategic. Modulating, he observes,

> cannot completely control the outcome. But it can inflect it, tweak it. So it is not strategic in the sense of preconceiving a specific outcome in all its detail and finding the means to arrive at that intended end. It is all means – all in the middle, in the midst, in the heat of encounter. (Massumi 2015a, 96)

Massumi challenges causality as such, but at the same time he does make room for the effects of 'accumulation', which are the potential impacts of retraining reflexes into more flexible and varying intuition. To return to a point first explored in the Introduction, Massumi sees reflex as a habit that has 'lost its adaptive power, its powers of variation, its force of futurity, that has ceased to be the slightest bit surprised by the world' (2015a, 66). Instead Massumi uses 'intuition' as a way to describe ‘a doing done more *through* me, self-relating, than *by* my I’, one that ‘brings a creative moment to life in a way that registers as a change in me that is also world-changing’ (2015c, 20–1, italics original). The effects of retraining reflexes to cultivate new ‘automaticities’ can, Massumi argues, ‘accumulate from one encounter to the next, and lead somewhere new’ (2015a, 96). Accumulating might ‘amplify, resonate or even bifurcate – potentially in ways that don’t coagulate into a power structure, but instead keep restructuring, keep the structuring alive’ (Massumi 2015a, 96).

The question ‘who is not here?’ – as we will explore in Chapter 6 – is one of museum constitution’s most potent kick-starters. It is the question that makes me feel more than a prick of shame. It is also the question that makes me take responsibility. Yet ‘who is not here?’ is also the question that, when considered in terms of the political ontologies of participatory worlding, has enormous capacities for different modes of ‘becoming-with’ (Haraway 2016, 12), ‘cutting together/apart’ (Barad 2010, 244) or of ‘difference without separability’ (Ferreira da Silva 2016). While it is a question that arises from the logics of inclusion, its affective and agential impacts are so potent as to also catalyse refusals (Lee-Crossett 2020; Ankenbrand, Fitzpatrick, Graham, Rees, Webb-Bourne forthcoming).

Ultimately Massumi’s orientations connect to questions of participatory and direct approaches to democracy that will be explored in Chapter 7. The ontology Massumi lays out is, in his own terms, ‘directly participatory, at no distance from the event under modulation’ (2015a, 96). Far from this being too abstract to act as a basis for political action, Massumi sees modulation as a:

> foundation for practices of direct democracy, lived democracy, democracy as essentially participatory and irreducibly relational […] This is a democracy whose base concept is not the supposed freedom of the individual from the collectivity, but the freedom of the collectivity for its becoming. It is the embodied freedom of bodies to come together in thinking-feeling, to participate in differentially attuned becoming, in all immediacy and with all urgency. (2015a, 97)

Modulating is one of the techniques this book seeks to develop because it offers a mode of being that enables, you could say *acts as the practice base for*, participatory worlding. Modulating is the *how* and *how much* (Grossberg 1992, 82) of organising; it is, to recall Kathleen Stewart’s phrase, the 'commonplace, labor-intensive process of sensing modes of living as they come into being' (Stewart 2010, 340). Modulating is the means by which we nourish practical, action-based experiments in how we might organise differently.

Writing as participatory worlding

Across the traditions of participatory and action research and theories of affect, materialism and the more-than-human, there has long been an interest in writing not as reflecting or representing but as doing or an enactment of the relational ontologies being explored. For example, in the *Historia doble de la Costa*, Fals Borda and the wider team combined two different modes of knowing: 'Logos / Mythos or core / cortex combining "hardcore" data with imaginative, literary and artistic "cortex" interpretation within cultural frames' (Fals Borda 2001, 31).[7] Or, to give another example, first person action researcher Judi Marshall describes the way in which writing form as arising from action research itself (Marshall 2008).

Poetics in affect theory has been a response to, and methodology for, its ontologies.[8] As Stewart puts it, 'analytic attention to the forms and forces of moving bodies and events invites experiments with description and with the conceptual' (Stewart 2017, 197). It starts from 'the state of being in the middle of attachments and threats, of what lingers and what jumps. This is a method that tries to move in the manner of things slipping in and out of existence' (2017, 197). As Ben Highmore suggests, such 'entanglements don't require critical untangling (the scholarly and bureaucratic business of sorting categories and filing phenomenon); instead what is required is a critically entangled contact with affective experience' (Highmore 2010, 119).

For Stewart – an anthropologist – this calls for a writing which, instead of fixing 'notions of agency, subjects, objects, bodies, and intentions' (2017, 197), can 'describe a world under pressure, the way a present moment can descend like a curtain on a place, the way a world elaborates in prolific forms, taking off in directions, coming to roost on people and practices' (2017, 197). Yet of course – in the political ontology of affect theory – in describing there is also a bringing into being. As Stewart puts it: 'The root process of things taking form is ordinary and pervasive: a process of making things matter (like it or not), a leaning in, a vigilance, a way of going on in the world' (Stewart 2014, 126). This goes for writing too.

Participatory worlding is being done through the writing experiments of this book, in particular through shifting modes of attention, through mixing proximities and distances and through giving words to things at the 'very edge of semantic availability' (Williams 1977, 134). Its descriptions are also its creations. In this book I have come to treat writing as a technique by which we develop technique – technique (Spatz 2015; see note 13 on page 24) for participatory worlding. The page offers a space and time where retraining happens. It is not away from life, but part of life. Writing offers the promise that giving form, crafting a phrase, a memory or a cadence, might get under your skin enough to be carried with you, and so disrupt the habitual reflex. We might think – to anticipate the next chapter – of the page as a time and space that does modulation to enable modulation. In turn, modulations done and tried will be returned to the page, heightened to be heightened.

Notes

1 We might think of political ontology in Arturo Escobar's terms as 'an open-ended ethical and theoretico-political proposition, rather than a hard-nosed claim on the real [and …] a way of telling stories differently, in the hope that other spaces for the enactment of the multiple ontologies making up the pluriverse might open up' (Escobar 2018, 218).

2 Before I go on, it must be noted that the word 'inclusion' is still very much used in the participatory and action research literature – not least being recently stated as a core challenge for participatory inquiry in the conclusion to a recent and highly significant reader, *The SAGE Handbook of Participatory Research and Inquiry* (Howard, Ospina and Burns 2021). However, almost as soon as the editors of *The SAGE Handbook of Participatory Research and Inquiry* (Jo Howard, Sonia M. Ospina and Danny Burns) name 'inclusion' as the first of the three big challenges for the future of participatory inquiry, they immediately reframe the challenge of inclusion in terms of decolonisation (2021, 1029). This opens up and requires, I would argue, a very different political ontology to inclusion.

3 Niels Bohr's quantum physics is crucial to Barad's agential realism. Bohr – 'contrary both to the ontology assumed by classical physics, wherein each entity (e.g., the electron) is either a wave or a particle, independent of experimental circumstances, and to the epistemological assumption that experiments reveal the pre-existing determinate nature of the entity being measured' – argues that 'the nature of the observed phenomenon changes with corresponding changes in the [experimental] apparatus' (Barad 2007, 106). The implication of this is that any attempt to know the world is involved in producing the world, an insight Barad develops as 'intra-actions' and agential separability. I will not attempt to give an account of Bohr's two slit experiments with electrons as waves and particles, but you can find Barad's account in Chapter 3 of her book *Meeting the University Halfway* (2007).

4 Worlding has an association with Martin Heidegger's phenomenology. Haraway is keen to draw a distinction between a Heideggerian use and the way she is using it through her term Terrapolis: 'Finished once and for all with Kantian globalizing cosmopolitics and grumpy human-exceptionalist Heideggerian worlding […] Never poor in world, Terrapolis exists in the sfweb of always-too-much connection, where response-ability must be cobbled together, not in the existentialist and bond-less, lonely, Man-making gap theorized by Heidegger and his followers' (Haraway 2016, 11).

5 Participatory research and action research act as umbrella terms for a multitude of different strands with different names, different nuances and associated with different researchers. 'Co-operative inquiry' is an approach associated with John Heron and Peter Reason which links

an action research process with 'extended' epistemologies and ontologies to include the ways experiential knowledge, practical knowledge and knowledge arising from how things are presented interact with more traditional forms of 'propositional knowledge' (Heron and Reason 1997; 2006; 2008; see also Gaya 2021). 'Participatory action research' became a term used by Orlando Fals Borda to emphasise the links between ways of being together – *vivencia*, described in this chapter – and transformative social and political change (Fals Borda 2001; see Díaz-Arévalo 2022 for a full account of the evolution of 'participatory action research').

6 Chris Whitehead, Tom Schofield and Gönül Bozoğlu, in their 2021 book *Plural Heritages and Community Co-production: Designing, walking and remembering*, convey a moving and rich sense of openness to being affected through their work with people around the walls in Istanbul. The book reads like a live grappling with the complex political ontology that participatory processes produce. Their argument – arising explicitly from putting themselves in the way of being affected – is to suggest that the 'real potential of thinking with plural heritages is *to understand relationalities*, to see the flow between and across minor and major, to catch a glimpse of how an unknown life story suddenly hinges on a famous historical moment. It is also to think with the vibrancy of heritage as an endless relationality of materials, bodies, affects, and memories' (Whitehead, Schofield and Bozoğlu 2021, 159, italics original). The desire these processes create for something else, for other ways of being, is conveyed through the final line of the book, in which the authors cite Erin Manning, 'there must be other ways of living?' (2021, 159).

7 Participatory action research has always been interested in full selves, challenging any residual Cartesian mind–body split. As Fals Borda puts it: 'through the actual experience of something, we intuitively apprehend its essence; we feel, enjoy and understand it as a reality, and we thereby place our own being in a wider, more fulfilling context' (1991, 4). At play here is the idea that participatory action research creates social conditions where you can 'think with the heart' (1991, 50), and that much is to be gained by using the 'affective logic of the heart and sentiments than the cold-headed analysis that comes from offices and laboratories' (1991, 8).

8 For Stewart worldings 'prompt', offering us 'a line, a refrain, a tendency, an icon, a colour, a groove of habit or hope, or a rhythm', which in turn we world. Our everyday labour of responsiveness becomes caught up in how 'qualities, a density, an aesthetic, become somehow legible, recognizable' (Stewart 2014, 119). Through becoming refrains that we might 'score' and 'rescore' (Stewart 2010, 339), it is this tipping – passing over a threshold into legibility – that is worlding: resonating with the ontological streams in the writings of Fals Borda and Reason. As Stewart puts it, 'disparate and incommensurate elements (human and non-human, given and composed) cohere and take on force as some kind of real, a world' (Stewart 2014, 119).

6
Modulating

Someone asks, '*Who isn't here?*'

You are immediately gripped. The baton of moral obligation passing as that question is asked. Asking that question creates a cut, a disruption, generating moral authority by it being taken off the peg. Now you find yourself galvanised, molten, guilty, determined, owning those absences as yours and energised to do something.

The cut produces a distribution, a making responsible.[1] That unpegged question now lives, dynamically morphing as it goes, making present an adapting structure of thought, a trajectory with a history, ideological, moving at speed through the meeting, opening it up and scattering in many directions and in varying tempos.

To be gripped now is to accept a premise. This place is in deficit. The question queasy with complexity.

Called forth most easily is the liberal reflex. To right those wrongs (Spivak 2004). The question, taken this way, generates only a certain type of agency. The responsibility of the mediator, the includer, the redeemer of the institutional ideals. Quick to take that on as your own, revealing and forging an alignment with the abstractions of the liberal horizon, straightening in their demands on you.

A cut that makes you agent while making others those-who-have-been-excluded and are to-be-included.[2] A cut that centres you as you scale yourself up. A cut that norms you, racialised, classed, self-possessed. Your conduct conducted to these ends, enlightenment running hot, pulsing with purpose.[3]

Knowing this question will be asked and that you will be called to account, you might have sought to stabilise the urgency, to plan for the moment the question will be asked. You might have technologised a response with stakeholder mapping, collecting postcodes, requiring demographic data so you can try and face the question with a grafted calm and tell yourself, and those assembled for your report, that you have done enough.

Yet, as you also already know, the question never allows for completion. It will never be satisfied, no matter how much you extract. No matter how much you require people to contort themselves into tick boxes and to become accountable to your accountability through trading in their personal data. The question will never be satisfied within the terms of the liberal museum constitution because it relies on a certain type of lack, one that motors an endless orientation to reform: *we are trying, we keep trying*. The museum constitutional lack joining with a lack in you, recruiting you to its task through this mirroring.

Each new iteration of this question recruits, each time a test of who finds this their responsibility. Who takes up its call, and how, and how much. Flushed at first. The agential hit always fades, leaving only belly truths, the impatient labour of contorted guts.[4]

In the wake of the question, unfolding through the meeting, dynamically now, are also other potentials, less habitual, harder to take up, requiring cultivation, rearrangement, practice.

Who is here?
A breath, pause-making, gap-making, detaching from the grippedness and its promise to your lack. Detaching from its promise to draw you out into the world, always failing and ever-righteous.

You try taking it in more slowly as the question travels away from the asker of the question and moves towards you. Instead of catching it, and then holding it, owning it, taking it up as your own, taking it away to be worked and finding groups to be drawn in. You stop the question and place it, arrested, in the centre of the room.

Everyone peers. In movement, the question has an inevitability in its speed, its velocity and its tendency away from some people towards other people. Stopped now it is a more complex question – vibrating, fused light and dark, many-sided, some sides shiny, reflective; other sides dull, absorbing.

Who isn't here?
Refusing that cut of self-possessed agency and seeking other modes. The meeting already a fullness. Ungripping, attending back to the room.

(What of) who (we are) isn't here?
Unbracketing those parts of ourselves bracketed by professional life and institutional participation, parts set aside and opening them up. Singularities. Vibrating with histories. The once invisibilities of whiteness to those occupying its norm appearing now to be constituted by things once treated as negative externalities and now coming into presence.

'I' fraying now, less decisively cut or at least cut with a less sharp and less practised blade. Fuzzier and more luminescent, caught less in the movement of progress or sequencing. A dwelling.

Unclenching and then feeling out for the type of conversation that has enough expansiveness and room for manoeuvre. The quiet shift that means that through something said you understand that something you had proposed was wrong, or had missed something important, or had made unhelpful assumptions. Or at least that what you proposed wasn't the only or richest possibility. And then to able to say so and adjust and adjust together. Old, semi-frozen modes of relating, thawing and creating different types of heat fuelled by less false intensity, more slowly and more carefully generated.

Yet still sometimes and unbidden, that old familiar defensive posture, curling through your body, maldistributing eye contact, a protecting harsh wall channelling you only in one direction. Or the tramlines of something more complacent remerging, steely and directional, taking us off and back, sweeping up excess, re-incorporating it into cynical institutional realism.

Trying to notice that and maybe slow things down a touch; or try bouncing it, up and down or across.

Who isn't here?
Trying instead to hold the idea that the 'we' we are crafting is necessary and also never sufficient. And that our 'we' has an integrity, a holding form, a basis for communion, for organising, for 'becoming-with' (Haraway 2016, 12). Our 'we' being the locale of our 'incompleteness'. 'Inclined towards each other', and cautiously hopeful (Harney and Moten 2021, 41).

A recomposition of what the work is. To hold in this space collapsed modernity. No longer to use the calculation of a distance gaze to maintain a horizon. No longer to see the past as a completed action, a debt already paid. To make a here and now. A here and now where the conditions of possibility of this museum, this project, of us having been gathered together, is not in ignorance.

Who is already here as we are elsewhere?
Finding ourselves anew, entangled. Not separable, not other-able, enmeshed. Already present. A thought-shift for modulation moment-by-moment, an expansive implication and generosity towards what is and might be on the cusp. Uncomplacent, stiller now and staying.

Following out

Pulses often rise in strip-lighted meeting rooms because someone has drawn attention to the question of who is missing. More often than not in meeting rooms like this – or via email, or online – the person asking this question feels their responsibility is discharged through the asking itself. In my experience it is often senior managers, or sometimes funders or policy people, who tend to ask the question. It is a facet of liberal governance to be concerned with this question, more than anything, as a question.

Karen Barad once said 'you can walk around in concepts'. They go on:

> I walk around in a sentence, I walk around in a word. A word, or even a letter, entails stories, different stories. *It is a phenomenon, an entire entangle spacetimemattering of particular kinds of configurations – and not others*. These are matters of ethics, of justice. (Barad in Barad and Gandorfer 2021, 32, italics original)

You can certainly walk around in the question 'Who is not here?'. This is what I tried to do in the experiments that led to the piece above.

The question 'Who is not here?' imagines others – never specific people but demographics (Morse 2020, 88). It is a question with a pointed history of who gets to define who else is a problem and in what ways. As W. E. B. DuBois observed about the 'flutter[ing]' of white people, 'between me and the other world there is an ever-unasked question [...] "how does it feel to be a problem?"' (2015 [1897], 67). In this case the problem being that 'they' are not yet here and that 'they' will have to be sought out and manifested somehow, a process that has led to many everyday atrocities.

It is a question which – like the question of inclusion generally – distributes subject positions and agency to different people, with some becoming already included and others becoming those-to-be-included (those not yet here). It is a question that devalues anyone already taking part in participatory processes and who are already present. The question demands that there are always some other people – not yet known – who are imagined to be more excluded, more worthy of resources and attention. The crucial bit being that 'they' are not yet known. As soon as they are, they will no longer be excluded enough to be so recognised.

The question also works in such a way as to appear to take responsibility for exclusion while also oddly alleviating the questioner from responsibility – especially, I would suggest, in the institutional conversation between white staff around race.[5] The question also – as I understood better through writing the piece above – has a momentum which always moves away from certain people towards others.

Through the writing experiments that led to this chapter, I wanted to play through the moment of the question 'Who is not here?' being asked and how it – the question and its many layers – might be affectively modulated in Massumi's terms. It was this movement between the tight loop and an entangled form that I wanted to try give form to – developing an alternative trajectory to replace the momentum of the question hurtling across the room, there to be caught by my ever-ready hands. While modulating is a way of experimenting in everyday modes of being, modulating also makes possible, and is also made possible, by experiments in everyday modes of organising – the focus of the next chapter.

Notes

1 'Cut' here is influenced by Karen Barad, Brian Massumi and Erin Manning. For Barad, 'intra-actions' create 'agential separability', which they describe as an 'agential cut' (Barad 2007, 140). Drawing on Alfred North Whitehead's process philosophy, Manning defines the cut as 'decisional' and 'not as external to the event but as the cut, in the event, through which new ecologies, new fields of relation are crafted' (Manning 2016, 19). I use 'cut' here to describe how a certain tendency – to ask the question 'Who is not here?' – shapes potential into certain types of differentiated agency.

2 Throughout this reimagination of the question 'Who is not here?', I am working with theorists who have drawn attention to the Western ontology at work in 'separability' (Ferreira da Silva 2016, 63). A separability that not only produces violence of all kinds, but also never finally achieves separation. Indeed, the desire for separation itself generates consequential entanglement. In the terms of Stefano Harney and Fred Moten, 'Europe is constantly disestablished by what it seeks to envelop, which, in and out of turn, envelops it' (2021, 28).

3 In Stefano Harney and Fred Moten's words: 'The moment you say it is mine because I worked on it and improved it, or you say that I am me because I worked on myself and improved myself, you start a War' (Harney and Moten 2021, 32).

4 See Chapter 4 for a discussion of Michel Foucault's 'What is Enlightenment?' (1984).

5 Aamir Darr reflects on attempts to open up a conversation about race as part of the Bradford's National Museum project (Darr 2021).

7
Organising

> The leaves, the roots, the trunk, the orchard, and the ecosystem?
> It is our Western conceit to focus on the apple.
> (Bollier 2003, 15)

Museum constitution's modern and representational ontology has a specific political organisational consequence – it calls into necessity 'on behalf of' governance. As argued in Chapter 1, museum constitution's horizon ideals generate deficits. These deficits in turn create competition over collections and exhibition space and produce differentiated political agency for those that act as includers – who are required to manage diversity – and those perceived to be in need of inclusion, who are required to perform their difference in acceptable ways. These deficits produce tensions between the interests of imagined and abstract constituencies. They also operate through ontological contradictions between the ability to exploit collections and make objects stand in for other things, people and ideas and the singularity of objects, meaning that they demand careful protection which, in turn, brings forth an entire institutional infrastructure. Together the looped constitutional structure works in justification of the need for professionals and trustees to make decisions that balance out interests between future generations and everybody here today, as well as *between* all of those here today.

If museum constitution's political ontology – to recall the argument made in Chapter 1 – creates ongoing problematics that have to be endlessly negotiated and require 'on behalf of' governance, participatory worlding – as introduced in Chapter 5 – seeks to draw on other ontologies that are produced by, and also make possible, different modes of political organising. In this chapter, one of our aims is to activate participatory worlding for participatory organising through a deliberate reworking of key terms of museum constitution: 'conserve', 'future', 'access', 'everyone', 'represent the world' and 'on behalf of'. While organising with a participatory ontology and through in-the-moment modulating does take us a long way, persistent political challenges related to decision-making, conflict, harm and differentiated rights of use and access also need to be addressed.

In developing political modes for a participatory worlding, what we are seeking are not only ways of organising that can both generate abundance and energy, and therefore minimise competition, but also ways of organising that can deal with overt conflict, differentiated interests and motivations, and experiences of harm – all in direct and participatory ways and all without falling back on the need for professional or trustee 'on behalf of' governance.

Museum constitution: a reminder of the political problems it is meant to solve

If you are accountable to abstract constituencies, some of which are not yet born, and you have a fragile and precious resource to which they all have an equal right, then – the political logic goes – you have an immense duty to protect the resource while balancing out interests fairly. It is through this political imagination that museum authority is generated, and it is sustained through the negotiation of the everyday problematics such a context produces. This is museum constitution. Adding participation – so drawing into play a specific group of people who will make decisions on their own behalf – is always going to trouble museum constitution because it demands the question: Are you being fair to everyone else and to future generations?

To appreciate the dynamics of museum constitution is to understand that the answer to this question will always be no.[1] After all, it is the greater calling beyond any group – to an idea of humanity, public, future generations and everyone – which is used in justification of museum 'on behalf of' governance. Then, having both called forth and de-legitimised participation, various management techniques are deployed to re-legitimise the participant group in representational terms. As explored in Chapter 1, these typically include limiting group-based decision-making power (so that professionals can ensure that all interests are considered), requiring those participants to stand in for/represent others from their locale or demographic (so participation can be justified within a representational framework), time-limited engagement (so that other groups can be worked with and so enable fair access to resources) and editing work produced through participatory processes (to make exhibits more acceptable or engaging for the wider public). The many, well-documented frustrations that groups have had in working with museums arise from museums activating the logics of museum constitution which, under current governance forms, is also the source of professional and trustee legitimacy. To put it another way, participation always has to be foreclosed.[2] This is why museum participation has constantly generated not very pretty pickles (e.g. Fouseki 2010; Kassim 2017; Lynch 2011a; 2011b; Lynch 2019; Lynch 2020; Morse 2020; von Oswald 2023).

Liberal democratic theory and liberal economic theory further illuminate the representational logics of museum constitution. In liberal democratic theory what makes something democratic is determined by the concept of 'all affected' – requiring all who are affected by a decision to be involved in its making.[3] If 'all affected' by a decision is a very large number of people or people who are not yet born, then forms of representation and delegation tend to be deployed to take decisions 'on behalf of' all those affected. In liberal economic theory, the question of democratic management of resources has been conventionally linked to questions of 'rivalry' – that use by one precludes use by another. If an object is thought of as scarce, fixed and non-renewable – rival – then some form of management is needed to balance out use fairly. As long as the 'all affected' for museums comprises future generations and everyone – or even everyone in a city or in a particular neighbourhood (it is the abstraction that is the issue, not the scale of the abstraction) – then the problem of 'all affected' remains. As long as abstract constituencies are paired with rivalry, then again 'on behalf of' re-emerges.

One of the effects of the political ontology of museum constitution is that it cleverly holds everyone equally at arm's length in the name of being fair. If any given object cannot be on open display and touched by everyone, no member of the public should be allowed to touch it. If you are allowed greater access, for instance by virtue of being a museum volunteer, then you have access not as a community or agent in your own right but as a servant of the governance logics of 'on behalf of' all. If you want to tell your story, you will receive help to ensure it is the right story, and then be assisted again to make this story work for visitors through various professional techniques of interpretive planning.

It is the case that over the last decades museums have started to break down this idea of being equally and fairly estranged from collections. There are now numerous examples of faith groups and source communities being able to use objects (for an early example, see Brown and Peers 2020). However – and while I am making no claim this happens in all instances – a danger here is if community use happens under the strictures of museum constitution. Even while enabling source community use of collections, any enforcement of abstract constituencies – 'all affected' – and the sense of the object as being scarce and fragile – 'rival' – is likely to have the effect of keeping the representational ontology of the museum in place, including 'on behalf of' governance.

To develop this point further, let's return to a discussion in Chapter 1 about the depth to which power is devolved in participatory projects. What I am suggesting is that it will not matter at all how much control is devolved to any given group if they remain required to serve the museum constitutional ontology of abstract constituencies and rivalry. To illustrate this for a moment it is useful to return to the classic ladder of participation developed by Sherrie Arnstein (2019 [1969]) and discussed in Chapter 1. At the bottom of Arnstein's ladder is 'Manipulation' and at the top is 'Citizen Control'. But in the event that a community of citizens took control of their museum, if they still placed abstract constituencies and rivalry at their organisation's heart then it will become a representational structure all over again. It would simply be different people enacting the same requirement to balance out interests fairly.

This is something to watch out for: thinking that the apex of the ladder or, more trendily, the right hand of the spectrum, can be achieved within a representational structure. If there are community partners on trustee boards – a move that is often seen as being at the 'leading and championing' right-hand end of the spectrum (Museums Association n.d., 13) – we might pay attention to whether they are being expected to stand in for others of their demographic or locality in some way, whether they are asked to account for the extent to which they are grassroots or excluded (and therefore not 'usual suspects') or whether they are called to speak to the question of others who are not yet included. We might also be attentive to whether the trustee boards themselves believe they are stewarding collections and legitimate representation on 'behalf of', and might therefore demand any community members do the same. Late liberal representational thinking is very powerful. The persistent nature of the late liberal and the representational is, after all, experienced by many of us as a reflex. This is why participatory governance also requires the cultivation of a participatory ontology, a participatory worlding.

Changing political problems

As has been argued so far in this chapter, the most important element in enabling direct, participatory self-constituting is that it is done in concert with a participatory ontology. In other words it is important to recognise that participation will never be able to act as an answer to the problems generated by a representational politics; instead participation offers – and requires – a change in the framing of political problems. In contrast to the representational politics of museum constitution, a participatory ontology – participatory worlding – disintensifies competition over scarce resources of objects and exhibitions. It shifts from constituencies as abstract ideas (future generations, everyone) in favour of particularity, and it foregrounds responsibility, to reinvoke Karen Barad, for the differences and entanglements created through everyday relating. A participatory worlding also generates potential for participatory and self-organising alternatives to 'on behalf of' governance. In short, it ends the sense that we need professionals and trustees to act as mediators.

Reframing 'conserve objects for future generations': conserving as participatory worlding

Before exploring how conserving might be figured as happening through participatory worlding, we can develop our understanding of the ways in which museum constitution operates as a liberal political and economic form by turning to Garrett Hardin's 1968 'The tragedy of the commons' and the various ways in which his thesis has since been contested.[4] Hardin argues that we live in a world of finite resources and if all 'men' [*sic*] are 'rational actors', they can be expected to want to 'maximize his [*sic*] gain' (Hardin 1968, 1244). As population growth continues, Hardin reasons, common use of land is no longer viable and other forms of management are required. Hardin deploys the examples of cattle grazing common land and of US National Parks. In terms of cattle grazing, Hardin uses a rational actor economic approach in which the only course of action for famers to take is constantly to increase the size of their herd:

> Ruin is the destination towards which all men rush, each pursuing his own best interest in a society that believes in the freedom of the commons. Freedom in a commons brings ruin to all. (Hardin 1968, 1244)

In terms of National Parks – an example that has similarities to museums and conservation – Hardin diagnoses that being 'open to all, without limit' sees visitors also 'grow without limit'. As a result, 'the values that visitors seek in the parks are steadily eroded (Hardin 1968, 1245). He argues that the Herdsman's Commons fails because it is not properly constructed as 'private property' – or, in other terms, as a 'private good' i.e. one which is rival (where use by one precludes use by another) and excludable (where others' use can be prevented). Similarly, Hardin argues that the National Parks fail to manage the parks effectively because they are governed as if they are 'open to all, without limits' – or, in other terms, as if they are a type of 'public good' (one which is neither rival nor excludable) when they are not.

Applying Hardin's argument, we might see museum constitution's 'on behalf of' governance as a means of turning material culture into something as close as it is possible to come to a public good, so that use by one does not preclude use by another and that no limit on use need be made. Glass cases that prevent touch (Henderson and Lingle 2023; Henderson, Lingle and Parkes 2023; Brenna 2014), limits on how long items can be displayed, use of gloves by museum staff, secure storage or attempts to find alternatives to touch for people who are blind or partially sighted (Henderson and Lingle 2023; Hetherington 2000; 2002; Candlin 2008), free entry and fixed visiting times are all practical expressions of an attempt to make museum objects if not actually public goods then at least quasi-public goods. This happens through turning 'use' wherever possible into 'access'.

The shift from use to access, and from commons to public governance, forms part of the story of the development of heritage in the UK. In the late nineteenth century when the London-based Commons Preservation Society – the precursor to the National Trust – started to create public access rights to land, they did so by using the law to convert commons rights to public access (Cowell 2012). This shift from commons rights to public rights continued throughout the twentieth century. The 1955 Royal Commission on Common Lands, as Peter Linebaugh notes, 'introduced a third legal party in addition to the landlord and the commoners, namely, the public' (Linebaugh 2014, 145); while the Commission recognised 'a universal right of public assess on common land', the implications were clear: 'the public significantly does not manage the land, as commoners used to do' (Linebaugh 2014, 145). This meant that those that lived on or near a common would no longer have traditional rights of pasture (to graze cattle or sheep) or estoves (picking up fallen branches) – but workers on public holidays could walk, picnic and use their leisure time in nature (Hill 1877, 8). In other words, like museums as a political-economic form, the shift from commons to 'public' encompassed a corresponding shift from rights of use to rights of access, and away from supporting livelihoods to supporting leisure.

Any reclassification from commons rights of use to public access demands quite different governance arrangements. As Sylvia Federici and George Caffentzis argue in the context of publicness in other contexts, 'the public, which is owned, managed, controlled, and regulated by and for the state, [has the effect of] constituting a particular type of private domain' (Federici with Caffentzis 2019, 96). In museum terms, Federici and Caffentzis draw our attention to how the generating of the '*quasi*-public good' I have posited is, in effect, a form of private good – the distinction being that it is a private economic form managed through public governance in our name and, to return to our key concern, 'on our behalf'. As this discussion about rivalry as an economic form has suggested, participatory approaches to governance are significantly aided by reworking rivalry and logics of scarcity. Debates concerning commons and commoning, as a particular form of participatory organising, share a desire to move attention from the specific object – or 'apple', in the terms David Bollier uses in the quote that opens this chapter – to emphasise instead the commons variously as significantly immaterial (and therefore not defined by rivalry and scarcity) or as a resource system (in which certain elements are rival, but the system as a whole replenishes).

In their collaborative writing Michael Hardt and Antonio Negri suggest that there is an emphasis in the post-Fordist economy on affective, biopolitical and immaterial labour. This in turn means that we can increasingly think of 'the common' not only materially, as 'natural resources' and 'the earth we share', but also immaterially as 'the languages we create, the social practices we establish, the modes of sociality that define our relationships, and so forth' (Hardt and Negri 2009, 138, 139).[5] While for the purposes of considering museum conservation we will need to keep working with the idea of a material object that might be used, and even used up, what we can take from Hardt and Negri are the ways in which their reading of 'the common' opens up alternative modes of political organisation – precisely because 'this form of the common does not lend itself to a logic of scarcity as does the first'. They argue that:

> The concepts of public goods and services were developed in the light of a legal theory that considered the public as patrimony

> of the state and the principle of general interest as attribute of sovereignty. (Hardt and Negri 2005, 206)

The commons, then, is comprised not only of a different approach to materiality, but also of a non-sovereign mode of political constitution, termed *self*-constitution:

> The common marks a new form of sovereignty, a democratic sovereignty (or, more precisely, a form of sovereignty which displaces sovereignty) in which social singularities control through their own biopolitical activity those goods and services ... This would constitute a passage from *Res-publica* to *Res-communis*. (Hardt and Negri 2005, 206, italics original)

To return to museums, reading conservation as a form of commoning – a form of participatory worlding – thus opens up both a different ontological basis (not primarily or even necessarily based in scarcity or rivalry) and different modes of governance (not based in the logics of 'on behalf of').

The etymology of 'conservation' – which we'll develop as 'conserving' to emphasise the active nature of commoning – holds rich potential for participatory worlding. Its etymology includes 'wise use', 'to use without using up', 'to keep from running out' (*Oxford English Dictionary*). Within its etymology lies the potential to see conserving not only as a material practice, but also as a practice that is both materially and socially dynamic. Indeed, conservators such as Mariam Clavir, Jane Henderson and Elizabeth Pye (Clavir 2020; Henderson 2020, 203; Pye 2016; see also Jones and Yarrow 2022 in the context of built environment) have consistently suggested that decontextualising and aesthetising practices of preservation and protection are contrary to conserving in a more expanded sense of ongoing relevance, going on to emphasise the particular and context-specific negotiations this recognition then requires. As Kevin Lynch has argued:

> Preservation is not simply the saving of old things but the maintaining of a response to those things. This response can be transmitted, lost or modified. It may survive beyond the real thing itself. (1972, 53)[6]

Linking conserving and 'commoning' as a form of participatory organising is to see heritage-making – or what Henric Benesch terms 'heritaging' – as a form where people and things co-constitute:

> The relation between commons and commoning, or as in this case – heritage and heritaging – is not fixed. Like any relation of care or love, it is not only about keeping or a preserving a status quo (what kind of love or care would that be?). It is about change and evolving together – in a respectful, loving and reciprocal way. In other words – care and caring are not only practices that change that which is cared for, but that also, while doing so, changes those who are doing the caring. (Benesch 2015, 246)

This allows for a shifting in focus from 'object' – as a product of a modern and representational ontology – to a social-material process of world-making (DeSilvey 2017, 186; Harrison 2018). It opens up the potential no longer to think of any given object as ontologically distinct from other objects, or from the people who made it, used it, might use it or might repair it. It allows us to attend – as Benesch evokes – to the ways in which people and things are made and changed through the very processes of conserving, and to understand that this as conserving in action.

Thinking about conserving in this way allows us to draw back into our discussion Karen Barad's relational ontology. In Barad's terms, for anything to exist is an ongoing act of creation through which 'it' as an entity is produced through intra-actions in an ongoing present. Any entity – such as a specific object – that is produced through agential separability also, through the same process, creates a set of entanglements. As Barad summarises, 'cutting together/apart' (Barad 2010, 244) entails 'the enactment of an agential cut together with the entanglement of what's on "either side" of the cut since these are produced in one move' (Barad in Barad, Juelskjær and Schwennesen 2012, 20). Part of what is being reconfigured here is the relationship between materiality and time. Barad's agential realist approach to materiality and time sees both as at once sedimented and open:

> The past is never closed, never finished once and for all, but there is no taking it back, setting time aright, putting the world back on its axis. There is no erasure finally. The trace of all reconfigurings is written into the enfolded materialisations of what was/is/to-come. Time can't be fixed. (Barad 2010, 264)

Through the concept of 'enfolded materalisations', Barad characterises memory as that which is sedimented through the ongoing intra-actions that make realities:

> Memory – *the pattern of sedimented enfoldings of iterative intra-activity – is written into the fabric of the world*. The world 'holds' the memory of all traces; or rather, the world *is* its memory (enfolded materialisation). (Barad 2010, 261, italics original)

What this offers to ideas of conserving is to take all entities as produced through 'iterative intra-activity' as being memory itself.[7] A participatory worlding makes it possible to see conserving not as taking things out of life but as life-enabling, and always part of ongoing responsibilities of worlding (DeSilvey 2017; Harrison 2018; Harrison et al. 2020; Whitehead, Schofield and Bozoğlu 2021), 'evolving together' (Benesch 2015, 246).[8] At the same time, which is my focus here, participatory worlding also opens up ways in which participatory non-sovereign self-constituting modes of organising actively facilitate conserving (keeping things from running out of relevance), rather than endanger it.

In developing our focus on modes of self-organising, commoning allows us to draw in mutually enabling (if not ontologically identical) thinking from the work of Elinor Ostrom on governing the commons that helps us to deal with the material element at play in commoning conserving. Ostrom draws a distinction between a 'resource system', which 'refers to a natural or manmade resource system' that is sufficiently large as to make it costly (but not impossible) to exclude potential beneficiaries from obtaining benefits from its use' (Ostrom 1990, 30), and a 'resource unit', which 'is what individuals appropriate or use from resource systems' (1990, 30). In Ostrom's terms what is 'common' is the resource system, governed through self-organising; 'the process of designing, implementing, and enforcing a set of rules to coordinate provision activities is equivalent to the provision of a local collective good' (1990, 32–3).

Many in this debate since have stepped away from the ways in which Ostrom considers the common so firmly in relation to liberal economic theory (e.g. Dardot and Laval 2019, 32; Kioupkiolis 2020, 15, 29) and there is certainly no perfect mapping from Ostrom's work onto our focus. Nevertheless, the distinction between system and unit helps us to develop conserving as a form of commoning. The distinction between system and unit scaffolds thinking of conserving as a social-material phenomenon generated through intra-actions that include the use of rival resource units (specific objects, in the case of museums) but as part of a generative and renewing resource of materiality and meaning. As with David Bollier's phrase used at the start of this chapter, a commoning conservation would be one that is interested in 'the leaves, the roots, the trunk, the orchard and the ecosystem' as well as the apple. The objects in the system of conserving might be used, broken, repaired or recycled – the apple could be eaten – yet all the while a healthy ecosystem of relevance and meaning is sustained precisely through these activities, done in the ethos of making common.

Getting this far with Ostrom's distinction then allows us to take another step further and activate participatory worlding to rethink the rivalry of any given object. In Ostrom's ontology it is rival units that are 'appropriated', like a fish that is caught and eaten, but it is the resource system – in this case an ecosystem – that makes the fish possible and is the common-based pool resource (Ostrom 1990, 43). However, activating participatory worlding, we might now rework any fixed distinction between unit and system (1990, 30). We might see that any object itself – through commoning – can become ontologically redistributed through use. Even as an object might in its singularity change, get broken, become chipped or in need of repair, it is the agential separability of each intra-action 'cutting together/apart' (Barad 2010, 244) – both distinct and entangled in evolving ways – that *is* a commoning conserving.[9] Or, to put this in the language of participation, conserving is ontologically participatory and is enabled through direct modes of self-organising.

Reframing 'accessible to everyone': community, commoning and participatory organising

Along with questioning the nature of an object, conserving as participatory worlding also requires us to shift away from abstractions of 'all affected'. A feature of the literature on commons is that they are not governed 'on behalf of' others, but by those not-at-all-abstract specific people who have a shared interest in producing a common. Indeed, it is often argued, 'community' is a term that benefits from being used in a very specific sense – as that which is produced through the active creation and collective management of a commons (de Angelis 2017; de Angelis and Harvie 2014; Gibson-Graham, Cameron and Healy 2013; 2016; Amin and Howell 2016; Dardot and Laval 2019).

This is significant for debates in critical museum and heritage studies, as community has often been seen as a weak descriptor of an abstract demographic group believed to be in need of inclusion or a nostalgic sop that hides class relations (e.g. Waterton and Smith 2010). This more active processual definition of community is key to participatory approaches to organising:

> For some, this idea of community is so tainted with nostalgia and romanticism that it is if not a dangerous concept, then at least a naive one. But the community that commons is not pregiven; rather, communities are constituted through the process of commoning. (Gibson-Graham, Cameron and Healy 2016, 196)

Given the necessarily non-abstract idea of a community that commons, there is an ongoing discussion about whether commoning requires processes of inclusions and exclusions – i.e. that you are either part of the commoning community and therefore have rights of use or you are not and do not. Hardt and Negri contest this:

> We […] endorse Ostrom's claim that the common must be managed through systems of democratic participation. We part ways with her, however, when she insists that the community that shares access and decision-making must be small and limited by clear boundaries to divide those inside from the outside.
> (2017, 99)

Hardt and Negri go on: 'We have greater ambitions and are interested instead in more expansive democratic experiences that are open to others' (Hardt and Negri 2017, 99). Yet others have more firmly emphasised the point that it is impossible to think of a process of commoning without some inclusions and exclusion by virtue of the requirement of collective effort. In Gibson-Graham's terms, commons are that which are 'negotiated by a community' and underpinned by responsibility which is 'assumed by a community' and care which 'is performed by members of a community' (Gibson-Graham, Cameron and Healy 2013, 132).[10] What this means in practice is:

> the willingness to spend much time in the work of cooperation, discussing, negotiating, and learning to deal with conflicts and disagreement. … Only in this way can a community in which people understand their essential interdependence be built … and [we can] build the skills necessary for self-government. (Federici with Caffentzis 2019, 94)

From the perspective of deconstituting museums, recognising the specificity of community is a crucial move. It challenges the sense that 'open' means 'universal', and therefore calls back into being abstract constituencies of future generations or 'everyone'. There might be a variety of different types of boundaries around a commoning community;[11] for instance, there might be examples which are more closed. There might also perhaps be commons that operate with the idea of being open to 'anyone', instead of to 'everyone'. Here 'anyone' can act as an ongoing open invitation, but one which is never abstract, as anyone once they approach will become someone in particular; 'semi-permeable membranes' in the terms of David Bollier and Silke Helfrich (2019, 130). A benefit of 'anyone' over 'everyone' is also that it is an idea not in perpetual deficit, as it carries no assumption about quantity or completeness.

Seeing a community as being brought into being through commoning opens a way for the new set of meanings relating to conserving as commoning in the sense of nourishing a resource system. J. K. Gibson-Graham, Jenny Cameron and Stephen Healy draw out the distinction between a desire to make access 'shared and wide' while still ensuring that a specific and particular community manages, uses, benefits from and cares for it. They suggest:

- *access* to property must be shared and wide
- *use* of property must be negotiated by a community
- *benefit* from property must be distributed to the community and possibly beyond
- *care* for property must be performed by community members
- *responsibility* for property must be assumed by community members.

(Gibson-Graham, Cameron and Healy 2016, 131–2)

In the case of conserving, it could well be that shared and wide access is understood as a generative and replenishing aspect of conserving. It could also be that only members of the commoning community can use, play, turn on, ride or wind the objects that are the rival parts of the wider system of conserving but that what is made more widely available is information, often known as 'knowledge commons' (Hess and Ostrom 2007).

In referring to 'benefit' being distributed, Gibson-Graham, Cameron and Healy also point to their wider focus in terms of 'taking back the economy' and developing 'community' and diverse economies'. As they put it:

> Encouraged by the idea that we can build the economies we live in, individuals and communities across the globe are taking economic matters into their own hands to help create worlds that are socially and environmentally just. (2013, xiii)

Their wider argument points to the ways in which heritage as commons – in shifting back from 'access' to 'use' – could also be a means of supporting livelihoods, as is pointed to by the community-led tourism movement, which seeks to distribute the economic outcomes of tourism more widely and more equally.

A final thought on the link between community and commoning and scarcity and rivalry. There is a specific dimension to the commons debate which suggests that commons are not identical to traditional ideas of property – because the kinds of 'use' they enable does not include full appropriation which includes 'The Right to the Capital – or the power to alienate, consume, spoil, or destroy a property' (Dardot and Laval 2019, 325). For example, Pierre Dardot and Christian Laval argue that the common is common precisely because it is not about appropriation:

> use of the common is not a right of ownership: it is the practical negation of property rights in all of its forms, and the only form in which the unappropriable can be properly managed. (Dardot and Laval 2019, 329)

On one view this claim seems consistent with the argument I have made, in part because we might see use of a specific object to destruction not as appropriation but – depending on the spirit with which it is done – as itself an act of replenishment, of generating relevance, of conserving beyond any one entity. Yet it is also the case that some might certainly not accept this. Instead they would see the use of a specific object to destruction precisely *as* destruction, and therefore as appropriation.

However, disputes of this nature return us back to the self-organising nature of the commons (Dardot and Laval 2019, 326).[12] A commoning community would need to decide if use to destruction of any specific object was an act of commoning and unappropriation – a contribution to wider systemic replenishment – or one of uncommoning and appropriation. Processual politics based in relationships are inevitably sites where there is a constant need for local negotiation. While participatory worlding offers a rich variety of ways of understanding conserving that are not based in abstraction and scarcity, there are no norms or rules beyond the contingency of commoning. That is one of the political implications of participation.

Reframing 'represent the world' and 'on behalf of': participatory worlding and participatory democracy

Museum constitution justifies the right to undertake 'on behalf of' professional and trustee decision-making in a number of ways. Taking on this delegated responsibility is meant to:

1) ensure fairness of representation within the space and time of exhibitions and programmes, given their high status and their role in broadcasting content to audiences
2) determine what counts as high-quality content for audiences
3) ensure the use of liberal norms to frame the acceptable range of expression both to prevent harm or offence and to minimise the risk to those sharing stories of being amplified through the institution
4) resolve any conflicts through taking final decisions.

In contrast this section is interested in how any of the issues that arise from people seeking to take action, use and make things and share ideas can be dealt with directly by those involved.

Museum constitution has been a bit stuck on this question of what political forms participatory work can take. Concepts such as 'panels' or 'boards' remain popular (Armin and Bowler 2022). This is not surprising because museum constitution is embedded within trustee and professional structures of legitimacy. Yet there are a range of democratic innovations that museums could be using to enable a transition towards greater devolved authority and participatory legitimacy. The shift here would be – as has been indicated in previous chapters – no longer to think of participation as engagement, but instead as governance (where governance means how things are done and decided legitimately).[13] The approaches explored below prioritise ways of maximising energy, action and divergence in ways that minimise the need for deliberation, decision-making and conflict resolution. The approaches explored also point to well-established techniques to deal with conflict, specifically direct consensus or consent decision-making approaches, restorative approaches to mediating harm and agonistic self-constitution to develop shared and revisable agreements.

As with reworking scarcity and 'accessible to everyone', reworking 'representing the world' and 'on behalf of' also requires a reworked political ontology. Participatory worlding happens through letting go of the idea of museums as trusted spaces for representation and high-quality broadcast of content to large audiences. This point includes the idea that #MuseumsAreNotNeutral, a campaign which challenges the way museums 'strive to remain "above" the political and social issues that affect our lives – embracing a myth of neutrality' (Murawski 2020 [2017]).[14] It also includes letting go of the notion that museums can be representative.

As explored in Chapter 1, in the context of museum constitution the concept of epistemic representation calls into necessity the representational politics of 'on behalf of'. If you are seeking to claim a story, a photo or an exhibition as representative, you are setting up a real world that you use as the arbiter of accuracy of the representation. This means you will then probably require whatever or whomever is being so judged then to adjust to fit this criteria. To enable this, crucially, you need to take up a vantage point – above or outside – from which representativeness can be judged (Scott 2003; Hage 2012). Instead of representations we might think of performative, enactive worlding. Saying, writing, drawing, curating, heritaging (Benesch 2015) or caring (Morse 2020) are all doings, active in making realities. Thought of in this way, there is no one-to-one relationship between a really real world and a representation. Instead there are only world-making intra-actions, bringing what matters into being.

Devaluing museums as high-status spaces opens up instead a blooming of varying activity – the kind of small-scale, self-organised cultural and heritage activity which is already under way in every city – across decentralised, semi-networked spaces (addae 2020; Ashley 2019; Illich 1971; McLaughlin 2023; Morse 2020, 211; Harrison and Sterling 2021; Lee-Crossett 2020). This could be seen as a living (Lawson, Cremin and Benson 2015), social (Benson and Cremin 2019) or systemic approach to heritage (Happy Museum 2022). Such a 'scaled-out' approach liberates museums from determining quality and allows what might be thought of as quality to be a contextual and emergent peer conversation between people interacting.

The shift away from 'on behalf of' decision-making is, of course, core to the meaning of participation in political theory (Pateman 1970) and in participatory and action research.[15] I want to nourish for participatory worlding some of the striking ways in which the relationship between decision and action is managed in certain strains of participatory and action research, in contrast to liberal democratic ideas of representativeness (politically and epistemically) and 'on behalf of' governance – not least as they are approached through the systemic action research approaches pioneered by Danny Burns.

The concept of representativeness does often arise in participatory process; it certainly does when participation is attempted in relationship to museum constitution. The dangers of this are well documented. Trying to add representativeness to participation forces people into an illegitimate role – speaking on behalf of others from that demographic without any elections or any of the other means by which representation achieves some sort of legitimacy in liberal democracy. As Burns asks:

> Can a young person really represent the experiences of all of the other young people in an area, a disabled person the experiences of all disabled people etc? (Burns 2007, 53)

With this observation Burns points to the ways in which these types of representational approaches are often activated and insisted on only because they appear to offer accountability to external forms of power, whether in terms of organisational governance or funders (i.e. we can say who was there, we can establish legitimacy through representation). But more crucially, in Burns's analysis, this type of representational mindset misses the sheer energetic potential of participation as action. Burns argues 'that a process (or a sample) is representative tells us who was there (who was included), but not who has power and what they care about' (Burns 2007, 53).

Burns offers an alternative. One of the impetuses that Burns cites for his systemic action research approach arose very far from institutional engagement of the type that enrols people into being representative. It derived from the experience of being an activist making decisions about a protest at the nuclear submarine base at Faslane in the west of Scotland. Burns reflects on a particular collective decision-making process:

> The dialogic process was sophisticated; the facilitators were highly skilled. The process was recognised by all to have worked, but in the end no action resulted because motivation was not there. I wrote in a journal at the time, 'the commitment to consensus was at the expense of desire'. (2007, 50)

Recognising the difference between consensus decision-making and energy and desire has led Burns to have 'steadily moved away from a focus on group consensus towards the idea of parallel action' and to 're-think the possibilities of participation', arguing that:

> the foundations for meaningful community engagement lie in the day-to-day acts of participation in community life, not in elaborate community decision-making processes. (Burns 2007, 50)

Instead of representativeness Burns looks for 'resonance' as a way of 'identifying issues of concern and possibilities for mobilisation' (2007, 64). What this means – unlike the de-energising effects of consensus decision-making that occurred at Faslane – is that 'people "see" and "feel" the connection between things', 'they "know" that it is related to their experience' and 'they are "energised" and motivated' (2007, 53). Resonance instead of representativeness opens the way to refigure ideas of accountability as something that happens not through establishing representative samples of people and making people speak on others' behalf, but rather through the clustering and intensity of activity.

As Burns and Stuart Worsley argue, this generates an alternative concept of democracy – neither as representative democracy (via elections) nor as consensus decision-making, but instead as 'democracy as attractor':

> When we talk about participation in this way we are describing a social process by which people take action and others either reject it or move towards it. If it is resonant enough – which means that it must be appropriate, work and be meaningful to people's lives – then it will act as an attractor. (Burns and Worsley 2015, 47)

Burns has developed an iteration of systemic action research named 'nurtured emergent development' (NED) which is deliberately experimental and emergent. Activity is kick-started and then it is noticed what attracts and what does not. Burns argues that this shifts the definition of the legitimacy of an activity away from its representativeness and from a focus on making decisions:

> This is an expression of the democratic will of the people. The participation is in the doing and the democratic legitimacy lies in their convergence on this form of activity. It does not require a vote or a consensus decision-making process. This is democracy in action and represents a distributed form of accountability which is not controllable or malleable in the same way as formal democratic deliberation. (Burns and Worsley 2015, 170)

The concept of 'attractor' is drawn from Burns's use of complexity theory, seeing 'systemic action research' and 'nurtured emergent development' as means by which action research can work with non-linearity and emergence – not simply as a strategy for generating new knowledge but as a strategy for whole system change:

> In order to change the dynamics of [a] system, it is necessary to create alternative attractors – deeper underlying shifts in perceptions, relationships and attitudes, to provide foundations for new points of convergence to emerge. Once these reach a critical mass, tipping points occur which allow a shift in the pattern of social relationships to a new attractor. So participation in this context is either the enactment of innovative action or its adoption, followed by adaptation of action catalysed by others. Participation is not just about sitting in meetings; it is about acting directly to shift system patterns. (Burns and Worsley 2015, 47)

Again – as with the participatory worlding we are seeking to elaborate – what is at stake here is not representing the world, or knowing the world, but worlding.

When taken as a participatory alternative to museum constitution this approach immediately offers abundance thinking, rather than thinking based in scarcity or deficit. It is enabled by doing whatever is possible not to think in terms of a fixed and non-renewable resource, which requires people to be in competition and therefore in need of some form of legitimate 'big D' decision-making moment. 'Democracy as attractor' enables shifting the logics that have prevented scaled-out approaches in museums. Museum constitution holds in place logics of 'scaling up' through treating collections as fixed and non-renewable, and through broadcast logics of generating high-quality, representationally appropriate content for large audiences. As noted above, this means attempts to scale out and do things at smaller scale are often questioned, either by asking (if collections are not involved) 'why are we the right people to do this?' or by applying criteria of quality and of representativeness even to small, low-stakes exhibitions and events. Scaled-out, 'democracy as attractor' approaches are made more possible by thinking of conserving as a material-social practice of ongoing mattering, and by de-centring the museum as a competitive space of valued representation. In response to the 'depth' critique of museums and participation – which is concerned that power is not devolved enough – this is a way of recognising that while there might be a need to use full participatory decision-making processes at certain points, a scaled-out participatory worlding limits how often this is required.

Where there is uncertainty or the potential for conflict, action research in general, and systemic action research more particularly, has minimised the need for decision-making by framing a process – not in terms of articulating opinions (which assumes people already know what they think) or of making decisions (which assumes that a decision will enable positive action) – but instead in terms of inquiry. Thinking of issues through questions, action and sense-making rather than through forums and decision-making loosens things up; it disintensifies fixed positions and creates potential. Crucially, inquiry as a technique of participatory worlding enables people and the issues to be made and to change through ongoing co-constitution. In the discussion above about conserving as participatory worlding, it was possible to see how an energetic and engaged worlding is enabled if conserving is a question and a process, not only or always a decision. This makes way for divergence, ensuing that wherever possible being locked into dispute is avoided.

Yet of course sometimes there is conflict, and sometimes decisions do need to be made. A participatory worlding enables a way of thinking who might need to be involved, not in terms of 'all affected' – which draws in abstraction and, with it, different forms of representation – but instead, as suggested above, in terms of 'anyone interested'. If there is agreement that those who want to take part all have the right to do so, then consensus or consent can be explored, using consensus decision-making processes (e.g. Baldwin and Linnea 2010) or consent decision-making process (e.g. Rau 2022). Consensus decision-making sometimes is misunderstood as meaning complete and full agreement, and therefore seen as a form of decision-making that can become coercive (Lynch and Alberti 2010, 30). Yet even within approaches that are aiming for consensus there are a variety of ways to enable dissent or neutrality – as 'consent decision-making' does – and to deal with the emotional fall-out of the process itself.[16]

If there is no agreement that those who want to take part in the decision-making have the right – or a person or group has 'called out' or 'called in' an action as harmful – then restorative processes could be used. Restorative justice is a well-established facilitated process that enables harm to be defined by those who have experienced it and named it. The use of restorative justice is not confined to a criminal justice context; it is a term being used widely now in schools, as well as now in a number of museums. Two examples of these are Kansas City Museum, through its RestoreKC programme which started in 2020 (Kansas City Museum 2020–), and Denver Museum of Nature and Science (Nash 2022; for context of the anthropology department's approach to repatriating see Colwell and Nash 2021).[17] A restorative justice approach to harm is described as 'an alternative approach to addressing and healing from harm', where 'harm can be traced back to an unmet need for food, shelter, safety, belonging, respect, and feelings of self-worth' (Cetoute et al., 2020, 26). Powerfully, it is a process in which those involved are able to become more aware of their actions and their impacts on others, as well as to see the issue at hand through other people's eyes. It is a practical facilitating technique for the kinds of ethics of 'intra-action' (Barad 2007; 2010), 'becoming-with' (Haraway 2016) and 'modulation' (Massumi 2015a; 2015c) that we have been exploring.

It is the case that those involved in restorative justice processes have to volunteer, and so there will always be a question of how to deal with those that do not. There is a tendency in museum practice and theorising to assume that conflict – and especially expression of views that are experienced by others as harmful – requires a pre-existing governance structure, based in norms such as human rights, that can step in, manage and ultimately exclude those not respecting normative values. Yet certain norms to guide everyday behaviour and agreed ways of dealing conflict can be constituted in participatory ways. The difference of constitution when done as participatory worlding is that such agreements are constituted by those who will be so bound and in ways that are revisable. 'Constitute yourself', as Hardt and Negri have put it (Hardt and Negri 2012, 43). This is the focus of the next section.

Reframing a representational constitution: revisable self-constitution

In order to clarify the important shift generated by making the very terms of legitimate engagement a matter for self-constitution, it is worth taking a swing through theories of agonism. Not least as agonism, usually via Chantal Mouffe, has featured in museums and heritage studies (Mouffe 2010; Lynch 2011b; Lynch 2019) and in recent debates concerning commoning (Kioupkiolis 2020, 219–22).

Concerned fully to recognise antagonism as part of the human condition, and concerned also that the consensus politics prevalent in the 1990s was in constant danger of marginalising in ways that produced extreme antagonism, Chantal Mouffe proposed agonism as a means of turning enemies intent on each other's destruction into 'friendly enemies' – able to disagree, free absolutely to try and create new hegemonies over institutions while also recognising the legitimacy of each other's positions, of their right to be in the fight (Mouffe 1993; Mouffe 2000).

Mouffe's definition of 'friendly enemies' is 'persons who are friends because they share a common symbolic space but also enemies because they want to organise this common symbolic space in a different way' (2000, 13).[18] For Mouffe the common symbolic space is 'constituted by the ethico-political principles of liberty and equality for all' (2000, 102). Crucially, for our purposes, the kind of 'constituted' she imagines is very similar to museum constitution. It is not a written document but a set of ideas. Indeed, Mouffe argues, 'profound disagreements' will then take place around what 'liberty and equality for all' might mean – fuelled precisely by what she conceives of as constitutive tensions between liberty and equality and between liberalism and democracy. Mouffe sees these high-level ideals acting as the common symbols through which antagonism is turned into agonism (Mouffe and Oppelt 2014, 271).[19] Needless to say, the concern I would have is that the 'ethico-political principles of liberty and equality for all' act as the same type of horizon ideals that kick-start museum constitution, and thus encourage the institutionalisation of different versions of freedom or equality being delivered on our behalf.

Mouffe has herself applied her theories of agonism to institutions including museums. For her, engagement with institutions is far preferable to the 'exodus' she associates with the horizontal, common, constituent power of Hardt and Negri. In making her case – writing in 2013 – she suggests that some of the then most recent horizontal movements such as Occupy are not a 'refusal of the post-political order'. Instead Mouffe chooses to read the protests as a 'call for a radicalization of liberal democratic institutions, not for their rejection' (Mouffe 2013, 120) and interprets their demands as being for 'better, more inclusive forms of representation':

> to satisfy their desire for a 'voice', existing representative institutions have to be transformed and new ones established, so as to create the conditions for an agonistic confrontation where the citizens would be offered real alternatives. Such a confrontation requires the emergence of a genuine left, able to offer an alternative to the social liberal consensus dominant in centre-left parties. (2013, 120)

Therefore – to return to the question of 'common symbolic space' – Mouffe argues that:

> The problem with modern democratic societies, in our view, is not their ethico-political principles of liberty and equality, but the fact that these principles are not put into practice. So the strategy of the left in these societies should be to act for the enforcement of these principles, and this does not require a radical break. Rather it requires what Gramsci calls 'a war of position' [trying to build a movement with a shared analysis], leading to the creation of a new hegemony. (Mouffe 2013, 134, definition by the author)

Mouffe's faith in calls for representation, liberty and equality as an entry point to institutional transformation, I would suggest, leads us straight back into the teeth of museum constitution and its very effective way of inviting and organising such claims.[20]

What I am more interested in is taking Mouffe's insight that some form of common symbolic space is needed for agonism and exploring how those directly involved can be involved in its self-constitution, without the use of horizon ideals. Constitutions are supposed to sit above the everyday churn of politics; they are only revisable irregularly and through the agreement of a large majority. Yet there are choices to be made about how far above the everyday constitutions need to be, how and how often they can be revisable and, crucially, the ways those agreements are articulated. Self-constitution is, in effect, the basis of any commoning process and could also be the basis for enabling agonistic processes of different kinds, what Alexandros Kioupkiolis has termed 'agonistic commons' (2020, 219).[21] In short, all aspects of commoning could be subject to ongoing contestation without relying on the assertion of ethical norms and without late liberal ideals and their self-reinforcing deficits, tensions and contradictions.

Speculative self-organising

Having changed the political problems from those that museum constitution generates and then seeks to solve (conserve for future generations, accessible to all, represent the world), we have drawn out alternative approaches and clarified the issues that participatory organising will need to address.

To emphasise the point again, participation is not an answer to the political problems framed by and created by representation. Rather, it refuses the premise of the liberal and representation paradigm via a different ontology and different governance forms. What this means is shifting from ideas of all affected, of rivalry, of unquestionable normative values and on behalf of governance. Participation is not engagement: participation is governance. More than governance – to underline the point: what I have been arguing is that participation is world-making. As a result, participation needs experimentation in modes of being to be matched with experiments in modes of organising.

What participation proposes for museums is to create activity which does not centre the museum as a valued space. Activity which is lower stakes, not expensive, not fixed, not seeking to represent all, not seeking to be for everyone and not broadcast. Exhibits that can be fixed and changed easily (Simon 2012). Approaches that can fail and make it possible to learn.

Participation also proposes that conserving happens through use, through dynamic social-material process. Where there is abundance, a replenishing of meaning and relevance, and where terms of use – and use that might damage or be seen as destruction – are collectively and locally negotiated.

Participation also proposes the need for agreements that are collectively developed and always revisable. That there is no need either for abstract values, handed down to us from human rights frameworks, nor 'on behalf of' governance that takes difficult decisions and the definition and mediation of harm out of our hands. Instead participation proposes that conflict over rights and experiences of harm can be directly negotiated between those involved.[22]

These issues now are the focus of three speculative writing experiments in self-organising which follow out participatory worlding as it might be enabled to flourish through varying forms of participatory organising.

Speculative self-organising I

In a museum, near the large open doors, there is a room that hums with potential. A room where the weight of the last centuries is in flux, electrified. In this room proposals, ideas, inquiries, calls for objects or discussions or to join protest groups are posted. Each is nailed to a high wall, marked forever with the denting of thousands of intentions.

No consensus is ever needed for any proposal to begin to take space, use objects, make claims. Mostly micro-negotiations of space and time happen between people. Timetables for certain spaces resolved around different requirements of work, the quality of light, childcare arrangements, acoustics or proximity to the toilets.

In these rooms it is not that there is no notion of representation. After all the spaces, each once a gallery, still carry that history. But representation here has become rescaled as part of use, enactment, making and the bringing forth of new realities.

Sometimes a proposal is formally contested as being beyond this loose, messy, productive but also shared symbolic space. Various things then happen. Sometimes, if those involved are open to it, discussion ensues. Challenging of the premise happens; new ideas are introduced that reframe. Sometimes the inquiry then simply adapts, the debate enriching, refiguring, cast now with more generative potentials.

Sometimes a project goes ahead in spite of the dispute – sometimes with a conflicting inquiry or position also staged at the same time. Dissenting opinions are posted, either within the gallery being used or, if that is refused by the convening group, outside. Plastering the corridor. Posters making the counter-argument are bluetacked on the back of toilet doors.

If a group wants to explore something that is experienced as harmful or life-denying to another group, and that is registered by that other group in those terms, the agonistic constitution is activated and an assembly is called. Anyone can come and take part. Not to adjudicate over the detail, but over the implications for their shared symbolic space and the intention to keep open the space for divergent articulating and exploration. Collectively adjusting the constitution in the light of discussions.

Alongside this restorative justice approaches to harm might be entered, circled, seeking deeper understanding, facing up to what might not have been thinkable before it was made so.

Always unstable and always emergent in these moments is where this tends. Hoovering always in the balance between reaffirmation of agonism and this museum as a space worth trying to hold in common. Or something else, more divergent, withdrawn and with different proximities of entanglement.

Speculative self-organising II

In a building, near the centre of town, there is a store house, an archive of things ready and waiting. Pared back. No longer an institution of interpretation or representation – it is there to enable use, by anyone interested.

Things vibrate on shelves – they are there for now, but not long before were part of life, and will be again.[23]

Things that have, depending …

> been taken on marches unfurled (Smith 2006, 262)
> turned on and played wondrously (Boon et al. 2015)
> brought back to where they were once in everyday use, with old friends, memories flowing,
> proudly sat on the corner of the bar to be pointed at and drank with or activated in worship by skilled hands.

Open to anyone – but anyone interested to take out objects becomes a member. The store house is governed through a collaboratively written and yearly renewed constitution, which confirms principles of use and principles of distributed decision-making for the following year.

Controversies always arise. If multiple groups are interested in a certain thing, rather than taking the decision off into a more distanced, decision-making structure, a facilitation process is used between the groups. The principle being to keep the decision with the people who care about it, rather than abstracting it or generalising it in ways that would result in the decision being taken by people who don't deeply care.

Sometimes one group wishes to stop another using a thing in a certain way. At stake here are often very different types of claim, including whether some people have any rights over a certain object. What is reached for then, in this case – if not always achieved – is deep respect for the entanglement that the dispute represents. The entanglement which is, too often, the processing of sedimented violence, still happening in the connections between us and between us and things.

Speculative self-organising III

Slow talk. Use the point. In a room in a large building shared with other commons, or in the backroom of a church, or in flight wherever can be found, temporarily autonomous, things once held apart are now jointly held. Commoning for livelihoods. Commoning, seeking interdependency.

Use leads to repair. Repair as 'an ethics of mutual care' done carefully and thoughtfully, documenting closely what is done and sharing knowledge with wider interested networks.[24] Any repair arises out of someone's desire. Then a sharing of ideas, perhaps a deliberation so more people in the commons can help to set a course.

Each community commoning manages itself differently. In many cases, things are locally embedded part of geographical communities or as part of trans-local communities of interest, forged in a powerful proximity of action and decision. Boundaries between the community-that-commons and other people also vary. For some commons there is a strong interest in keeping open for an 'anyone' who might be interested to join; other commons are not motivated by this and focus more inwardly. However, it is the commoning community that can use, a right generated by involvement but always negotiated.

No consensus has ever arisen among heritage commons on what they do or how they run. The commons structure enables plurality of formation. Recognising that commons is embedded in a European tradition, 'commons' is used when a group identifies with it and other formations are used in other cultural traditions such as 'meeting house' or 'custom house' (Kreps 2003, 45). Sometimes commons, meeting houses and custom houses are federated when there are connections. When commons and keeping houses or custom houses are federated, they are likely to be things that are shared and things which are not shared (Tulalip Tribes of Washington 2003).

Fully realised, this is a completely different world. In transition, commoning started to happen anywhere where people sought interdependencies instead of the clean boundaries of user, visitor, professional. Yet it can also be glimpsed whenever an abstraction is refused and when something was done without evoking anyone else's behalf. Or when the desire to share in responsibility stirs, as it so often does.

Speculative trajectories

These speculative narratives are not utopian. They are neither 'educative' nor producing norms.[25] Having stuttered the reflex – modulating modes of being and now also of 'constitution' – this chapter has been about cracking open the rich variety of ways in which organising might be done. The chapter started in critical mode – using the same type of hyper-tone as in Chapter 1 – to clarify what is at stake in deconstituting museums in terms of modes of organising. In doing so it reworked the key concepts at play in museum constitution, indicating how these concepts combine to reinforce rivalry and 'on behalf of' governance. The chapter has ended with reworking the insights gained through the critical into speculative trajectories. Clearly there can be no leap from where we are now to the fully realised ideological infrastructures of these three narratives. The point is rather that they can jostle here, not as fully realised possibilities but as interferences to map dependences of the usual structures of boards, panels and forums. Both the critical and speculative together contribute towards retraining the late liberal reflex – elaborating alternatives for organising heritage that may mean new forms of participatory governance should be tried. Or at least felt in those moments in strip-lighted meeting rooms to be a possibility that disrupts the immediate kick-starting of museum constitution.

The three pieces are tonally influenced by William Morris's *News from Nowhere* (2012 [1890]). As with *News from Nowhere*, there are explanatory elements to the narratives that join dots and which try to satisfy the 'how' question, at least in part. However, the sentences I have carried with me most clearly are not the bits that I felt had to be there in order to point back to the theory I have introduced. The images that have got under my skin and are offering retraining work are the dents in the wall, the bluetack on the toilet doors, the idea of an object being borrowed to prop up a bar and the phrases 'things once held apart are now jointly held' and 'when the desire to share in responsibility stirs'.

These images operate a little like the House of Commons being used for a dung market in *News from Nowhere* (Morris 2012 [1890], 64) in its world of participatory democracy (2012 [1890], 74–5). They work as a condensed signal of how things are different. The form in the speculative pieces is hoping to be evocative. It is trying hold together different political theories with how this might feel, not as embodied emotion precisely – indeed the emotions of anger, hurt, pain are held at a certain aesthetic distance in this form. Rather, it is a gesture to how quantities and qualities of affecting and being affected might be entangled with different modes of organising. It is more that the dents in the wall or the object on the bar hold in a sentence a different world that is starting to bloom within this now.

Notes

1 I think here of Dougald Hine's reflection that there is 'a more general tendency to treat specific human relationships as interfering with the equality of individuals, as envisioned by the logic of the public: to avoid such interference, friendship should be confined (or at least be seen to be confined) to the private sphere' (Hine 2015, 195).

2 Nuala Morse gives an excellent example and analysis of this dynamic in her account of conversations about communities at Tyne and Wear Archives and Museums: 'The absent community was imagined entirely through the need to manage its expectations rather than through any discussion of how to raise its aspirations or ambitions'. This 'frames the process, from the very start, not in terms of an ethics of collaboration, but in terms of risk management where communities are viewed as antagonistic, and engagement is necessarily confrontational. Framed in this way, managing expectations becomes the main way in which the idea of community engagement is operationalised in the museum' (Morse 2020, 114).

3 'The Principle of Affected Interests' requires that 'everyone who is affected by the decisions of a government should have the right to participate in that government' (Dahl 1990, 64) or 'all those who will be bound by a rule should have a say in making the rule' (Goodin 2007). Yet if museum constitution claims to be accessible, and for everyone now and everyone in the future then, as Robert E. Goodin puts it, 'this expansive conception of "all possibly affected interests" causes the franchise to balloon dramatically and the scope for legitimate exclusions to shrink accordingly' (2007, 55). This is known in democratic theory as 'the boundary problem' (Dahl 1990, 60–1; Whelan 1983).

4 Needless to say, since its publication in 1968 many people have taken issue with Hardin's analysis. For example, David Harvey has pointed out that if the cattle were also owned collectively rather than privately then the very issue Hardin outlines in relation to the Herdsman's Commons would simply not arise (Harvey 2011, 101). Gibson-Graham reports that Hardin later recognised there had been a word missing in the article's title: 'unmanaged' (Gibson-Graham, Cameron and Healy 2013, 131). Although, as theorists of commons tend to agree, there can be no such thing as an 'unmanaged commons'.

5 The sense of 'commons' being expanded from dealing with specific material resources to knowledge, practices and ideas has been taken up in discussions of how ideas of commons might relate to galleries, libraries, archives and museums (Avdikos, Dragouni, Michailidou and Pettas 2024).

6 This approach to conserving might have also found its moment in part because of the impossibility of collecting itself. Harald Fredheim, Sharon Macdonald and Jennie Morgan convey a sense of overwhelm in museum staff and the various pragmatic approaches taken to managing a sense of 'too many things' (2020, 186–8).

7 Barad's experiments in academic writing include subverting the ontology of time implied by writing itself. In their 2010 article 'Quantum entanglements', they write, 'I aim to provide the reader with an opportunity to engage in an imaginative journey that is akin to how electrons experience the world: that is, a dis/orienting experience of the dis/jointedness of time and space, entanglements of here and there, now and then, a ghostly sense of dis/continuity, a *quantum dis/continuity*, which is neither fully discontinuous with continuity or even fully continuous with discontinuity, and in any case, surely not one with itself. There is no overarching sense of temporality, of continuity, in place' (2010, 244, italics original). One of the ways Barad does this elsewhere is by adding a footnote to the article itself, as if the article precedes itself and is at the same time 'a gesture to include what is also coming from the future' (2014, fn.64, 187).

8 For example, Caitlin DeSilvey suggests: 'At the moment, our comportment toward heritage objects tends to cleave to a relatively narrow register of possible responses – appreciation, contemplation, concern. A postpreservation model of heritage would open up many more, and many of them in an active rather than a passive mode of engagement – creation, cultivation, improvisation, renewal' (DeSilvey 2017, 187). Harrison argues 'that fundamental to understanding the value of these alternative heritage ontologies is the recognition of ontological plurality, that *different* forms of heritage practices operate in *different* ontological fields and hence work to assemble *different futures*. … [This opens up] an ontological politics of and for heritage, a sense of how heritage could be oriented toward composing "common worlds" and "common futures", while maintaining a sensitivity to the ways in which different

domains of heritage practice relate to different modes of existence … and thus produce their own worlds and their own specific pasts, presents, and futures' (Harrison 2015, 28, 29).

9 There are clear resonances here with the recent discussions in conservation studies in terms of 'disruptive conservation', which emphasises making visible interventions rather than making interventions seem natural (Sweetnam and Henderson 2021).

10 'Care' is how Nuala Morse frames an alternative to the 'logic of contribution' in museum participatory projects. Morse draws on an ontologically expansive definition of care as 'a species activity that includes everything we do to maintain, continue and repair our 'world' so that we can live in it as well as possible. That world includes our bodies, ourselves and our environment, all of which we seek to interweave in a complex, life-sustaining web' (Tronto, cited in Morse 2020, 200). Ultimately, Morse argues, 'A care-ful museology would develop through the application of care ethics to a range of museological questions and practice' (2020, 213). In many ways the arc Morse traces and the arc of this book are similar: that participation produces a need for a different ontology. I hope I can complement Morse's work with the emphasis I offer here.

11 As Pierre Dardot and Christian Laval elucidate the limited constituencies of 'common' in relationship to universal: 'the universality of the common is of a strictly practical type: its universality only includes those who take part in the common's governance, those who co-produce the rules of use and who transform these rules when needed. Notions of abstract universality will only lead to a confiscation of the common by the only actors recognised by international public law, namely states. We are thus left with something of a paradox: while certain resources, substances, etc. are "common" by virtue of the universal character of their purpose or end, they are nonetheless reserved in practice to a very limited category of "users".' (Dardot and Laval 2019, 328).

12 As Dardot and Laval put it: 'the establishment of rules of common use through the exercise of instituent praxis, and its extension into a form of instituent use that is based on the ongoing revision of these rules – common use must be linked to co-decision concerning the rules, and the resulting co-obligation that flows from this process. Without this link, common use cannot be considered truly common, or – what amounts to the same thing – the resource being used cannot be considered to be a true common' (2019, 327–8).

13 As noted in the Introduction when first introducing this idea that participation is a form of governance, the intervention here is to wrestle back the idea of governance from government and its representational and 'on behalf of' logics (see also Gould 2017, 173). As David Bollier and Silke Helfrich put it: 'government and governance are different things. One could say, there is governance in the commons, but no government'. Bollier and Silke Helfrich modify the term governance with the term 'peer' to draw out the distinction (Bollier and Helfrich 2019, 120). The core of their intervention is to articulate the ways in which 'Peer Governance amounts to an artful political dialectic between culture and structure'. In other words that 'the shared motivations and visions that commoners wish to enact must have sufficient structure in law, formal organization and finance to be protected and nurtured. But there must also be sufficient open space for individual creativity, deliberation and action to flourish, which in turn recursively improves the structures of law, organization and finance that guide a commons forward' (2019, 121).

14 The relationship between whiteness and the universal is identified by the founders of Museums Are Not Neutral in a published exchange: 'White supremacy thrives within this tyranny of the universal, the neutral, the apolitical, the fair and balanced, and the objective. Acknowledging that museums are not neutral is a meaningful and urgent step toward gaining awareness of the powerful role that White supremacy and White dominant culture play within our institutions. It is a crucial step toward recognizing one's own role in questioning it, interrupting it and being a part of taking transformative action to replace it' (Mike Murawski in Autry and Murawski 2019, n.p). Or as Sumaya Kassim puts it: 'Museums are not neutral in their preservation of history. In fact, arguably, they are sites of forgetfulness and fantasy' (Kassim 2017, n.p.).

15 Carole Pateman puts it in this way: 'One might characterise the participatory model as one where maximum input (participation) is required and where output includes not just policies (decisions) but also the development of the social and political capacities of each individual, so that there is "feedback" from output to input' (Pateman 1970, 43). Pateman is very concerned to see democratic process as also a process of human development and flourishing (1970, 25). I should also note that Pateman sees participation as linked to better representational

democracy at a national level: 'The ordinary man might still be more interested in things nearer to home, but the existence of a participatory society would mean that he was better able to assess the performance of representatives at the national level, better equipped to take decisions of national importance when called upon to do so, and better able to weigh up the impact of decisions taken by national representatives on his own life and immediate surroundings' (Pateman 1970, 110).

16 There are a wide range of techniques to establish consensus and that have enough sophistication to manage discensus within a consensus process. To give a flavour from 'The Circle Way', which has become an internationally used approach, Christina Baldwin and Ann Linnea argue that 'consensus is a process in which all participants have come to agreement before a decision goes forward or action is taken. Consensus is applied when a group wants or needs to take collective responsibility for actions. [...] Consensus doesn't require that everyone has the same degree of enthusiasm for each action or decision, but it does require that each person approve the group action or is willing to support the action the group is about to take. Consensus provides a stable, unifying base. Once consensus is reached, the circle can speak of its actions as "we". [...] Consensus can also hybridize according to a circle's needs. Some groups operate with a consensus-minus-one philosophy. Group members listen carefully to the dissenting voice, and if the group remains confident in its decision, they honor the principle to move ahead so that no single person can stop a decision' (Baldwin and Linnea 2010, 32). There is also the 'sociocracy' 'consent approach', which seeks to deal with some of the perceived limitations of consensus – for example, that it stifles new ideas or fails at a larger scale. The way Ted Rau puts it is: 'If you want to put a slogan on it that makes the difference clear, one could say that in consensus, we ask everyone "do you agree?". In consent, we ask "do you object?"' (Rau 2022, n.p.).

17 The term 'restorative justice' is used sometimes quite loosely and sometimes very specifically to describe the approach developed in a criminal justice context. I am interested in the facilitation technique that has developed under the name 'restorative justice' for institutions such as schools. The case studies in *Restorative Justice in Schools: Whole-school implementation process* (Cetoute et al. 2020) are powerful. The case studies are focused on how everyday conflicts are connected to systemic issues of racism and misogyny. I am interested in how the question of convening 'anyone interested' could itself be a harmful process, both in terms of who might want to take part and in terms of whether those involved recognise each others' right to do so. Sophisticated ways of dealing with harm will be necessary as part of participatory experimentation.

18 Mouffe notes the 'paradox' generated between the liberal and the democratic in generating a common symbolic space: 'democratic logics always entail drawing a frontier between "us" and "them", those who belong to the "demos" and those who are outside it. This is the condition for the very exercise of democratic rights. It necessarily creates a tension with the liberal emphasis on the respect of "human rights", since there is no guarantee that a decision made through democratic procedures will not jeopardise some existing rights. In a liberal democracy limits are always put on the exercise of the sovereignty of the people. Those limits are usually presented as providing the very framework for the respect of "human rights" and as being non-negotiable. In fact, since they depend on the way "human rights" are defined and interpreted at a given moment, they are the expression of the prevailing hegemony and thereby contestable. What cannot be contestable in a liberal democracy is the idea that it is legitimate to establish limits to popular sovereignty in the name of liberty. Hence its paradoxical nature' (Mouffe 2000, 4). While Mouffe's hope is that this paradox can be productive, the concern of the arguments developed in this book is that paradoxes such as these – when institutionalised – actively foreclose participatory ways of being.

19 Mouffe's argument is: 'There is not one single interpretation of the common good that all citizens would have to accept. That doesn't mean that we don't need a reference to the common good, but this common good is always contested' (Mouffe in Mouffe and Oppelt 2014, 272–3). In essence, the idea of the common good can act as a container for contestation even as it itself is contested. Yet the requirement of the idea of a common good to mobilise abstractions makes such a concept, as always, in danger of justifying 'on behalf of' governance.

20 The quotations referring to calls for greater representation are in Mouffe's response to debates concerning the politics of Occupy and other movements of the early 2010s in the context of the financial crisis. When Mouffe writes directly about museums, she emphasises more that they

can act as sites for 'subverting the ideological framework of consumer society. Indeed, they could be transformed into agonistic public spaces where this hegemony is openly contested' (Mouffe 2013, 101), with a focus on public sphere, debate and contest.

21 In the terms of Alexandros Kioupkiolis, '*agonistic commons* [...] share not only particular resources and synergies, but the very conflict over the constitution of the commons as a collective activity of reflection, challenge, renegotiation and revision which should go on over time in order to amplify the commons itself. Sharing dissent and dispute leans on particular ethical and affective relations, which mitigate aggression and breed political friendship amidst difference' (Kioupkiolis 2020, 219, italics original).

22 If a museum could deconstitute itself enough to be 'constituent' (Byrne et al. 2018; Armin and Bowler 2022) then these might be the type of self-organising processes that could be used.

23 Inspirations here are Media Archaeology Lab and *Medienarchäologische Fundus*. Both are archives of media technology where active experimentation *is* the conservation.

24 In this iteration, repair is an act that draws on '[the] very old but routinely forgotten relationship of humans to things in the world: namely, an ethics of mutual care and responsibility' (Jackson 2014, 231). This is the type of future-making which is committed to in this Federated Commons iteration: small acts of care from which the ongoing present emerges.

25 A point of discomfort with the utopian relates to the ideas of utopia as educative. For both Ernest Bloch and Miguel Abensour there is an idea of utopia as respectively the 'education of hope' (Bloch 1986 [1959]) or 'education of desire' (Abensour 1991). While this is, I think, not the only way of interpreting Abensour's notion of 'education of desire' (not least due to the texture of his writing), for Ruth Levitas the implication is that for either of these educative terms to be operative there is a normative, evaluative dimension (e.g. anticipatory, concrete, disciplined) (Levitas 1990, 24, 25). Coming at utopia from a critical stance, Toni Cade Bambara also draws attention to the assumption of 'a common set of values' in much avowedly utopian literature (Bambara, cited in Gordon 2018, 35). This more normative and didactic dimension of utopia, as I have discussed above, does not fit the orientation to the present of the speculative narratives I have crafted. The speculative narratives do offer methodological elements that resonate with Levitas's 'utopia as method' (Levitas 2013) – archaeological, ontological, architectural. They have aspects of the archaeological (in that they excavate potentials in the present). They are certainly ontological (in that they imagine how ways of being might unfold otherwise). And at times they are architectural (institutional and economic designs are evoked). However, they are not meant to be seen as alternatives to be evaluated.

International museology III: ecomuseums – can 'museum' be deconstituted?

Ecomuseum, integral museum and community museum pioneers of the late 1960s, 1970s and 1980s – mentioned in International museology II – experimented in ontologically participatory approaches to museums. This can be seen very clearly in a special issue on ecomuseums from 1985 and in a PhD thesis written by Andrea Hauenschild and later published (2022 [1988]; see also Davis 2011).

There are claims of 'autonomous participation in the development of their traditional culture' (Kinard 1985, 223). Objects, it is suggested, 'may be eliminated as a result of continuing use' – or documented and returned. More 'safeguarding of skills' than [...] 'museification' of artefacts' (Querrien 1985, 199). There are glimpses of participatory worlding: 'a twofold temporal mode: in continuing time [...] and in the moment, [...] "the right time" for each action' (Bellaigue-Scalbert 1985, 195). 'Not self-enclosed: [the ecomuseum] receives and it gives' (Rivière 1985, 183).

Democratic structures are evoked via 'a well-developed network of citizens' committees and self-help organizations' (Hauenschild 2022 [1988], 206), or through promises of electing the museum director, 'whoever the people in the neighbourhood choose' (Marsh, cited in Hauenschild 2022 [1988], 170).

A sense of political contingency pervades, of having to work through what museums have been and whether they can be something else. 'Born of contradiction, the ecomuseum thrives on it' (Querrien 1985, 198). Contradictions defined by 'breaks, moments when things stop, leap [...] forward, undercurrents, work that is sometimes long and imperceptible' (Mayrand, cited in Hauenschild 2022 [1988], 140). Ecomuseums are described as being 'a process that is continually in question' and 'an open question for a population'. An open question which includes posing 'even whether there is a need for it' (Mayrand, cited in Hauenschild 2022 [1988], 140).

Lurking in these same accounts, however, is the pull of a museum constitutional dynamic. 'Of', 'for' and 'by' slip around, each suggesting a slightly varying – and not always consistent – position on whether the museum was offered as an act or service or as a space of participatory creation. 'Instead of a museum "of" [...] a museum "for"' (Gomez de Blavia 1985, 229). 'Not for a *public* but by *community*' (*Museum International* 1985, fn.2, 184, italics original). 'Local museums, for all, by all' (Mayrand 1985, 200). Sometimes they form part-concepts in dynamic tension, in the sense used by Brian Massumi (2015b, 214) and discussed in Chapter 1, although very palpably seeking release.

A question raised by these ecomuseum descriptions – and by the arguments in this book – is whether 'museum' as a word can be occupied, reinfused with a new political ontology. The arguments for this may lie in the ways in which museums are already failing to enact a representational political ontology (Witcomb 2003, 12). There are profusions (Fredheim, Macdonald and Morgan 2020), derelictions, decomposition, rotting and decay (DeSilvey 2017). There are also – perhaps especially in participatory practices – expansions, being-variously and potentials always arising that exceed museum constitution.

Indeed, many have also consciously tried – and continue to try – to occupy 'museum' differently. Not least the ecomuseum pioneers cited above, who sought to make 'museum' so entangled with people and place and ecologies and economies that it obliterated the dynamics this book has named museum constitution – even if renewed efforts were always required to make 'museum' open again. As argued in Chapter 7, there are ways in which richer experiments in participatory organising are there for the trying. Ways that scale out and disintensify competition, and therefore the need for decision-making – and that, where conflict arises and decision-making does becomes necessary, ways that use consensus, consent, restorative justice or agonistic self-constituting processes.

In its etymology, 'museum' carries connotations of separation and distinctiveness. In ancient Greek it meant the place 'holy to the Muses' and in classical Latin 'a building set apart for study' – a place, of course, for preservation and display, a place where there is a 'change in pace or style from the surrounding area' (Candlin and Larkin 2020, 125). There is within its etymology a type of distance that museum constitution creates and relies on. If there remains a desire to rehabilitate the word 'museum', we might want to attend carefully to why we feel so attached to it: what it is in the term 'museum' and its apartness that still calls to us. To return to Karen Barad, we may need to consider whether there is a way for 'museum' to account for – and to attend to – the entanglements created through the separation the term 'museum', for now at least, seems to require.

Conclusions

Participation – grafted onto museums – has created messy, fertile joins. Margins of epochal, conjunctural shifts. Generating a proliferation of instances that may seem small, peripheral to the institution, often involving junior and precariously contracted staff but that are, I have been suggesting, highly significant. Participation is where political theory is lived, in endless practical clashes created by the different logics of representational and direct forms of democratic praxis. Participation is where institutional late liberalism is waning, as those expected to service its inclusion and recognition deficits are no longer gripped to do so in the same way. Participation is where whole selves deal with the generational impacts of colonialism and the ongoing sorting work of racialisation in ways that cannot be personally sustained in a reformist mode. Practising participation in museums has been where I've attended to the tectonic conjunctural grinding because it was loud there, increasingly unignorable. And, after all, that's where I found myself.

Participation – its affective work, its worlding – is also extraordinary richness, a replenishing excess. Participation always offers something unexpected, a magic kind of sociality. Participation is laughter, in-jokes that build over time, odd tensions, disagreements, gossip, cleaning up at the end, energies rising and falling and wanting to leave but also trying again. Participation is where public service fairness becomes illegitimate coldness and those involved find themselves, without always realising it, choosing the relational, the horizontal, the directly negotiated. Facilitating participation in museums is to be a 'street-level' (Lipsky 1980) political philosopher – dealing with the contradictions of modernity alongside making sure you have enough teabags.

This book has called into being 'museum constitution'. This status of this knowledge claim is rather specific. I have not been claiming I know some kind of general truth about 'the museum' or 'all museums' – nor, for that matter, unveiling the power structures at work in any specific museum at any specific time. Rather, I have been intent on describing the political formation in which I seemed to have become trained and have trained myself. I have found myself over and over again responding to the call to address access, representation and inclusion, fired up and righteous. Long after participation started to work on me, causing me to feel a certain slackening, I still endlessly surprise myself – finding myself kick-starting the constitutional cycle again and again, all urgency, starter fuel and individualising sugar rush; pulse always rising. The intention of naming museum constitution is that of reconditioning, writing myself out of the grip of late liberalism, retraining my reflexes so I need not always react in the same way. I did need to wake which, like all important changes, personal and political, happened achingly slowly, slowly and then – once the page found me the words – if not all at once, then at least with an increased momentum. Many people won't need this type of writing out, never inducted as I was or never caught up in the desire to be needed in quite this way. After all, this book is a lot to do with the non-coincidental links between late liberalism and whiteness, as well as other gendered and classed normativities. But I hope my writing out of museum constitution might be useful to some people whose participatory work is also making them tug at the conjuncturally fraying and loosening knots.

Participation's affective work has been to open us up to each other, in ways which slacken that late liberal investment to include, to represent and to strive righteously on others' behalf. Participation's affective work has also been to lean more actively into the ways in which participation 'induces the creation of its own field', in the terms of Orlando Fals Borda (1991, 6). Participation creates its own realities, changes who you are and what you understand the world to be and through this, aided by experimenting in modes of organising and governance, makes worlds; it is worlding.

Not taking up the role of institutional includer does not, of course, let you off the hook. It is necessary instead to try 'heightening' and intensifying 'contradictions' (Moten, Harney and Shukaitis 2021, n.p.) or to explore 'loosening' and making 'different [recombinations] available from within the scene of attachment' (Berlant 2022, fn.25, 181). It is instead to detach from museum constitution through modulating, seeking in everyday ways no longer to reproduce the political and economic structures that have supported the concept of 'professional' and the differencing and othering on which it relies. It is instead to give yourself more fully to mutual accountability and its negotiation, constantly to try out new approaches and then to see where that takes you.

The conclusions continue the three registers that have made up this book's methods and forms – critical, affective, speculative. 'Critically' draws out the 'so what' in relation to museum practice. 'Affectively' highlights the shifts in attachments and intensities that may enable deconstitution and participatory worlding. 'Speculatively' prises wider and leaves open.

Towards abolition

When I began this book, I didn't know where I'd end up. For a very long time the Introduction used to end with the phase: 'But still I can't deny that right now – as this book opens – it somehow still remains easier to imagine the end of the world than the end of museums.' This was a reference to the oft-quoted phrase 'It is easier to imagine the end of the world than the end of capitalism', generally attributed to Fredric Jameson, who himself attributed it to 'someone' (Jameson 2003).[1] This felt too pat, so I removed it later on in the editorial process. However, there was a truth there. It has taken this writing and writing out for me to imagine a world without museum constitution.

This book has ended up being towards abolition.[2] Abolition in Stefano Harney and Fred Moten's sense: 'the abolition of a society that could have prisons, that could have slavery, that could have the wage, and therefore not abolition as the elimination of anything but abolition as the founding of a new society' (Harney and Moten 2013, 42). A term that I do want to say very 'quietly', in the spirit of Jemma Desai (2020), 'so as not to empty it of meaning'. In particular with awareness of how not-fully-thinkable abolition might be, for me.

Forged in overturning the violence of enslavement that is definitional of colonial-modernity, abolition has become increasingly understood as abolition of the underlying political ontology that holds our world of division and hierarchy in place. As Marquis Bey has observed, what abolition seeks to abolish is 'the ontological order that has bestowed a fundamental sense of being onto anything that must be said to properly exist' (2022a, 24). It is necessary to find different ways of being and being together, 'to attempt a (collective, critically reflective) praxis of human being *against the alienated, coercive universalization of white/Western/Civilizational human being*' (Rodríguez 2019, 1608–9, italics original). As Ruth Wilson Gilmore puts it, 'abolition is a fleshly and material presence of social life lived differently'. Abolition, Gilmore goes on, 'is a theory of change, it's a theory of social life. It's about making things' (2018, n.p.).

Prisons – the site of activism where abolition has expanded and elaborated its practical meanings, not least through the work of Ruth Wilson Gilmore and Angela Davis – have long been connected to museums in Museum Studies. In Tony Bennett's 1995 work *The Birth of the Museum*, which draws on Michel Foucault's unfolding of power, prisons and museums exemplify two directions within the same nineteenth-century trajectory that held together and apart disciplinarity (which operated through individuation and directly applied force) and liberal governmentality (which, among other techniques, used public spaces and techniques of display to encourage, at a distance, the production of a self-regulating self) (1995, 99). Prisons and museums can be seen as two sites of a shared and mutually reliant worlding. The logics of the carceral are different, calibrating modes of authority in different ways. Yet both are modes that determine, conduct, individuate and produce norms, as well as generate and maintain hierarchies.

A world that has museum constitution in it is a world that supports a certain kind of definitional and boundaried political ontology. That there are people and there are objects. That there is a discreteness. That each person is separate from each other and each object is different from every other object. That there is an inside and an outside. That there are margins and a centre. That there is a completed past and a future, in continuity, that is yet to come. That people can be known, and that they can know themselves. That people can be gendered, raced and classed; and that they can represent and be represented. That the world can be taken in, classified, known, interpreted and visited – with all of the still unfinished violence of this idea (Hicks 2021). Abolition in this 'broad sense' is 'the making impossible – and creating a sociality indexed to the impossibility – of carcerality, any form of captivity, which can include categorial taxonomies, agential circumscription, and the like' (Bey 2022a, 22).

A world where museum constitution continues to exist is a world in which this political ontology continues to be nourished. The climate and ecologically urgencies of our planet in this conjuncture are as they are because of the very same colonial and capitalist extractions that enabled museums and museums enabled (Harrison and Sterling 2021, 9).

The same urgencies require of us a redirection of political attention away from the reform of the very institutions brought into being to hold calmly in place a catastrophic worlding. We need to shift our eyes from the liberal horizon whose greatest hopes are always to-be-worked towards and always suspended. A horizon that leaves us caught endlessly in the compulsion to define with every greater resolution who must be included and how. In contrast, 'abolition is an undefinitional project, an attempt to undefine, radically, toward no definition' (Bey 2022b, 139). A 'jailbreak of imagination' (Kaba and Hayes 2018), which comes from the grounded work of finding different ways of being and being together.

The book is written *towards* abolition of museum constitution. *Towards* because it is not a completed action. It is not a completed action not only because museum constitution is not yet abolished, nor just because abolition of museum constitution is ongoing in its fleshy sociality. It is not a completed action in the context of this book in respect of the leap that abolition is *for me*, from whiteness and from classed and gendered normativity. Dylan Rodríguez writes:

> There is thus a frightening beauty to historical abolitionist praxis, to the extent that it hinges on assertions of collective forms of being as (criminalized, systemically pathologized) acts of insurgent self-determination, security, and communal reproduction — without the sturdy guarantees, epistemological presumptions, and material entitlements of social futurity that characterize Western Euroamerican (white) civil subjectivities. (Rodríguez 2019, 1607)

Towards is in recognition of the 'study guarantees' and 'material entitlements' that I have had and still have and that museums have also offered me and still offer me – though in the complex and ambivalent ways that have affectively conditioned me to seek out abolitionist praxis. *Towards* signals that 'participation's affective work' has taken us so far in desiring something else beyond the late liberal circuit, but in ways that will require certain kinds of affective-ideological scaffolding. It is to such affective-ideological scaffolding that this book seeks to contribute – offering, as it does, conclusions in its three registers.

Conclusions I: critically

The big 'so what' of this book is to say this: it is not possible to add participation to the representational logics of museum constitution without causing pain for everyone involved. Pain for a simple reason – liberal and representational politics and participation arise from distinct and different political genealogies and hold incompatible logics of legitimacy.

Two courses of action then present themselves. The first is to deconstitute museums – to undo the ideals, the abstractions and the motor of deficits. This is clearly my preferred course of action and is the focus of Part III. It involves taking participation seriously – not as a mode of engagement but as a mode of governance in its own right and, more than that, taking participation seriously as a mode of world-making, of worlding. A mode of worlding – to draw attention to its recursivity – scaffolded and extended precisely through seeking different ways of organising, of being together and of conceiving governance. In Chapter 7 deconstitution is undertaken through reworking the key concepts of museum constitution – 'conserve', 'future', 'access', 'everyone', 'represent the world' and 'on behalf of'. The purpose of reworking these concepts was to make way for a participatory political ontology that minimised scarcity and deficit thinking – and therefore minimises the need for formal decision-making. It was also to indicate that where and when there is conflict and harm there may also be direct and self-constituting means of address. The 'on behalf of' justification for professional and trustee governance can be weakened through taking seriously the many innovations in participatory governance and restorative justice. To pay more attention to what is possible in terms of self-constitution is to add further grit to the reflex that kick-starts museum constitution.

That all said, if participatory worlding and direct forms of organising have not taken your fancy – or indeed it all seems like a ridiculous flight of fancy, given current museum governance and funding arrangements – that is understandable. In such a case, another course of action is possible. This is to recognise fully that if you believe – or are institutionally required to believe – in public service, and in an inclusive space which representationally offers recognition and validation, then gains might come from owning the implications of your position fully.

If you are committed to producing 'high-quality content' – which in museums is a descriptor generally used to describe stories that nourish an inclusive or plural world-view, told simply and clearly – then this is very probably not best achieved through participation. Ontologically participation is not meant to bear scaling up or being broadcast. Consider instead falling back to approaches that were so common before participation was mainstreamed, for example interviews confirmed through clear, informed processes of checking and consent.

If you want to listen to more voices to help you make decisions through your current governance structure then this is consultation or engagement, not participation. A panel is just a panel; it is not participation unless decision-making power is actually devolved. Adding community members to your trustee board is not participation, especially if you ask them – whether explicitly or implicitly – to represent others from their demographic or neighbourhood, or if you ask them also to steward museum constitution ideals and abstractions.

My point here is that it is crucial at this juncture to tie participation to its political genealogy and to underscore its logics of legitimacy, so it can stop being a synonym for engagement or taking part. Not being clear about this has meant a constant stream of participatory invitations which are then followed by persistent institutional efforts of delegitimisation through deploying representational logics. Efforts to delegitimise generally include both those involved in the process – *they are the usual suspects, they are not representative* – and its results – *this is not the right story, this is not accessible to visitors*.

Alternatively there are, perhaps, possibilities for action that take the core point of not confusing the representational and the participatory, but go on to evolve a variety of practical and experimental responses, approaching this – in an action research way – as an inquiry.

You could imagine – and there are examples of this – a museum service doing representation in its permanent, city-centre displays, but then doing lower-stakes participation in its satellites.

You could imagine enabling energy and enthusiasm and letting it run. This could lead to more imaginative governance structures in which a trustee-type model retained an overarching view while decisions about certain collections were devolved to people who care and sustain its relevance and meaning in a way professionals never could (Boon et al. 2015). This would probably create contradictions, but contradictions that could be entered into knowingly, to be heightened (Moten, Harney and Shukaitis 2021, n.p.) and with a view to further democratic innovation.

You could imagine a museum of members where a constitution is collectively set and revised – after all, community groups do this all the time.

You could imagine restorative justice approaches being used around questions of rights over collections – when the rights of a certain group over a specific object are contested, for instance, or when harm is experienced. There are examples of this practice in both schools and in museums (Kansas City Museum 2020–; Nash 2022; Cetoute et al. 2020).

Probably the most widely recognised of the techniques of democratic innovation – beyond consultation and engagement process – is the Citizens' Assembly, Citizen Jury or other forms of 'mini public' deliberative democracy. There is widespread recognition of the significant contribution that mini-publics can make – and there are some widely acknowledged and celebrated success stories, such as in framing the abortion referendum in Ireland (Palese 2018). There is also a recent example in museums (Birmingham Museums Trust and Shared Future 2025). Thinking in terms of participatory worlding, an important aspect of Citizens' Assemblies is the undeniable beauty that arises when you treat people like citizens and proper partners in decision making. People step up, they educate themselves, they listen, they co-constitute.

Yet it should also be noted that Citizens' Assemblies are representative in two ways. They are based in ideas of demographic representativeness, so people stand in for (if not formally represent) other people 'like them', where the concept of 'like them' is based on race, gender, sexuality, disability, income and neighbourhood. They are also a form of 'on behalf of' decision-making. The difference is that the decision-making (or making of recommendations) is being done by a selection of the public on behalf of the wider public – but without the logics of legitimacy offered by elections. What I'd prefer to see is to take the transformatory magic that happens when people are taken seriously – which Citizens' Assemblies have clearly demonstrated – and use that in genuinely participatory processes, those where big D decision is minimised and action generates both its own legitimacies and realities.

In politics, as an area of academic study, there is now a long-running debate about applying ideas of systems either to deliberation or to democratic governance more generally. One of the motivations for the early Deliberative Systems debates was to see deliberation not as confined to the 'mini-publics' associated with Citizens' Assemblies but as a capacity distributed everywhere, from 'everyday talk' via media to parliaments (Mansbridge et al. 2012). The idea of applying a systems view to democratic governance has been developed more recently by Michael Saward (2021). The aspect of Saward's argument that might be especially useful to museums seeking democratic innovation is the fact that he shows how different democratic components with different logics of legitimacy can be designed together, in order to deal with specific issues.

This inspires the thought that museums could – much more clearly than typically happens – articulate participatory work as a devolved part of a governance system that also includes trustee authority. The point here, to underline an argument made more than once in Part III, would be to see participation not as engagement but rather as part of a designed, distributed and devolved approach to governance. Retaining trustee authority alongside participation is not where I would want museums' deconstitution to end. However, it seems a useful way of taking a step on from where we presently are, especially if undertaken, inquiry-style, as a question for collective and open exploration.

That said, and to take us back to this book's core argument, as the colonial and liberal fuel that has powered museums is now running out, the issue is not better trustee and professional decision-making – nor just adding different voices to this structure. The issue is rather one of experimenting with no longer retaining that right to decide. Without the abstractions of museum constitution – without all affected and rivalry as constraining political underpinnings – a world of participatory innovation opens up. And not – as I have now often said – only of participatory governance, but of participatory worlding.

Conclusions II: affectively

Your pulse still rises, unbidden, even after all this work. The reflex runs deep, but has perhaps now enough of a performative gap. Body meeting enough resistance from mind. Working still for the reflex to become hollowed, distant enough almost to be pleasant in its pastness, like remembering an often-shared joke long after heartbreak has healed.

Detaching is from what museums promised you, which has only become easier – and perhaps possible – as it is also not what they can promise anyone any more. The material base, its 'sturdy guarantees' (Rodríguez 2019, 1608), has fallen out of liberalism's personal contract with professionals: that they will be comfortable, own houses, have holidays, be able to retire. The loss of continuity futures serves to undermine traditional approaches to museum conservation and investments in late liberalism alike.

Detaching is taking up that space of interference that you've been training yourself to make possible. All those repetitions – speeding up, slowing down, trying stolidly, paying attention to your desire for escape. All for that micro-second where you find yourself not immediately raising your hand. All for a slight standing back for a different kind of commitment to the present, less on autopilot and all the more frightening for it. A terrifying kind of calm in the face of history as your pulse slows, if only slightly.

You try to modulate, knowingly unable to appreciate consciously all the potentials jostling, but at least knowing they are there. That many different things could actually happen, even if they still don't this time.

You try organising. Embracing more than you could before the rub of a facilitation approach that changes the atmosphere, disrupts cultural norms and seeks to enlarges the call of the present. You try taking things less personally, as you know whatever you experiment with will not always work. You 'will have been wrong' (Povinelli 2002, 33) as you try staying, both stiller and more actively, with your own constellation of trouble (Haraway 2016). You know you will have to expose yourself. You will have revealed who you are, even as you hope that will change. In this you try finding liberty (Foucault 1984).

Conclusion III: speculatively

Wilder now (Halberstam 2013). Without circuited tramlines and without anyone else to blame. Unfired up, seeking an ever-richer responsive range. Mixing up forms of being together, feeling out how to organise, carrying the weight of responsible world-making while also accepting its ethically imperfect mess. The centre withering, energy and attention distributing more evenly as different entities are brought into being and with them different entanglements. Accountability not via abstractions of ideals or values, but summoned between. Called in and coming as prepared as possible for unwinding. On the cusp and grafting for something else.

Notes

1 Matthew Beaumont traces the genealogy and argues that Jameson 'is probably misremembering some comments made by H. Bruce Franklin about J. G. Ballard' (Beaumont 2014, fn.1, 79).

2 I want to acknowledge and give thanks for a fascinating discussion I had with Kyle Lee-Crossett when acting as PhD examiner for 'Collecting Change/Changing Collections: Diversity and friction in contemporary archive and museum collecting in London'. Lee-Crossett argues: 'Without arguing for the exclusion of these options, what I have been struck by when reading the literature on museum reform and critique is that no one appears to be willing to consider refusing the museum. Partly because of this absence of work, this is the form of refusal I end my thesis by exploring. I have not been able to find any published work that deals with, by name or otherwise, the abolition of the archive or the museum as a response to the neoliberal perpetuation of its colonial, racist and exclusionary structures' (Lee-Crossett 2020, 214).

In the concluding paragraph to the thesis Lee-Crossett suggests: 'The benefits of utilising an abolitionist framework, besides offering a way out of the cycle of institutional critique and reform, include being able to learn from the forty years of work grappling with what it means to refuse reform' (2020, 218). This has been my exploration of what it might mean to 'refuse the museum', specifically museum constitution.

Appendix

I have worked on a series of collaborative museum and heritage research projects that are drawn on in this book.

The History of Day Centres in Croydon
2006–8
(Open University/HLF)

Art on Tyneside: Redeveloping a permanent display about art, place and identity at the Laing Art Gallery, Newcastle
2008–11
Led by Rhiannon Mason (PI, Newcastle University) and Chris Whitehead (CI, Newcastle University) in collaboration with Tyne and Wear Archives and Museums. I acted as the project's research associate.
(Arts and Humanities Research Council, AH/G000654/1)

Museums for Us: Exploring museums with people with learning disabilities
2012
(Smithsonian Fellowship)

Ways of Knowing: Exploring the different registers, values and subjectivities of collaborative research
2013–14
With Professor Sarah Banks (Durham University), Michelle Bastian (University of Edinburgh), Catherine Durose (University of Birmingham), Katie Hill (Sheffield Hallam University), Tessa Holland (West End Housing Co-op), Ann McNulty (HAREF: Health and Race Equality

Forum), Niamh Moore (University of Manchester), Kate Pahl (University of Sheffield), Steve Pool (artist), Johan Siebers (University of Central Lancashire).
(Arts and Humanities Research Council, Connected Communities Programme, AH/K006568/1)

How Should Decisions about Heritage Be Made?
2013–15
With Martin Bashforth (York's Alternative History and Radical Historian), Mike Benson (Director, Bede's World), Tim Boon (Head of Research and Public History, Science Museum), Karen Brookfield (Deputy Director, Strategy, Heritage Lottery Fund), Peter Brown (Director, York Civic Trust), Danny Callaghan (Independent Consultant and Co-ordinator for Prescot Townscape Heritage Initiative: 'Building Stories' and 'The Potteries Tile Trail' (HLF All Our Stories)), Richard Courtney (University of Leicester), Alex Hale (Royal Commission of Ancient and Historic Monuments Scotland), Paul Manners (Director, National Co-ordinating Centre for Public Engagement), Jennifer Timothy (Senior Building Conservation Officer, Leicester City Council), Rachael Turner (MadLab and 'The Ghosts of St Pauls' project (HLF All Our Stories)).
(Arts and Humanities Research Council, Connected Communities Programme, Co-design Development Grant Programme, AH/K006 754/1)

Developing a Co-produced, Digital, and Living Archive of Learning Disability History: An exploration of ethics, ownership and new connectivities
2014–17
Led by Elizabeth Tilley (PI, Open University) with Andy Minnion (CI, UEL), Victoria Green (Open University), Kassie Headon (UEL), Nigel Ingham (Open University), Sue Ledger (Open University) and Row Richards (Open University).

Bradford's National Museum: Connecting Bradford and the National Science and Media Museum
2017–21
With Jo Quinton Tulloch and Vicky Clifton (National Science and Media Museum), Mary Dowson (Bradford Community Broadcasting), Nima Poovaya-Smith (Alchemy), Will Gould (History), Seán McLoughlin (PHRS), Lynn Wray (Project Researcher, FAHACS), Caroline Carr (Project Administrator, FAHACS), Tim Smith (photography and curator),

Aamir Darr (Kahani Reading Project), Lynn Wray and Julia Ankenbrand (University of Leeds).
(Arts and Humanities Research Council AH/P008585/1)
A full list of collaborators can be found here: https://bradfordsnationalmuseum.org/conclusion/acknowledgements/.

The Congruence Engine: Digital tools for new collections-based industrial histories
Led by Tim Boon (Science Museum Group). This a very large and multi-partner project, but I worked most closely with Arran Rees, Katerina Webb-Bourne, Julia Ankenbrand, Alex Fitzpatrick, Tim Boon, Jane Winters and Alex Butterworth.
(Arts and Humanities Research Council AH/W003244/1)

References

Abensour, Miguel. 1991. 'William Morris: The politics of romance'. In *Revolutionary Romanticism*, edited by Max Blechman, 125–61. San Francisco, CA: City Lights.

Abungu, George, Margaret Anderson, Jette Sandahl and W. Richard West, Jr. 2020. 'Reflections on our resignation from the ICOM MDPP2'. Accessed 29 April 2025. https://www.museumsassociation.org/museumsjournal/news/2020/07/icommuseumdefinitionrowrumbleson/#.

addae, yaa. 2020. 'Reimagining museums as portals'. Accessed 29 April 2025. https://medium.com/afrotectopia-imagineer-fellowship-2020/re-imagining-museums-as-portals-de1dd3d6dc1.

Adotevi, Stanislas Spero. 2022 [1971]. 'Museums in contemporary educational and cultural systems'. Translated from the French by Zoë Stilpass. In *Museums, Transculturality and the Nation-State: Case studies from a global context*, edited by Susanne Leeb and Nina Samuel, 39–52. Bielefeld: Transcript Verlag.

Agyris, Chris. 2004. *Reasons and Rationalizations: The limits to organizational knowledge*. Oxford: Oxford University Press.

Ahmed, Sara. 2007. 'A phenomenology of whiteness', *Feminist Theory* 8(2): 149–68.

Ahmed, Sara, 2012. *On Being Included: Racism and diversity in institutional life*. Durham, NC and London: Duke University Press.

Ahmed, Sara. 2017. *Living a Feminist Life*. Durham, NC: Duke University Press.

Alliance for American Museums. 2000. *AAM Code of Ethics for Museums*. Accessed 30 April 2025. https://www.aam-us.org/programs/ethics-standards-and-professional-practices/code-of-ethics-for-museums/.

Alves, Vânia Maria Siqueira and Maria Amélia Gomes de Souza Reis. 2013. 'Tecendo relações entre as reflexões de Paulo Freire e a MesaRedonda de Santiago do Chile, 1972', *Revista Museologia e Patrimônio, MAST* 6(1): 113–34.

American Association of Museums. 1993. 'Code of Ethics'. Accessed 29 April 2025. https://www.aam-us.org/programs/ethics-standards-and-professional-practices/code-of-ethics-for-museums/.

Ames, Michael M. 1999. 'How to decorate a house: The renegotiation of cultural representations at the University of British Columbia Museum of Anthropology', *Museum Anthropology* 22(3): 41–51.

Amin, Ash and Phil Howell. 2016. *Releasing the Commons: Rethinking the futures of the commons*. London: Routledge.

Anderson, Ben. 2014. *Encountering Affect: Capacities, apparatuses, conditions*. Farnham and Burlington, VT: Ashgate.

Anderson, Ben. 2021. 'Affect and critique: A politics of boredom', *EPD: Society and Space* 39(2): 197–217.

Anderson, Ben. 2023. 'Media promises on attachment and detachment with Berlant', *Media Theory* 7(2): 209–24.

Anderson, Ben and Paul Harrison. 2010. 'The promise of non-representational theories'. In *Taking-Place: Non-representational theories and geography*, edited by Ben Anderson and Paul Harrison, 1–36. London: Routledge.

Ankenbrand, Julia, Alex Fitzpatrick, Helen Graham, Arran Rees and Katherina Webb-Bourne (forthcoming). 'This project is very white'. In *Emerging Histories*, edited by Tim Boon. London: UCL Press.

Appiah, Kwame Anthony. 2020. 'The case for capitalizing the B in Black', *The Atlantic*, 18 June. Accessed 9 July 2025. https://www.theatlantic.com/ideas/archive/2020/06/time-to-capitalize-blackand-white/613159/.

Armin, Janine and Denise Bowler. 2022. *The Constituent Museum Cookbook*. Manchester: The Whitworth.

Arnstein, Sherry R. 2019 [1969]. 'A ladder of citizen participation', *Journal of the American Planning Association* 85(1): 24–34.

Ashley, Susan L. T. 2019. *A Museum in Public: Revisioning Canada's Royal Ontario Museum*. London: Routledge.
Audience Spectrum. n.d. 'The most powerful tool for segmenting UK cultural audiences'. Accessed 29 April 2025. https://audiencespectrum.org/en.
Autry, La Tanya S. and Mike Murawski. 2019. 'Museums are not neutral: We are stronger together', *Panorama: Journal of the Association of Historians of American Art* 5(2). https://journalpanorama.org/article/public-scholarship/museums-are-not-neutral/.
Avdikos, Vasilis, Mina Dragouni, Martha Michailidou and Dimitris Pettas. 2024. 'Rethinking GLAMs as commons: A conceptual framework [version 2; peer review: 2 approved]', *Open Research Europe* (3): 157. Accessed 29 April 2025. https://doi.org/10.12688/openreseurope.16473.2.
Bal, Mieke. 2004. 'Telling objects: A narrative perspective on collecting'. In *Grasping the World: The idea of the museum*, edited by Donald Preziosi and Claire J. Farago, 461–73. London: Routledge.
Baldwin, Christina and Ann Linnea. 2010. *The Circle Way: A leader in every chair*. San Francisco, CA: Berrett-Koehler Publishers, Inc.
Baldwin, James. 2017 [1984]. 'Preface to the 1984 edition'. In *Notes of a Native Son*, xi–xviii. London: Penguin.
Barad, Karen. 2007. *Meeting the Universe Halfway: Quantum physics and the entanglement of matter and meaning*. Durham, NC and London: Duke University Press.
Barad, Karen. 2010. 'Quantum entanglements and hauntological relations of inheritance', *Derrida Today* 3(2): 240–68.
Barad, Karen. 2014. 'Diffracting diffraction: Cutting together-apart', *Parallax* 20(3): 168–87.
Barad, Karen and Daniela Gandorfer. 2021. 'Political desirings: Yearnings for mattering(,) differently', *Theory & Event* 24(1): 14–66.
Barad, Karen, Malou Juelskjær and Nete Schwennesen. 2012. 'Intra-active entanglements – An interview with Karen Barad', *Kvinder, Køn & Forskning* 21: 10–23.
Barnes, Marian, Janet Newman and Helen Sullivan. 2007. *Power, Participation and Political Renewal: Case studies in public participation*. Bristol: Policy Press.
Beaumont, Matthew. 2014. 'Imagining the end times: Ideology, the contemporary disaster movie, *Contagion*'. In *Žižek and Media Studies*, edited by Matthew Flisfeder and Louis Paul Willis, 79–89. New York: Palgrave Macmillan. https://doi.org/10.1057/97811373615167.
Bellaigue-Scalbert, Mathilde. 1985. 'Actors in the real world', *Museum International* 37(4): 194–7.
Benesch, Henric. 2015. 'Future ecologies'. In *Heritage as Common(s), Common(s) as Heritage*, edited by Henric Benesch, Feras Hammami, Ingrid Holmberg and Evren Uzer, 243–9. Gothenburg: Makadam.
Benkler, Yochai. 2006. *The Wealth of Networks: How social production transforms markets and freedom*. New Haven, CT and London: Yale University Press.
Bennett, Tony. 1995. *The Birth of the Museum*. London: Routledge.
Bennett, Tony. 1998. *Culture: A reformer's science*. London: Sage.
Bennett, Tony. 2006. 'Exhibitions, difference and the logic of culture'. In *Museum Frictions: Public cultures/global transformations*, edited by Ivan Karp, Corinne A. Katz, Lynn Szwaja and Tomas Ybarra-Frausto, 46–69. Durham, NC: Duke University Press.
Bennett, Tony. 2018. *Museums, Power, Knowledge: Selected essays*. London: Routledge.
Benson, Mike and Kathy Cremin. 2019. 'A social museum by design'. In *Connecting Museums*, edited by Mark O'Neill and Glenn Hooper, 17–32. London: Routledge.
Berlant, Lauren. 2011. *Cruel Optimism*. Durham, NC and London: Duke University Press.
Berlant, Lauren. 2015. 'Structures of unfeeling: Mysterious skin', *International Journal of Politics, Culture and Society* 28: 191–213.
Berlant, Lauren. 2022. *On the Inconvenience of Other People*. Durham, NC and London: Duke University Press.
Berlant, Lauren and Kathleen Stewart. 2019. *The Hundreds*. Durham, NC and London: Duke University Press.
Berman, Ari and Jacob Rosenburg. 2024. 'Democrats need to stop defending a broken democratic system', *MotherJones*, 21 November. Accessed 29 April 2025. https://www.motherjones.com/politics/2024/11/defending-democracy-failed-message-dnc-biden-harris-trump-stop-defending-broken-system/.
Berman, Marshall. 1982. *All that Is Solid Melts into Air: The experience of modernity*. New York: Simon and Schuster.

Bey, Marquis. 2021. 'AnarchoBlackness: A conversation with Marquis Bey', *Ill Will*, October. Accessed 29 April 2025. https://illwill.com/anarchoblackness.

Bey, Marquis. 2022a. *Black Trans Feminism*. Durham, NC and London: Duke University Press.

Bey, Marquis. 2022b. *Cistem Failure*. Durham, NC and London: Duke University Press.

Birmingham Museums Trust and Shared Future. 2025. 'Birmingham Museums Citizen Jury'. Accessed 23 February 2025. https://www.birminghammuseums.org.uk/about/what-we-do/citizens-jury.

Bloch, Ernest. 1986 [1959]. *The Principle of Hope*, Volume 1. Translated by Neville Plaice, Stephen Plaice and Paul Knight. Cambridge, MA: MIT Press.

Boast, Robin. 2011. 'Neocolonial collaboration: Museum as contact zone revisited', *Museum Anthropology* 34(1): 56–70.

Bollier, David. 2003. *Silent Theft: The private plunder of our common wealth*. London: Routledge.

Bollier, David and Silke Helfrich. 2019. *Free, Fair and Alive: The power of the insurgent commons*. Gabriola Island, Canada: New Society Publishers.

Bonilla-Merchav, Lauran. 2019. 'Letting our voices be heard: MDPP Roundtables on the future of museums', *Museum International* 71(1–2): 160–9. DOI: 10.1080/13500775.2019.1638073.

Boon, Tim, Jean-Paul Calvin, Richard Courtney, Helen Graham, David Robinson, John Stanley and Martin Swan. 2015. 'The Science Museum: An experiment in democratising collecting'. In *How Should Decisions about Heritage Be Made?: Increasing participation from where you are*, edited by Martin Bashforth et al. Accessed 29 April 2025. https://heritagedecisions.leeds.ac.uk/publications/.

Bourdieu, Pierre. 2000 [1997]. *Pascalian Meditations*. Cambridge: Polity Press, in association with Blackwell Publishers.

Brenna, Britta. 2014. 'Nature and texts in glass cases: The vitrine as a tool for textualizing nature', *Nordic Journal of Science and Technology Studies* 2(1): 46–51.

British Museum. n.d. 'About Us'. Accessed 29 April 2025. https://www.britishmuseum.org/about-us.

Brown, Alison, K. and Laura Peers. 2020. 'The Blackfoot shirts project: "Our ancestors have come to visit"'. In *Museum Transformations: Decolonization and democratization*, edited by Annie E. Coombes and Ruth B. Phillips, 263–87. Oxford: Wiley Blackwell. https://doi.org/10.1002/9781118829059.wbihms993.

Brown, Wendy. 2000. 'Suffering rights as paradoxes', *Constellations: An international Journal of Critical and Democratic Theory* 7(2): 208–29.

Brulon Soares, Bruno. 2020. 'Defining the museum: Challenges and compromises of the 21st century', *ICOFOM Study Series* 48(2): 16–32. https://doi.org/10.4000/iss.2295.

Bunning, Katy. 2020. *Negotiating Race and Rights in the Museum*. London: Routledge.

Burke, Edmund. 2008 [1790]. *Reflections on the Revolution in France*, edited by Frank M. Turner. New Haven, CT: Yale University Press.

Burns, Danny. 2007. *Systemic Action Research: A strategy for whole system change*. Bristol: Policy Press.

Burns, Danny, Jo Howard and Sonia M. Ospina, eds. 2021. *The SAGE Handbook of Participatory Research and Inquiry*. London: Sage.

Burns, Danny and Stuart Worsley. 2015. *Navigating Complexity in International Development: Facilitating sustainable change at scale*. Rugby: Practical Action Publishing.

Byrne, John, Elinor Morgan, November Paynter, Aida Sánchez de Serdio and Adela Železnik. 2018. *The Constituent Museum: Constellations of knowledge, politics and mediation*. Amsterdam: Valiz.

Callon, Michel, Pierre Lascoumes and Yannick Barthe. 2011. *Acting in an Uncertain World: An essay on technical democracy*. Cambridge, MA: MIT Press.

Canadian Museums Association (CMA). 2006 [1999]. 'Code of ethics'. Accessed 29 April 2025. https://www.museums.ca/.

Candlin, Fiona. 2008. 'Touch and the limits of the rational museum or can matter think?', *Senses and Society* 3(3): 277–92.

Candlin, Fiona. 2015. *Micromuseology: An analysis of small independent museums*. London: Bloomsbury.

Candlin, Fiona and Jamie Larkin. 2020. 'What is a museum? Difference all the way down', *Museum and Society* 18(2): 115–31.

Carpentier, Nico. 2011. *Media and Participation: A site of ideological-democratic struggle*. Bristol: Intellect.

Cetoute, Mischae et al. 2020. *Restorative Justice in Schools: Whole-school implementation process*. New York: Center for Court Innovation.

Clarke, John. 2019. 'A sense of loss? Unsettled attachments in the current conjuncture', *New Formations: A Journal of Culture/Theory/Politics* 97–98: 132–46.

Clavir, Miriam. 2020. 'Conservation and collaboration: A discussion'. In *Heritage Conservation and Social Engagement*, edited by Renata F. Peters, Iris L. F. den Boer, Jessica S. Johnson and Susanna Pancaldo, 30–45. London: UCL Press.

Clifford, James. 1988. *The Predicament of Culture: Twentieth-century ethnography, literature and art*. Cambridge, MA: Harvard University Press.

Clough, Patricia Ticineto. 2000. 'Comments on setting criteria for experimental writing', *Qualitative Inquiry* 6(2): 278–91.

Clunas, Craig. 2004. 'China in Britain: The imperial collections'. In *Grasping the World: The idea of the museum*, edited by Donald Preziosi and Claire J. Farago, 461–73. London: Routledge.

Coates, Ta-Nehisi. 2015. *Between the World and Me*. New York: Spiegel & Grau.

Colwell, Chip and Stephen E. Nash. 2021. 'Why we repatriate: On the long arc towards justice at the Denver Museum of Nature & Science'. In *Working with and for Ancestors: Collaboration in the care and study of ancestral remains*, edited by Chelsea H. Meloche, Laure Spake and Katherine L. Nichols, 79–90. London: Routledge.

Cooke, Bill and Uma Kothari. 2001. *Participation: The new tyranny?* London: Zed Books.

Cornwall, Andrea. 2002. 'Making spaces, changing places: Situating participation in development', *IDS Working Paper Series* 170. Brighton: IDS.

Cornwall, Andrea, Vera Schattan and P. Coelho, eds. 2007. *Spaces for Change? The politics of participation in new democratic arenas*. London: Zed Books.

Cowell, Ben. 2012. 'The Commons Preservation Society and the campaign for Berkhamsted Common, 1866–70', *Rural History* 13(2): 145–61.

Crang, Mike and Divya P. Tolia-Kelly. 2010. 'Nation, race, and affect: Senses and sensibilities at national heritage sites', *Environment and Planning A* 42: 2315–31.

Crooke, Elizabeth. 2008. *Museums* and *Community*: *Ideas, issues and challenges*. London: Routledge.

De Angelis, Massimo. 2017. *Omnia Sunt Communia: On the commons and the transformation to postcapitalism*. London: Zed Books.

De Angelis, Massimo and David Harvie. 2014. 'The commons'. In *The Routledge Companion to Alternative Organizations*, edited by Martin Parker, George Cheney, Valerie Fournier and Chris Land, 280–94. London: Routledge.

Dahl, Robert A. 1990. *After the Revolution?* New Haven, CT: Yale University Press.

Dalal-Clayton, Anjalie and Ilaria Puri Purini. 2021. *Doing the Work: Embedded antiracism and decolonisation into museum practice*. London: UAL: Decolonising Arts Institute and Contemporary Art Society.

Dardot, Pierre and Christian Laval. 2019. *Common: On revolution in the 21st century*. Translated by Matthew MacLellan. Preface by Imre Szeman. London: Bloomsbury Academic.

Darr, Aamir. 2021. 'Moment'. Accessed 29 April 2025. Available at: https://bradfordsnationalmuseum.org/moment/aamir-darr/.

Davis, Ann. 2020. 'Defining Museum'. ICOFOM Study Series 482. Accessed 29 April 2025. https://journals.openedition.org/iss/2630.

Davis, Peter. 2011. *Ecomuseums: A sense of place*. London: Bloomsbury.

Desai, Jemma. 2020. 'What do we want from each other after we've told our stories?', *Art Papers* 45.03. Accessed 29 April 2025. https://www.artpapers.org/what-do-we-want-from-each-other/.

DeSilvey, Caitlin. 2017. *Curating Decay: Heritage beyond saving*. Minneapolis, MN: University of Minneapolis Press.

DeSilvey, Caitlin and Rodney Harrison. 2020. 'Anticipating loss: Rethinking endangerment in heritage futures', *International Journal of Heritage Studies* 26(1): 1–7.

Desvallées, André. 1992. *Vagues: une antologie de la Nouvelle Muséologie*, Volume 1. Collection Museologia. Savigny-le-temple: Éditions W.M.N.E.S.

de Varine, Hugues. 2017. *L'écomusée singulier et pluriel: Un témoignage sur cinquante ans de muséologie communautaire dans le monde*. Paris: Éditions L'Harmattan.

Díaz-Arévalo, Juan Mario. 2022. 'In search of the ontology of participation in participatory action research: Orlando Fals Borda's participatory turn, 1977–1980', *Action Research* 20(4): 343–62.

Dibley, Ben. 2005. 'The museum's redemption: Contact zones, government and the limits of reform', *International Journal of Cultural Studies* 8(1): 5–27.
Dick, Bob. 2021. 'Facilitating participatory research'. In *The SAGE Handbook of Participatory Research and Inquiry*, edited by Danny Burns, Jo Howard and Sonia M. Ospina, 207–19. London: Sage.
Douglas, Stacy. 2017. *Curating Community: Museums, constitutionalism, and the taming of the political*. Ann Arbor, MI: University of Michigan Press.
Du Bois, W. E. B. 2015 [1897]. 'Strivings of the Negro People'. In *The Problem of the Colour Line At the Turn of the Twentieth Century: The essential early essays*, edited by Nahum Dimitri Chandler, 67–75. Oxford: Oxford University Press.
Duncan, Carol. 2004. 'The Museum of Modern Art as capitalist ritual: An iconographic analysis'. In *Grasping the World: The idea of the museum*, edited by Donald Preziosi and Claire J. Farago, 483–500. London: Routledge.
Escobar, Arturo. 2018. *Designs for the Pluriverse: Radical interdependence, autonomy, and the making of worlds*. Durham, NC and London: Duke University Press.
Fals Borda, Orlando. 1987. 'The application of participatory action research in Latin America', *International Sociology* 2(4): 329–47.
Fals Borda, Orlando. 1991. 'Some basic ingredients'. In *Action and Knowledge: Breaking the monopoly with participatory action research*, edited by Orlando Fals Borda and Muhammad Anisur Rahman, 3–12. New York: Apex Press.
Fals Borda, Orlando. 1999. 'Kinsey dialogue series #1: The origins and challenges of participatory action research', *Participatory Research & Practice* 10, Center for International Education, University of Massachusetts Amherst, iv–30.
Fals Borda, Orlando. 2001. 'Participatory (action) research in social theory: Origins and challenges'. In *Handbook of Action Research: The concise paperback edition*, edited by Peter Reason and Hilary Bradbury, 27–37. London: Sage.
Farrell-Banks, David. 2023. *Affect and Belonging in Political Uses of the Past*. London: Routledge.
Federici, Silvia with George Caffentzis. 2019. 'Commons against and beyond capitalism'. In *Re-Enchanting the World: Feminism and the politics of the Commons*, edited by Silvia Federici, 85–94. Oakland, CA: PM Press.
Felski, Rita. 2015. *The Limits of Critique*. Chicago, IL and London: University of Chicago Press.
Ferreira da Silva, Denise. 2007. *Towards a Global Theory of Race*. Minneapolis, MN: University of Minnesota Press.
Ferreira da Silva, Denise. 2016. 'On difference without separability', Catalogue 32a São Paulo Art Biennial, 'Incerteza viva' ('Living uncertainty'), 57–65.
Foucault, Michel. 1984. 'What is Enlightenment?'. In *The Foucault Reader*, edited by Paul Rabinow, 32–50. New York: Pantheon Books.
Foucault, Michel. 1997 [1994]. 'The masked philosopher'. In *Ethics: Subjectivity and truth. The essential work of Michel Foucault: 1954–1984. Volume 1*, edited by Paul Rabinow, translated by Robert Hurley and others, 521–8. New York: New Press.
Fouseki, Kalliopi. 2010. '"Community voices, curatorial choices": Community consultation for the 1807 exhibitions', *Museum and Society* 8(3): 180–92.
Frankenburg, Ruth. 1986. 'Introduction: Local whitenesses, localizing whiteness'. In *Displacing Whiteness: Essays in social and cultural criticism*, edited by Ruth Frankenburg, 1–33. Durham, NC and London: Duke University Press.
Fredheim, Harald, Sharon Macdonald and Jennie Morgan. 2020. 'Curating museum profusion'. In *Heritage Futures: Comparative approaches to natural and cultural heritage practices*, edited by Rodney Harrison et al., 169–89. London: UCL Press.
Freire, Paulo. 2015 [1970]. *Pedagogy of the Oppressed: 30th anniversary edition*. Translated by Myra Bergman Ramos. London: Continuum.
Gaventa, John. 2021. 'Linking the prepositions: Using power analysis to inform strategies for social action', *Journal of Political Power* 14(1): 109–30.
Gaya, Patricia Carolina. 2021. 'Towards ever more extended epistemologies: Pluriversality and decolonisation of knowledge in participatory inquiry'. In *The SAGE Handbook of Participatory Research and Inquiry*, edited by Danny Burns, Jo Howard and Sonia M. Ospina, 169–84. London: Sage.

Geoghegan, Hilary and Alison Hess. 2015. 'Object-love at the Science Museum: Cultural geographies of museum storerooms', *Cultural Geographies* 22(3): 445–65.
Gibson-Graham, J. K. 2008. 'Diverse economies: Performative practices for "other worlds"', *Progress in Human Geography* 32(5): 613–32.
Gibson-Graham, J. K., Jenny Cameron and Stephen Healy. 2013. *Take Back the Economy: An ethical guide for transforming our communities*. Minneapolis, MN: University of Minnesota Press.
Gibson-Graham, J. K., Jenny Cameron and Stephen Healy. 2016. 'Commoning as a postcapitalist politics'. In *Releasing the Commons*, edited by Ash Amin and Philip Howell, 192–212. London: Routledge.
Gilbert, Jeremy. 2019. 'This conjuncture: For Stuart Hall', *New Formations: A Journal of Culture/Theory/Politics* 96–7: 5–37.
Gilmore, Ruth Wilson. 2018. 'Prisons and class warfare: An interview with Ruth Wilson Gilmore'. Interview with Clément Petitjean. Verso Books. Accessed 29 April 2025. https://www.versobooks.com/engb/blogs/news/3954prisonsandclasswarfareaninterviewwithruthwilsongilmore.
Girard, Emilie. 2020. 'Définir une juste ambition pour les professionnels et une identité pour l'ICOM', ICOFOM Study Series 482. Accessed 29 April 2025. https://journals.openedition.org/iss/2630.
Goetz, Anne Marie and John Gaventa. 2001. 'Bringing citizen voice and client focus into service delivery'. IDS Working Paper 138.
Golding, Viv and Wayne Modest. 2013. 'Introduction'. In *Museums and Communities: Curators, collections and collaboration*, edited by Viv Golding and Wayne Modest, 1–9. London: Routledge.
Gomez de Blavia, Milagro. 1985. 'The Barquisimeto Museum: Invent or drift?', *Museum International* 37(4): 224–9.
Goodin, Robert. E. 2007. 'Enfranchising all affected interests, and its alternatives', *Philosophy & Public Affairs* 35(1): 40–68.
Gordon, Avery. 2018. *The Hawthorn Archive: Letters from the utopian margins*. New York: Fordham University Press.
Gould, Peter G. 2017. 'Considerations on governing heritage as a commons resource'. In *Collision or Collaboration: Archaeology encounters economic eevelopment*, edited by Peter G. Gould and K. Anne Pyburn, 171–87. New York: Springer.
Graham, Helen. 2016. 'The "co" in coproduction: Museums, community participation and science and technology studies', *Science Museum Group Journal* 5. Accessed 29 April 2025. https://journal.sciencemuseum.ac.uk/article/thecoincoproduction/.
Grossberg, Lawrence. 1992. *We Gotta Get Out of This Place: Popular conservatism and postmodern culture*. New York: Routledge.
Grossberg, Lawrence. 1997. *Dancing in Spite of Myself: Essays on popular culture*. Durham, NC and London: Duke University Press.
Gustavsen, Bjørn. 2008. 'Action research, practical challenges and the formation of theory', *Action Research* 6(4): 421–37.
Gustavsen, Bjørn. 2017. 'Action research and the promotion of democracy', *International Journal of Action Research* 1.3(2): 101–11.
Gustavsen, Bjørn, Agneta Hansson and Thoralf U. Qvale. 2008. 'Action research and the challenge of scope'. In *The SAGE Handbook of Action Research*, 2nd ed., edited by Peter Reason and Hilary Bradbury, 63–76. London: Sage.
Gustavsen, Bjørn and Thoralf U. Qvale. 2014. 'Norwegian industrial democracy movement'. In *The SAGE Encyclopaedia of Action Research*, edited by David Coghlan and Mary Brydon-Miller, 561–2. London: Sage.
Hafeez, Nabeelah. 2021. '"An open door", Bradford's National Museum'. Accessed 29 April 2025. https://bradfordsnationalmuseum.org/moment/nabeelah-hafeez/.
Hage, Ghassan. 2012. *White Nation: Fantasies of white supremacy in a multicultural society*. London: Routledge.
Halberstam, Jack. 2013. 'Go Gaga: Anarchy, chaos, and the wild', *Social Text* 31(3): 123–34.
Hall, Budd L. 2005. 'In from the cold? Reflections on participatory research from 1970–2005', *Convergence* 38(1): 5–24.
Hall, Budd L. 2014. 'International participatory research network'. *In The SAGE Encyclopaedia of Action Research*, edited by David Coghlan and Mary Brydon-Miller, 453–5. London: Sage.

Hall, Budd. L. and Rajesh Tandon. 2017. 'Participatory research: Where have we been, where are we going? – A dialogue', *Research for All* 1(2): 365–74.

Hall, Stuart. 1986. 'The problem of ideology: Marxism without guarantees', *Journal of Communication Inquiry* 10(2): 28–44.

Hall, Stuart. 2003. 'New Labour's double-shuffle', *Soundings* 24, 1–14.

Hall, Stuart. 2021 [1988]. *The Hard Road to Renewal: Thatcherism and the crisis of the left*. London: Verso.

Hall, Stuart, Doreen Massey and Michael Rustin, eds. 2015. 'Framing statement: Analysing the present'. In *After Neoliberalism? The Kilburn manifesto*. London: Soundings, Lawrence and Wishart.

Happy Museum. 2022. 'Manifesto'. Accessed 29 April 2025. https://happymuseumproject.org/ourhappymuseummanifesto/.

Haraway, Donna. 1988. 'Situated knowledges: The science question in feminism and the privilege of partial perspective', *Feminist Studies* 14(3): 575–99.

Haraway, Donna. 2013. *When Species Meet*. Minneapolis, MN: University of Minnesota Press.

Haraway, Donna. 2016. *Staying with the Trouble: Making kin in the Chthulucene*. Durham, NC and London: Duke University Press.

Hardin, Gareth. 1968. 'The Tragedy of the commons', *Science* 162(3859): 1243–8.

Hardt, Michael and Antonio Negri. 2005. *Multitude: War and democracy in the age of empire*. London: Penguin.

Hardt, Michael and Antonio Negri. 2009. *Commonwealth*. Cambridge, MA: Harvard University Press.

Hardt, Michael and Antonio Negri. 2012. *Declaration*. New York: Argo Navis Author Services.

Hardt, Michael and Antonio Negri. 2017. *Assembly*. Oxford: Oxford University Press.

Harney, Stefano and Fred Moten. 2013. *The Undercommons: Fugitive planning and Black study*. New York: Minor Compositions.

Harney, Stefano and Fred Moten. 2021. *All Incomplete*. Brooklyn: Minor Compositions.

Harrison, Rodney. 2013. *Heritage: Critical approaches*. Routledge: London.

Harrison, Rodney. 2015. 'Beyond "natural" and "cultural" heritage: Toward an ontological politics of heritage in the age of Anthropocene', *Heritage & Society* 8(1): 24–42.

Harrison, Rodney. 2018. 'On heritage ontologies: Rethinking the material worlds of heritage', *Anthropological Quarterly* 91(4): 1365–84.

Harrison, Rodney. 2020. 'Heritage as future-making practices'. In *Heritage Futures: Comparative approaches to natural and cultural heritage practices*, edited by Rodney Harrison et al., 20–50. London: UCL Press.

Harrison, Rodney et al., eds. 2020. *Heritage Futures: Comparative approaches to natural and cultural heritage practices*. London: UCL Press.

Harrison, Rodney and Colin Sterling, eds. 2020. *Deterritorializing the Future: Heritage in, of and after the Anthropocene*. London: Open Humanities Press.

Harrison, Rodney and Colin Sterling. 2021. 'Museums otherwise: A compendium of possible futures'. In *Reimagining Museums for Climate Action*, edited by Rodney Harrison and Colin Sterling, 6–15. London: Museums for Climate Action.

Harvey, David. 2011. 'The future of the commons', *Radical History Review* 109: 101–7.

Hauenschild, Andrea. 2022 [1988]. *Claims and Reality of the New Museology: Case studies in Canada, the United States and Mexico*, edited by Oscar Navajas Corral and Sofía Sánchez Giménez. Universidade Lusófona de Humanidades e Tecnologias e Autor.

Hein, Hilde. 2011. 'The responsibility of representation: A feminist perspective'. In *The Routledge Companion to Museum Ethics: Redefining ethics for the twenty-first century museum*, edited by Janet Marstine, 112–26. London: Routledge.

Henderson, Jane. 2020. 'Beyond lifetimes: Who do we exclude when we keep things for the future?', *Journal of the Institute of Conservation* 43(3): 195–212.

Henderson, Jane and Ashley Lingle. 2023. 'Touch decisions: For heritage objects', *Journal of the American Institute for Conservation* 63(1): 1–13.

Henderson, Jane, Ashley Lingle and Phil Parkes. 2023. 'Reflexive autoethnography': Subjectivity, emotion and multiple perspectives in conservation decision-making'. In *Working towards a Sustainable Past. ICOMCC 20th Triennial Conference preprints, Valencia, 18–22 September 2023*, edited by J. Bridgland, 1–10. Paris: International Council of Museums.

Heron, John and Peter Reason. 1997. 'A participatory inquiry paradigm', *Qualitative Inquiry* 3(3): 274–94.
Heron, John and Peter Reason. 2006. 'The practice of cooperative inquiry: Research "with" rather than "on" people'. In *Handbook of Action Research: The concise paperback edition*, edited by Peter Reason and Hilary Bradbury, 144–54. London: Sage.
Heron, John and Peter Reason. 2008. 'Extending epistemology within a cooperative inquiry'. In *The SAGE Handbook of Action Research*, 2nd ed., edited by John Heron and Peter Reason, 366–80. London: Sage.
Hess, Charlotte and Elinor Ostrom. 2007. *Understanding Knowledge as a Commons: From theory to practice*. Cambridge, MA: MIT Press.
Hetherington, Kevin. 2000. 'Museums and the visually impaired: The spatial politics of access', *Sociological Review* 48(3): 444–65.
Hetherington, Kevin. 2002. 'The unsightly: Touching the Parthenon frieze', *Theory Culture Society* 19: 187–205.
Hicks, Dan. 2021. *The Brutish Museum*. London: Pluto.
Highmore, Ben. 2010. 'Bitter after taste: Affect, food and aesthetics'. In *The Affect Theory Reader*, edited by Melissa Gregg and Gregory J. Seigworth, 118–37. Durham, NC and London: Duke University Press.
Highmore, Ben. 2018. 'Aesthetic matters: Writing and cultural studies', *Cultural Studies* 32(2): 240–60.
Hill, Octavia. 1877. *Our Common Land (and Other Short Essays)*. London: Macmillan and Co.
Hine, Dougald. 2015. 'The Friendly Society: On cooperation, utopia, friendship and the contrasting logics of the public and the commons'. In *Heritage as Common(s), Common(s) as Heritage*, edited by Henric Benesch, Feras Hammami, Ingrid Holmberg and Evren Uzer, 187–200. Gothenburg: Makadam.
Holtorf, Cornelius. 2015. 'Averting loss aversion in cultural heritage', *International Journal of Heritage Studies* 21(4): 405–21.
Hooper-Greenhill, Eilean. 2000. *Museums and Interpretation of Visual Culture*. London: Routledge.
Howard, Jo, Sonia M. Ospina and Danny Burns. 2021. 'Participatory research and the need for transformations in a world in crisis'. In *The SAGE Handbook of Participatory Research and Inquiry*, edited by Danny Burns, Jo Howard and Sonia M. Ospina, 1019–32. London: Sage.
Hudson, Alistair. 2017. 'Building a user-generated museum: A conversation with Alistair Hudson', *Open Democracy*. Accessed 29 April 2025. https://www.opendemocracy.net/en/buildingusergeneratedmuseumconversationwithalistairhudson/.
Humboldt Forum. 2021. 'About'. Accessed 29 April 2025. https://www.humboldtforum.org/en/about/mutual-understanding-and-goals/.
Hyman, Peter. 2024. 'Labour's swamp – Keir Starmer resets', *New Statesman* podcast, 5 December.
ICOM. 2017. *ICOM Code of Ethics for Museums*. Accessed 29 April 2025. https://icom.museum/en/resources/standards-guidelines/code-of-ethics/.
ICOM. 2022a. 'Final Report from the Standing Committee for Museum Definition, ICOM Define', published as part of the agenda for the ICOM Extraordinary General Meeting: Wednesday 24 August 2022, 12.30–14.00, 311. Accessed 29 April 2025. https://icom.museum/en/resources/standardsguidelines/museumdefinition/.
ICOM. 2022b. 'Museum definition'. Accessed 29 April 2025. https://icom.museum/en/resources/standards-guidelines/museum-definition/.
Illich, Ivan. 1971. *Deschooling Society*. New York: Harper & Row.
Invisible Committee. 2017. *Now*. Accessed 29 April 2025. https://theanarchistlibrary.org/library/theinvisiblecommittenow.
Jackson, Steven J. 2014. 'Rethinking repair'. In *Media Technologies: Essays on communication, materiality and Society*, edited by Tarleton Gillespie, Pablo J. Boczkowski and Kirsten A. Foot, 221–307. Cambridge, MA: MIT Press.
Jaitli, Namrata. 2014. 'Citizen participation'. In *The SAGE Encyclopaedia of Action Research*, edited by David Coghlan and Mary Brydon-Miller, 94–6. London: Sage.
Jameson, Fredric. 2003. 'Future city', *New Left Review*, 21 (May/June): 65–79. Accessed 29 April 2025. https://newleftreview.org/issues/ii21/articles/fredricjamesonfuturecity.
Jancovich, Lelia and David Stevenson. 2023. *Failures in Cultural Participation*. Switzerland: Palgrave Macmillan Cham.

Janes, Robert R. and Richard Sandell. 2019. 'Posterity has arrived: The necessary emergence of museum activism'. In *Museum Activism*, edited by Robert R. Janes and Richard Sandell, 1–22. London: Routledge.

Jones, Siân and Thomas Yarrow. 2022. *The Object of Conservation: An ethnography of heritage practice*. London: Routledge.

Jubb, David. 2018. 'Update: Co-creating change'. Accessed 29 April 2025. https://batterseaartscentreblog.com/2018/04/25/update-co-creating-change-25-apr/.

Kaba, Mariame and Kelly Hayes. 2018. 'A jailbreak of the imagination: Seeing prisons for what they are and demanding transformation', *truthout*. Accessed 29 April 2025. https://truthout.org/articles/a-jailbreak-of-the-imagination-seeing-prisons-for-what-they-are-and-demanding-transformation/.

Kahn, Aksana. 2021. 'Collective care is different from self care: Rethinking engagement in art museums and galleries'. In *Doing the Work: Embedded antiracism and decolonisation into museum practice*, edited by Anjalie DalalClayton and Ilaria Puri Purini, 10–20. London: UAL: Decolonisating Arts Institute and Contemporary Art Society.

Kansas City Museum. 2020–. 'RestoreKC'. Accessed 29 April 2025. https://kansascitymuseum.org/restore-kc/.

Kassim, Sumaya. 2017. 'The museum will not be decolonised'. *Media Diversified*. Accessed 29 April 2025. https://mediadiversified.org/2017/11/15/the-museum-will-not-be-decolonised/.

Kendall Adams, Geraldine. 2019. 'ICOM unveils new museum definition', *Museums Association*. Accessed 29 April 2025. https://www.museumsassociation.org/museumsjournal/news/2019/07/31072019icomrevealsupdatedmuseumdefinition/.

Kill, Cassie. 2022. 'The cruel optimism of co-production', *Qualitative Research Journal* 22(1): 56–66.

Kinard, John R. 1985. 'The neighbourhood museum as a catalyst for social change', *Museum International* 37(4): 217–23.

Kioupkiolis, Alexandros. 2020. *Heteropolitics: Refiguring the common and the political*. Brussels: European Research Council.

Kirshenblatt-Gimblett, Barbara. 2006. 'World heritage and economics'. In *Museum Frictions: Public cultures/global transformations*, edited by Ivan Karp, Corinne A. Kratz, Lynn Szwaja and Tomás Ybarra-Frausto, 161–202. London and Durham, NC: Duke University Press.

Kratz, Corinne A. and Ivan Karp. 2006. 'Introduction: Museum frictions: Public cultures/global transformations'. In *Museum Frictions: Public cultures/global transformations*, edited by Ivan Karp, Corinne A. Kratz, Lynn Szwaja and Tomas Ybarra-Frausto, 1–31. London and Durham, NC: Duke University Press.

Kreps, Christina. 2003. *Liberating Culture: Cross-cultural perspectives of museums, curation and heritage preservation*. London: Routledge.

Lash, Scott. 2007. 'Power after hegemony: Cultural studies in mutation?', *Theory, Culture & Society* 24(3): 55–78.

Latour, Bruno. 1983. 'Give me a laboratory and I will raise the world'. In *Science Observed*, edited by Karin Knorr Cetina and Michael Mulkay, 141–70. London: Sage.

Latour, Bruno. 1991. *We Have Never Been Modern*. Cambridge, MA: Harvard University Press.

Latour, Bruno. 2004. 'Why has critique run out of steam? From matters of fact to matters of concern', *Critical Inquiry* 30(2): 225–48.

Latour, Bruno. 2005. *Reassembling the Social: An introduction to action-network-theory*. Oxford: Oxford University Press.

Latour, Bruno. 2010. 'An attempt at a "Compositionist Manifesto"', *New Literary History* 41(3): 471–90.

Latour, Bruno and Anselm Franke. 2010. 'Angels without wings: A conversation between Bruno Latour and Anselm Franke', *Animism* 1: 86–96.

Law, John and Annemarie Mol. 2002. 'Complexities: An introduction'. In *Complexities: Social Studies of Knowledge Practices*, edited by John Law and Annemarie Mol, 1–22. Durham, NC and London: Duke University Press.

Lawson, John, Kathy Cremin and Mike Benson. 2015. 'Heritage as a living stream: Distributed decision-making and leadership at Bede's World'. In *How Should Decisions about Heritage Be Made?: Increasing participation from where you are*, edited by Martin Bashforth et al. Accessed 29 April 2025. https://heritagedecisions.leeds.ac.uk/publications/.

Lee-Crossett, Kyle. 2020. 'Collecting Change/Changing Collections: Diversity and friction in contemporary archive and museum collecting in London'. PhD thesis, UCL.

Lehmannová, Martina. 2020. '224 years of defining the museum', ICOM Czech Republic.

Levitas, Ruth. 1990. 'Educated hope: Ernst Bloch on abstract and concrete utopia', *Utopian Studies* 1(2): 13–26.

Levitas, Ruth. 2013. *Utopia as Method: The imaginary reconstitution of society*. London: Palgrave Macmillan.

Lewin, Kurt. 1946. 'Action research and minority problems', *Journal of Social Issues: A Journal of the Society for the Psychological Study of Social Issues*, 2(4): 34–46.

Lipsky, Michael. 1980. *Street-level Bureaucracy: Dilemmas of the individual in public services*. London: Russell Sage Foundation.

Lindqvist, Sven. 2014. 'Dig where you stand movement'. In *The SAGE Encyclopaedia of Action Research*, edited by David Coghlan and Mary Brydon-Miller, 265–6. London: Sage.

Linebaugh, Peter. 2014. *Stop, Thief! The Commons, enclosures and resistance*. Binghamton, NY: PM Press.

London-Edinburgh Weekend Return Group. 1980. *In and Against the State*. London: Pluto Press.

Lynch, Bernadette. 2011a. *Whose Cake Is It Anyway?* London: Paul Hamlyn.

Lynch, Bernadette T. 2011b. 'Collaboration, contestation and creative conflict: On the efficacy of museum/community partnerships'. In *The Routledge Companion to Museum Ethics: Redefining ethics for the twenty-first century museum*, edited by Janet Marstine, 146–63. London: Routledge.

Lynch, Bernadette. 2019. 'Notes from the frontline: Partnerships in museums'. In *Connecting Museums*, edited by Mark O'Neill and Glenn Hooper, 33–47. London: Routledge.

Lynch, Bernadette. 2020. 'Introduction: Neither helpful nor unhelpful – a clear way forward for the useful museum'. In *Museums and Social Change: Challenging the unhelpful museum*, edited by Adele Chynoweth, Bernadette Lynch, Klaus Petersen and Sarah Smed, 1–31. London: Routledge.

Lynch, Bernadette. 2023. 'The solidarity in action network', *Museum Worlds: Advances in research* 1(1): 199–201.

Lynch, Bernadette T. and Samuel J. M. M. Alberti. 2010. 'Legacies of prejudice: Racism, co-production and radical trust in the museum', *Museum Management and Curatorship* 25(1): 13–35.

Lynch, Kevin. 1972. *What Time Is This Place?* Cambridge, MA: MIT Press.

Macdonald, Sharon. 2020 [2002]. *Behind the Scenes at the Science Museum*. London: Routledge.

Macdonald, Sharon. 2023a. 'Doing diversity, making differences: Multi-researcher ethnography in museums and heritage in museums'. In *Doing Diversity in Museums and Heritage: A Berlin ethnography*, edited by Sharon Macdonald, 13–56. Bielefeld: Transcript.

Macdonald, Sharon. 2023b. 'Diversity Max*: Multiple differences in exhibition making in Berlin global'. In *Doing Diversity in Museums and Heritage: A Berlin ethnography*, edited by Sharon Macdonald, 173–92. Bielefeld: Transcript.

Macdonald, Sharon. 2023c. 'Making differences to diversity in museums and heritage: An afterword'. In *Doing Diversity in Museums and Heritage: A Berlin ethnography*, edited by Sharon Macdonald, 315–18. Bielefeld: Transcript.

Mackewn, Jenny. 2008. 'Facilitation as action research in the moment'. In *The SAGE Handbook of Action Research, Participatory Inquiry and Practice*, 2nd ed., edited by Peter Reason and Hilary Bradbury, 615–28. London: Sage.

Mairesse, François. 2020a. 'Definitions and missions of museums'. In *What Definition Do Museums Need? Proceedings of the ICOM Committees*, 31–42. Paris: ICOM.

Mairesse, François. 2020b. 'Museum diversity through the lens of the Kyoto Definition', *Muzealnictwo* 61: 75–9.

Mairesse, François and Olivia Guiragossian. 2020. 'Définir le musée à travers le monde', *ICOFOM Study Series 482*. Accessed 29 April 2025. https://journals.openedition.org/iss/2630.

Manning, Erin. 2016. *The Minor Gesture: Thought in the act*. Durham, NC and London: Duke University Press.

Mansbridge, Jane et al. 2012. 'A systemic approach to deliberative democracy'. In *Deliberative Systems: Deliberative democracy at the large scale*, edited by John Parkinson and Jane Mansbridge, 1–26. Cambridge: Cambridge University Press.

Maranda, Lynn. 2020. 'Is it possible to tie down a universal museum definition?', *ICOFOM Study Series* 482. Accessed 29 April 2025. https://journals.openedition.org/iss/2630.

Marshall, Judi. 2008. 'Finding form in writing for action research'. In *The SAGE Handbook of Action Research*, 2nd ed., edited by Peter Reason and Hilary Bradbury, 682–94. London: Sage.

Marstine, Janet. 2017. *Critical Practice: Artists, museums, ethics*. London: Routledge.
Massumi, Brian. 2015a. *Politics of affect*. Cambridge and Malden, MA: Polity.
Massumi, Brian. 2015b. *Ontopower: War, powers, and the state of perception*. Durham, NC and London: Duke University Press.
Massumi, Brian. 2015c. *The Power at the End of the Economy*. Durham, NC and London: Duke University Press.
Mayrand, Pierre. 1985. 'The new museology proclaimed', *Museum International* 37(4): 200–1.
McCarthy, Conel. 2018. *Te Papa: Reinventing New Zealand's national museum*. London: Routledge.
McKittrick, Katherine. 2021. *Dear Science and Other Stories*. Durham, NC and London: Duke University Press.
McLaughlin, Anna. 2023. 'Decentralising the museum: The need for a new institutional form'. Unpublished paper presented at 'Loosening the difficulty: Museums and participation workshop', University of Leeds, 14–15 June 2023.
Media Archaeology Lab. Accessed 29 April 2025. https://www.mediaarchaeologylab.com/.
Medienarchäologische Fundus. n.d. Accessed 29 April 2025. https://www.musikundmedien.huberlin.de/de/medienwissenschaft/medientheorien/fundus.
Mignolo, Walter D. and Catherine Walsh. 2018. *On Decoloniality: Concepts, analytics, praxis*. Durham, NC and London: Duke University Press.
Morgan, Jennie. 2013. 'Examining the "flexible museum": Exhibition process, a project approach and the creative element', *Museum and Society* 11(2): 158–71.
Morgan, Jennie. 2018. 'Assembling the new: Studying change through the "mundane" in the museum as organization', *Museum and Society* 16(2): 157–70.
Morgan, Elinor et al., eds. 2018. *The Constituent Museum: Constellations of knowledge, politics and mediation*. Amsterdam: Valiz.
Morris, William. 2012 [1890]. *News from Nowhere, or an epoch of rest being some chapters from a utopian romance*, edited by James Redmond. London: Routledge.
Morse, Nuala. 2020. *The Museum as a Space of Social Care*. London: Routledge.
Morse, Nuala and Ealasaid Munro. 2018. 'Museums' community engagement schemes: Austerity and practices of care in two local museum services', *Social & Cultural Geography* 19(3): 357–78.
Moten, Fred, Stefano Harney and Stephen Shukaitis. 2021. 'Refusing completion: A conversation', *e-flux*, 116. Accessed 29 April 2025. https://www.e-flux.com/journal/116/379446/refusingcompletionaconversation/.
Mouffe, Chantal. 1993. *The Return of the Political*. London: Verso.
Mouffe, Chantal. 2000. *The Democratic Paradox*. London: Verso.
Mouffe, Chantal. 2010. 'Chantal Mouffe'. Accessed 29 April 2025. https://www.artforum.com/features/chantal-mouffe-194635/.
Mouffe, Chantal. 2013. *Agonistics: Thinking the world politically*. London: Verso.
Mouffe, Chantal and Martin Oppelt. 2014. '"Thinking the world politically": An interview with Chantal Mouffe', *ZPTh – Zeitschrift für politische Theorie* 5(2): 263–77.
Munro, Ealasaid. 2014. 'Doing emotion work in museums: Reconceptualising the role of community engagement practitioners', *Museum and Society* 12(1): 44–60.
Murawski, Mike. 2017, updated 2020. 'Museums are not neutral', *Art Museum Teaching*. Accessed 29 April 2025. https://artmuseumteaching.com/2017/08/31/museums-are-not-neutral/).
Museums Aotearoa. 2013. *Code of Ethics and Professional Practice*. Accessed 29 April 2025. www.museumsaotearoa.org.nz.
Museums Association. 2016. *Code of Ethics*. Accessed 29 April 2025. https://www.museumsassociation.org/campaigns/ethics/codeofethics/.
Museums Association. n.d. *Power to the People Framework*. Accessed 29 April 2025. https://www.museumsassociation.org/campaigns/museumschangelives/powertothepeople/.
Museum International. 1985. 'Editorial'. *Museum International* 37(4): 184–5.
Naidoo, Roshi. 2016. 'All that we are: Heritage inside out and upside down', *International Journal of Heritage Studies* 22(7): 504–14.
Nash, Stephan. 2022. 'Repatriation: The arc of restorative justice at the Denver Museum of Nature & Science'. Accessed 29 April 2025. https://www.aiawestchester.org/events/repatriation-the-arc-of-restorative-justice-at-the-denver-museum-of-nature-science/.
National Trust. 2020. 'For everyone, for ever: Our strategy to 2025'. Accessed 29 April 2025. https://www.nationaltrust.org.uk/who-we-are/our-strategy.

Noce, Vincent. 2019. 'What exactly is a museum? ICOM comes to blows over new definition', *The Art Newspaper*, 19 August. Accessed 29 April 2025. https://www.theartnewspaper.com/2019/08/19/whatexactlyisamuseumicomcomestoblowsovernewdefinition.

O'Brien, D. 2019. 'The cultural policy puzzle: Is cultural policy a problem or a solution for social inequality?', *IPPR Progressive Review* 26(2): 134–43.

O'Brien, D., D. Laurison, A. Miles and S. Friedman. 2016. 'Are the creative industries meritocratic? An analysis of the 2014 British Labour Force Survey', *Cultural Trends* 25(2): 116–31. https://doi.org/10.1080/09548963.2016.1170943.

Of/By/For All. n.d. 'It started here'. Accessed 30 April 2024. https://www.ofbyforall.org/our-story

Onciul, Bryony. 2015. *Museums, Heritage and Indigenous Voice: Decolonizing engagement*. London: Routledge.

O'Neill, Mark. 2006. 'Essentialism, adaptation and justice: Towards a new epistemology of museums', *Museum Management and Curatorship* 21(2): 95–116.

O'Neill, Mark. 2012. 'Keynote', 8 November. Museums Association, Edinburgh. https://www.museumsassociation.org/museums-journal/news/2012/11/09112012-mark-oneill-museum-conference-access-combating-inequality/.

O'Neill, Mark, Pete Seaman and Ducan Dornan. 2019. 'Thinking through health and museums in Glasgow'. In *Connecting Museums*, edited by Mark O'Neill and Glenn Hooper, 95–111. London: Routledge.

Ostrom, Elinor, 1990. *Governing the Commons: The evolution of institutions for collective action*. Cambridge: Cambridge University Press.

Ostrom, Elinor, Roger B. Parks, Gordon P. Whitaker and Stephen L. Percy. 1978. 'The public services production process: A framework for analyzing police services', *Policy Studies Journal* 7(1): 381–9.

Palese, Michela. 2018. 'The Irish abortion referendum: How a Citizens' Assembly helped to break years of political deadlock'. Accessed 1 September 2024. https://www.electoral-reform.org.uk/the-irish-abortion-referendum-how-a-citizens-assembly-helped-to-break-years-of-political-deadlock/.

Palmar, Helen and Vicky Hunter. 2018. 'Worlding'. Accessed 29 April 2025. https://newmaterialism.eu/almanac/w/worlding.html.

Pateman, Carole. 1970. *Participation and Democratic Theory*. Cambridge: Cambridge University Press.

Pateman, Carole. 2012. 'Participatory democracy revisited', *American Political Science Association*, 10 March 2012(1): 7–19.

Paur, Jasbir. 2007. *Terrorist Assemblages: Homonationalism in queer times*. Durham, NC and London: Duke University Press.

Paur, Jasbir. 2012. '"I would rather be a cyborg than a goddess": Intersectionality, assemblage, and affective politics', *philoSOPHIA* 2(1): 49–66.

Paur, Jasbir. 2017. *The Right to Maim: Debility, capacity, disability*. Durham, NC and London: Duke University Press.

Phillips, Anne. 1993. *Democracy and Difference*. University Park, PA: Penn State University Press.

Povinelli, Elizabeth A. 2002. *The Cunning of Recognition: Indigenous alterities and the making of Australian multiculturalism*. London and Durham, NC: Duke University Press.

Povinelli, Elizabeth A. 2011. *Economies of Abandonment: Social belonging and endurance in late liberalism*. London and Durham, NC: Duke University Press.

Povinelli, Elizabeth A. 2016. *Geontologies: A requiem to late liberalism*. London and Durham, NC: Duke University Press.

Povinelli, Elizabeth A. 2018. 'Horizons and frontiers, late liberal territoriality and toxic habitats'. Accessed 29 January 2025. https://www.e-flux.com/journal/90/191186/horizons-and-frontiers-late-liberal-territoriality-and-toxic-habitats/.

Povinelli, Elizabeth A. 2021. *Between Gaia and Ground: Four axioms of existence and the ancestral catastrophe of late liberalism*. London and Durham, NC: Duke University Press.

Preservative Party and Abigail Harrison-Moore. 2024. 'New perspectives on participation', *Whose Power?* podcast, 6 August.

Preziosi, Donald and Claire J. Farago, eds. 2004. *Grasping the World: The idea of the museum*. London: Routledge.

Pye, Elizabeth. 2016. 'Challenges of conservation: Working objects', *Science Museum Journal*. Autumn, n.p. Accessed 29 April 2025. https://dx.doi.org/10.15180/160608.

Querrien, Max. 1985. 'Taking the measure of the phenomenon', *Museum International* 37(4): 198–9.

Rahman, Muhammad Anisur and Orlando Fals Borda. 1991. 'A self-review of PAR'. In *Action and Knowledge: Breaking the monopoly with participatory action research*, edited by Orlando Fals Borda and Muhammad Anisur Rahman, 24–34. New York: Apex Press.

Ramamurthy, Anandi. 2021. 'Moment', Bradford's National Museum. Accessed 29 April 2025. https://bradfordsnationalmuseum.org/moment/anandi-ramamurthy/.

Rau, Ted. 2022 'Consent decision-making', *Sociocracy for All*. Accessed 29 April 2025. https://www.sociocracyforall.org/consent-decision-making/.

Reason, Peter. 1998. 'A participatory world', *Resurgence* 168: 42–4.

Reason, Peter. 2005. 'Living as part of the whole: The implications of participation', *Journal of Curriculum and Pedagogy* 2(2): 35–41.

Rivard, René. 1985. 'Ecomuseums in Quebec', *Museum International* 37(4): 20–5.

Rivière, Georges Henri. 1985. 'The ecomuseuman evolutive definition', *Museum International* 37(4): 18–23.

Rodríguez, Dylan. 2019. 'Abolition as a praxis of human being: A foreword', *Harvard Law Review* 132: 1575–1612.

Rodríguez, Dylan. 2021. *White Reconstruction: Domestic warfare and the logics of genocide*. New York: Fordham University Press.

Round Table of Santiago. 2014 [1972]. 'Basic principles of the integral museum', *Museum International* 66(14): 175–82.

Ruskin, John. 1849. *The Seven Lamps of Architecture*. London: Smith, Elder and Co.

Saad, Layla F. 2020. *Me and White Supremacy: How to recognise your privilege, combat racism and change the world*. London: Quercus.

Sánchez-Juárez, Alejandro Sabido. 2015. 'Tres momentos en la actividad museológica de Mario Vázquez', *Gaceta de Museos* 60: 40–51.

Sandahl, Jette. 2019. 'The museum definition as the backbone of ICOM', *Museum International* 71(12): vi–9.

Sandell, Richard. 2007. *Museums, Prejudice and the Reframing of Difference*. London: Routledge.

Sandell, Richard. 2016. *Museums, Moralities and Human Rights*. London: Routledge.

Sarah, Sonia. 2021. No title. Accessed 29 April 2025. https://bradfordsnationalmuseum.org/moment/sonia-siddique/.

Saward, Michael. 2021. *Democratic Design*. Oxford: Oxford University Press.

Schugurensky, David. 2014. 'Paulo Freire'. In *The SAGE Encyclopaedia of Action Research*, edited by David Coghlan and Mary Brydon-Miller, 367–70. London: Sage.

Schumacher, E. F. 1972. *Small Is Beautiful: A study of economics as if people mattered*. London: Vintage.

Scott, David. 2003. 'Culture in political theory', *Political Theory* 31: 92–115.

Scott, David. 2004. *Conscripts of Modernity: The tragedy of colonial enlightenment*. London and Durham, NC: Duke University Press.

Scott, David. 2014. 'The tragic vision in postcolonial time', *PMLA* 129: 799–808.

Scott, David. 2017. *Stuart Hall's Voice: Intimations of an ethics of receptive generosity*. Durham, NC and London: Duke University Press.

Sedgwick, Eve Kosofsky. 2003. *Touching Feeling: Affect, pedagogy, performativity*. Durham, NC and London: Duke University Press.

Seigworth, Gregory J. and Melissa Gregg. 2010. 'An inventory of shimmers'. In *The Affect Theory Reader*, edited by Melissa Gregg and Gregory J. Seigworth, 1–28. Durham, NC and London: Duke University Press.

Shaffii, Wahida. 2021. No title. Accessed 29 April 2025. https://bradfordsnationalmuseum.org/moment/wahida-shaffi/

Sharpe, Christina. 2023. *Ordinary Notes*. London: Daunt Books.

Simon, Nina. 2006. *Museum 2.0*. Accessed 29 April 2025. http://museumtwo.blogspot.com/.

Simon, Nina. 2010. *The Participatory Museum*. Accessed 29 April 2025. https://www.participatorymuseum.org/.

Simon, Nina. 2012. 'Dreaming of perpetually beta: Making museums more incremental', *Museums 2.0*. Accessed 29 April 2025. http://museumtwo.blogspot.com/2012/10/dreaming-of-perpetual-beta-making.html.

Smith, Laurajane. 2006. *The Uses of Heritage*. London: Routledge.

Smith, Laurajane and Emma Waterton. 2009. *Heritage, Communities and Archaeology*. London: Duckworth.

Spatz, Ben. 2015. *What Can a Body Do?* London: Routledge.

Spivak, Gayatri Chakravorty. 1985. 'The Rani of Sirmur: An essay in reading the archives', *History and Theory* 24(3): 247–72.

Spivak, Gayatri Chakravorty. 2003. *Death of a Discipline*. New York: Columbia University Press.

Spivak, Gayatri Chakravorty. 2004. 'Righting wrongs', *The South Atlantic Quarterly* 103: 523–81.

Spivak, Gayatri Chakravorty. 2013. *An Aesthetic Education in the Era of Globalization*. New Haven: Harvard University Press.

Stewart, Kathleen. 2007. *Ordinary Affects*. Durham, NC and London: Duke University Press.

Stewart, Kathleen. 2010. 'Worlding refrains'. In *The Affect Theory Reader*, edited by Melissa Gregg and Gregory J. Seigworth, 339–54. Durham, NC and London: Duke University Press.

Stewart, Kathleen. 2014. 'Tactile compositions'. In *Objects and Materials: A Routledge companion*, edited by Penny Harvey and Eleanor Casella, 119–27. London: Routledge.

Stewart, Kathleen. 2017. 'In the world that affect proposed', *Cultural Anthropology* 32(2): 192–8.

Stewart, Kathleen. 2023. 'Worldings', University of Leeds, 13 December. Accessed 29 April 2025. https://www.youtube.com/watch?v=UW_a0D4Qkbg.

Strauss, Melissa. 2023. Unpublished paper, presented at 'Loosening the difficulty: Museums and participation workshop', University of Leeds, 14–15 June.

Sweetnam, Eleanor and Jane Henderson. 2021. 'Disruptive conservation in the material transmission of past to the future', *Studies in Conservation* 67(1–2): 63–71.

Tate. 2020. 'Our vision'. Accessed 29 April 2025. https://www.tate.org.uk/about-us/our-priorities.

Tinius, Jonas. 2023. 'Dis-othering diversity: Troubling differences in a Berlin-Brussels Afropolitan'. In *Doing Diversity in Museums and Heritage: A Berlin ethnography*, edited by Sharon Macdonald, 157–72. Bielefeld: Transcript.

Tolia-Kelly, Divya P., Emma Waterton and Steve Watson. 2016. *Heritage, Affect and Emotion: Politics, practices and infrastructures*. London: Routledge.

Tuckett, Alan. 2014. 'International council of adult education'. In *The SAGE Encyclopaedia of Action Research*, edited by David Coghlan and Mary Brydon-Miller, 452–3. London: Sage.

Tulalip Tribes of Washington. 2003. 'Statement by the Tulalip Tribes of Washington on folklore, indigenous knowledge, and the public domain, 9 July 2003'. Intergovernmental Committee on Intellectual Property and Genetic Resources, Traditional Knowledge and Folklore, fifth session, Geneva, 5–17 July.

Turner, Fred. 2006. *From Counterculture to Cyberculture: Stewart Brand, the Whole Earth network, and the rise of digital utopianism*. Chicago, IL: University of Chicago Press.

Velázquez, Yaiza María Hernández. 2019. 'Imagining curatorial practice after 1972'. In *Curating after the Global: Roadmaps for the present*, edited by Paul O'Neill, Simon Sheikh, Lucy Steeds and Mick Wilson, 255–70. Cambridge, MA: MIT Press.

Vergo, Peter. 1997. 'The reticent object'. In *The New Museology*, edited by Peter Vergo, 41–59. London: Reaktion Books.

Von Oswald, Margareta. 2023. 'Being affected: Shifting positions at the Ethnology Museum of Berlin'. In *Doing Diversity in Museums and Heritage: A Berlin ethnography*, edited by Sharon Macdonald, 77– 95. Bielefeld: Transcript.

Ware, Vron and Les Back. 2002. *Out of Whiteness: Color, politics and culture*. Chicago. IL: University of Chicago Press.

Warner, Michael. 2002. 'Publics and counterpublics', *Public Culture* 14(1): 49–90.

Waterton, Emma and Laurajane Smith. 2010. 'The recognition and misrecognition of community heritage', *International Journal of Heritage Studies* 16(1–2): 4–15.

Watson, Shelia. 2007. *Museums and Their Communities*. London: Routledge.

Weiser. M, Elizabeth. 2020. 'The definition debate: From paradigm shift to bend in the road'. *ICOM Study Series*, 247–63. https://doi.org/10.4000/iss.2922.

Whelan, F. G. 1983. 'Democratic theory and the boundary problem'. In *Nomos XXV: Liberal Democracy*, edited by J. R. Pennock and J. W. Chapman, 13–47. New York: New York University Press.

White, Hayden, 1973. *Metahistory: The historical imagination in nineteenth-century Europe*. Baltimore, MA: The John Hopkins University Press.

Whitehead, Chris, Tom Schofield and Gönül Bozoğlu. 2021. *Plural Heritages and Community Coproduction: Designing, walking and remembering*. London: Routledge.

Williams, Raymond. 1977. *Marxism and Literature*. Oxford: Oxford University Press.
Witcomb, Andrea. 2003. *Re-imagining the Museum: Beyond the mausoleum*. London: Routledge.
Wynter, Sylvia. 2003. 'Unsettling the coloniality of being/power/truth/freedom: Towards the human, after man, its overrepresentation – An argument', *CR: The New Centennial Review* 3(3): 257–337.
Zahoor, Pakeezah. 2021. 'Moment'. Accessed 29 April 2025. https://bradfordsnationalmuseum.org/moment/pakeezah-zahoor/.
Zwart, Inge. 2023. *Beyond the Participatory Project: Practices of organising, planning and doing participation in museums*. Uppsala: Uppsala Universitet.

Index

Notes are indicated by 'n' after the page reference.